Southern
California
and the World

Southern California and the World

Edited by
Eric J. Heikkila
and Rafael Pizarro

Westport, Connecticut
London

F
867
.S697
2002

Library of Congress Cataloging-in-Publication Data

Southern California and the world / edited by Eric J. Heikkila and Rafael Pizarro.
    p. cm.
    Includes bibliographical references and index.
    ISBN 0–275–97112–0 (alk. paper)
    1. California, Southern—Civilization. 2. Pluralism (Social sciences)—California,
Southern. 3. California, Southern—Relations—Foreign countries. 4. Globalization. 5.
Civilization, Modern—American influences. I. Heikkila, Eric John. II. Pizarro, Rafael,
1958–
F867.S697 2002
303.48'27949—dc21   2001133087

British Library Cataloguing in Publication Data is available.

Library of Congress Catalog Card Number: 2001133087
ISBN: 0–275–97112–0

First published in 2002   *C.1*

Praeger Publishers, 88 Post Road West, Westport, CT 06881
An imprint of Greenwood Publishing Group, Inc.
www.praeger.com

Printed in the United States of America

The paper used in this book complies with the
Permanent Paper Standard issued by the National
Information Standards Organization (Z39.48–1984).

10 9 8 7 6 5 4 3 2 1

47849533

Contents

List of Illustrations

Acknowledgments

This book is an outgrowth of an exposition held January 1 through June 30, 2000, at the University of Southern California (USC) on the theme "Southern California in the World and the World in Southern California" (SC/W).[1] Although the SC/W exposition and this book are quite distinct undertakings, many of the authors represented here were participants in the exposition, and both endeavors probe the same theme regarding the extensive and intensive nature of Southern California's interaction with the rest of the world. Our involvement as coeditors of this book also derived from our positions as director and assistant director, respectively, of the SC/W exposition. Moreover, were it not for the SC/W exposition, this book would not have materialized, and so we owe a large debt of gratitude to those who made the exposition possible.

Dean Robert Biller of the School of Policy, Planning, and Development at USC was the guiding light for the exposition, and as chair of the university's International Affairs Committee in 1997–1998, he set in place an organizational nucleus that anticipated the exposition. Vice Provost for International Affairs Richard Drobnick was a catalyst for mobilizing support within the university's administration, and with Dean Biller led the SC/W Managing Council. Provost Lloyd Armstrong's personal endorsement and funding made the exposition a reality. His support was based on the university's long-standing commitment to a proactive international agenda as formally expressed within the university's Strategic Plan and articulated persuasively by President Steven Sample and others. Deans from across the academic spectrum provided early endorsement for the exposition, making it a truly campuswide undertaking. The campuswide commitment to the exposition—and to the SC/W theme—was perhaps best exemplified by a keynote event held February 10, 2000, hosted by John Argue, now chair of the USC board of trustees, and whose keynotes were vocalized by USC trustee and chair of Hong Kong's Hung Lung Development Corporation Ronnie Chan; renowned architect Jon Jerde, who is chair of the Jerde Partnership International; chair and chief executive officer of Parsons Corporation James McNulty; and California state librarian and USC university professor Kevin Starr. They generated a special moment that crystallized in vivid form the SC/W theme for the university, for Southern California, and indeed for the rest of the world.

Detailed management and oversight for the entire effort were provided by SC/W managing council members Professor Robbert Flick of the School of Fine Arts; Assistant Dean Alan Baker of the School of Cinema-Television; Professor Michael Dear of the College of Letters, Arts and Sciences[2]; Director of Community Programs Michael Johnson of the Annenberg School of Communication; and Adjunct Professor Rocky Tarantello of the School of Business. This group collectively devoted many hours of effort in reviewing the more than fifty proposals for the exposition, selecting those to be awarded funding, and monitoring the progress of those funded. The two dozen principals thus selected contributed to the exposition in a most visible and tangible way through their creative and expository efforts. Those efforts have now been skillfully preserved in the SC/W electronic archives created by Mark Sorenson and his colleagues at Geographic Planning Collaborative, Inc.

Regarding the book project more specifically, we are most grateful to our contributing authors who have complied conscientiously with our many requests and deadlines and to Cynthia Harris and Frank Saunders of Greenwood Press who have been unfailingly encouraging, helpful, and patient throughout the year it has taken to pull this manuscript together. David Sumi and Laila Heikkila provided reformatting and editing assistance, and staff from the School of Policy, Planning, and Development including Anna Sai, Melissa Azarcon, and Jean Nguyen lent regular support to the effort. Finally, as coeditors, we are most grateful to each other for a most collegial and congenial experience.

NOTES

1. The SC/W exposition is archived electronically at http://sppdserver.usc.edu/scw/archives/index/index.html.

2. Michael Dear is also director of the Southern California Studies Center, or SC2 as it is more familiarly known. While the SC/W exposition (as a one-time event) and SC2 (as a more permanent institutional structure within the university) are quite distinct, SC2's support of SC/W was of fundamental importance.

1

Introduction

Eric J. Heikkila

Much has been written about Los Angeles as the emerging urban paradigm for the twenty-first century. If a single term might be used to summarize what distinguishes the Southern California urban region from earlier forms, it may be *restructuring*. This restructuring is evident in many dimensions, including economic, geographic, and demographic. The overall unifying element to this restructuring process, however, is that of *identity*. It is the identity of the region as understood by those who live and work in it, and as perceived by those outside the region, that is undergoing remarkable transformation, and it is the dynamic of identify transformation—rather than any fixed identity or image—that sets Southern California apart. In this sense, Los Angeles is the quintessential process postmodern metropolis.[1]

Geographer David Harvey concludes his compelling and influential account of space-time compression with an emphatic endorsement of the importance of becoming as opposed to being.[2] His reference is a counter to Martin Heidegger, who argues that being is the proper philosophical basis for human society in the modern age.[3] While this is not the forum to resolve or even intervene in such a debate, it is both useful and important to recognize its relevance for Southern California. The process of identity transformation distinguishes it from other places, and that process is clearly an act of becoming. However, *plus ça change plus c'est la même*, and so this very process of dynamic identity transformation is, ironically, one of the more permanent and telling aspects of the region's being.

This book explores different facets of the process of Southern California's identity transformation in the context of space-time compression. In particular, we explore how the local and the global are interfused with one another. This is more than a process of globalization. Referring again to Harvey, space-time compression focuses specifically on the tension between "the spatialization of time (Being)" and "the annihilation of space by time (Becoming)."[4] Identity transformation in Southern California is increasingly undetered by spatial constraints. We are increasingly able to become whomever we want, whenever we want, wherever we want. This is true at the level of the individual and also at more aggregate levels of identity. As S. Friedman describes it, postmodern identities "shift within a changing context, dependent upon the point of reference. . . . Identities are fluid sites that can be understood differently depending on the vantage point of their formation and function."[5] Such is Southern California.

Another framework for understanding the multiple levels of transformation in Southern California is drawn from twentieth-century French social philosopher Henri Lefebvre, whose *La production de l'espace* has richly influenced the works of Harvey, Soja, and other contemporary geographers.[6] Our understanding of Southern California may be enhanced by reference to Lefebvre's three aspects or dimensions of space:[7]

- Material space—the realm of spatial practices, corresponding to the physical space of everyday life
- Representations of space—the realm of spatial perception, corresponding to socialized or institutionalized space
- Spaces of representation—the realm of spatial imagination, corresponding to surreal, poetic, or spiritualized space

The transformation of Southern California's identity entails each of these dimensions, but not in any neat or tidy fashion. It is fascinating to see how the various chapters in this multifaceted study of *Southern California and the World* draw on Lefebvre's dimensions of space, explicitly or otherwise. They also bring to light three distinct aspects of Southern California's relationship to the rest of the world:

- Southern California as a nexus *to* the world
- Southern California as a microcosm *of* the world
- Southern California's projection *into* the world

In effect, these are the aspects by which space-time compression manifests itself in the context of Southern California's ongoing identity transformation. While the chapters of this book defy ready placement into such neat categories, these three aspects do provide a useful starting point for an introduction to the book.

SOUTHERN CALIFORNIA AS A NEXUS TO THE WORLD

No discussion of Southern California and its relationship to the rest of the world is complete without reference to the filmed entertainment and related industries known collectively as "Hollywood," and many chapters touch on its remarkable global influence as a fount of symbols and images. It is altogether fitting therefore that Chapter 2, "Globalization, Digitalization, and Hollywood," by Michael Clough, focuses directly on the industry itself. Globalization and digitalization are two intertwined forces that are having a driving effect on restructuring of the filmed entertainment industry. Thus, ironically, the machinery that is at the heart of producing a globally dominant space of representation is itself subject to changes wrought by economic and technological changes in material space. In this sense, Hollywood, and by implication Southern California, is an important nexus to the world: it is a major node of both transmission and receipt within a wider network of information and economic flows.

As Clough shows, and as Stanley Rosen illustrates in Chapter 3 via his fascinating account of the Hollywood industry's travails in China, markets are globalizing on both the supply side and the demand side of the filmed entertainment industry. On the supply side, competing production sites are springing to life throughout the world. While some of these are attached linguistically, politically, culturally, and otherwise to domestic markets overseas, others, particularly those in Canada, are viewed by Hollywood as "runaway production" centers that compete directly on the basis of cost and quality for the same consumer markets in the United States and abroad as does Hollywood.

Changes in technology, especially digitalization, accelerate this decentralizing trend while simultaneously (and somewhat paradoxically) fostering fears abroad of increasingly centralized American cultural hegemony within the industry worldwide. Clough portrays the process of digitization in terms of four kinds of convergence. Converging *content* arises as digitally stored content derived from one entertainment medium is swapped with others. Converging *pipes* come into play as the distinctions between content delivery methods blur. The *platforms* for receiving such data flows are increasingly convergent. Finally, a convergence of *commerce* is increasingly apparent as companies are compelled by market forces to span the range of services associated with packaged entertainment.

As Clough's chapter illuminates, Hollywood's position as a nexus to the world also reflects Southern California's unique position as a microcosm of the world. The many cultures and identities present in Southern California provide a natural testing ground for and conduit to global entertainment markets, and Clough urges industry leaders to build on such linkages. More broadly but from a similar perspective, Clough argues that the restructuring process within the filmed entertainment industry presents as many opportunities as it does threats for Hollywood. Its role as a nexus works both ways. Globalization and digitalization expand consumer markets as well as producer markets. They allow for the import of new ideas and fresh talent as well as for reexport of the same. Hollywood as an industry is well poised to participate in, lead, and benefit from the restructuring process. Recognizing and building on the process is preferable to ignoring or resisting it.

Stanley Rosen's chapter, "The Wolf at the Door: Hollywood and the Film Market in China," provides a poignant counterpoint to Clough's. Rosen uses a familiar Chinese idiom in describing the relationship between the Hollywood film industry and its Chinese governmental counterparts as one of "same bed, different dreams." Here, the tables are turned on the perceived threat posed by globalization forces to Hollywood. Instead, we see the latter—as the Chinese government does—as a potential menace economically, culturally, ideologically, and politically. Unlike the case of the former Soviet Union, China's systematic opening to the rest of the world since 1978 has assigned priority to economic engagement while keeping the political realm well under wraps. There is no *glasnost* in China to accompany *perestroika*.[8]

China is clearly committed to seriously engaging the world within the framework of the World Trade Organization (WTO), which it is poised to join in 2002. Its challenge in this context is how to admit the economic dimensions of the global filmed entertainment industry while excluding the more pernicious ideological and political dimensions. The ideological wolf at the door is dressed in the WTO's clothing, and this poses a challenge to an open-door policy. Superimposed on these ideological concerns are more mundane but no less crucial considerations of economic protectionism to allow time for China's domestic film industry to establish a viable market presence before having to compete head-on with the Hollywood behemoth.

On an economic level, the issues in the film industry are similar to those in the markets for other mass-marketed consumer commodities. China is still very much in the midst of its transition from a nonmarket to a market economy. State-supported film producers can no longer rely on the distribution monopoly of the China Film Corporation to ensure captive markets. These are concerns similar to those that confronted Canadian companies as the North American Free Trade Agreement (NAFTA) went into effect in 1994.[9] Technological changes contribute to the dissolution of state control over production and distribution in China, and this fact also bedevils Hollywood in the context of pirated digital video disks (DVDs) and other media. Why would one pay good money for a name-brand shirt or genuine Hollywood film when one can easily purchase a perfectly good pirated copy for a mere fraction of the price? China's enforcement of intellectual property rights has been spotty.

Ideological concerns are directly linked to economic ones, because the politically mandated objective of the domestic film industry to help build a socialist society with Chinese characteristics is typically at odds with a revenue-driven objective to produce commercial entertainment that appeals to the broadest possible market. If the domestic film industry is to compete with Hollywood on the latter basis, then it must be untethered from its ideological mandate. Here again we see a fascinating intermingling of Lefebvre's spaces of representations (as conjured up Hollywood), representations of spaces (as delineated by WTO turf rules and by national jurisdictional boundaries), and the material space of everyday life.

In both Rosen and Clough's chapters, we see Hollywood in the context of globalizing markets and digitalization. Gregory F. Treverton's "Making the Most of Southern California's Global Engagement" (Chapter 4) analyzes the Southern California economy more broadly in the context of these same driving forces. Of central concern to Treverton is how governance in the region can help to manage the political trade-offs that arise in response to the economy's increasingly global engagement. Treverton points to two issues here. One is whether the net benefits to the region as a whole from such infrastructure investments outweigh the costs. The second issue concerns the distribution of costs and benefits within a region where, as Treverton notes, the benefits of trade tend to be highly diffused spatially while the costs are often highly concentrated.

A case in point is the massive infrastructure required to support the flows of cargo and people into and out of the region. The Alameda Corridor project, for example, is an ambitious undertaking that is intended to provide a streamlined, grade-separated corridor for the rapid movement of goods by rail from San Pedro Harbor north to the major terminals on the eastern edge of downtown Los Angeles that provide rail links to the rest of the country. These investments, funded largely by long-term bonds backed by future port revenues, are designed to enhance the attractiveness of Southern California ports to shippers bringing goods into and out of the country. Much of the goods movement is in the form of transshipments to regions of the country well outside Southern California. As the intermodal links become increasingly well engineered, the transshipment process becomes more highly automated, with containerized cargo plucked by crane from the cargo decks of ships and speedily transplanted onto waiting flatbeds for rail transport to inland or eastern seaboard states. The port system itself clearly benefits from its role as a nodal point or nexus for these trade flows, and the combined San Pedro Harbor Ports of Los Angeles and Long Beach are well positioned to continue to dominate this West Coast transshipment activity, but the presence of a port in the region may not necessarily stimulate trade-related activity in Southern California beyond the ports any more than it does for other regions of the country. The question, then, is how much trade-related activity "sticks to the ribs" of the region in which a major port is located.

While much effort has been made to mitigate negative impacts due to noise, congestion, and physical barrier effects, it is nonetheless clear that the residual impacts stemming from the Alameda Corridor project are borne most directly by those communities through which the corridor runs. Whether by coincidence or design, most of these communities are also poor, black, or Hispanic and suffer from high rates of unemployment and other social ills, thereby raising a host of environmental justice issues. Similar concerns arise in the context of airport expansion; the neighborhoods that lie in the shadow of incoming flights are seldom the ones that benefit directly from the global links personified by the passengers who gaze out their windows at the communities below. The challenge is to help communities that carry the burden of negative impacts to share in a meaningful way from the regionwide benefits that derive from those investments. Treverton sees more effective regional governance as the key to this objective. He is concerned about the possible detrimental effects of increasing fragmentation on the ability of the region as a whole to make the most of its global engagement.

In addition to investments in physical capital to support global trade links to the region, the development of human capital is also essential. Treverton examines various dimensions of this, including education and immigration—activities that entail active forms of identity reconstruction. Immigration policy (including, in the broadest sense, how communities receive and accommodate immigrants), in particular, is a self-conscious act by which communities compose themselves in a most explicit way, while education helps to shape a community's view of itself relative to the world it inhabits. These two aspects of identity formation merge in the classrooms of Southern California, where from kindergarten to graduate school recent migrants sit side by side. The question is whether this is a case of—to paraphrase the familiar Chinese dictum quoted by Stanley Rosen—"same classroom, different daydreams." Within schools, immigration presents a host of issues regarding language training and other aspects of assimilation, and these are mirrored by similar issues in the communities outside the classroom.

Of particular importance is the issue of employment, and Treverton addresses some of the tensions that arise when recent immigrants are seen to be "taking jobs away" from more long-standing local residents. In a highly competitive market-driven society, most consumers—regardless of their professed political orientation—tend to be keenly price conscious, and this puts tremendous pressure on employers to utilize expensive labor sparingly. To a certain extent, a continuous immigration inflow provides a kind of intermediate solution between relatively expensive domestic production versus production abroad. Again, David Harvey's notion of space-time compression is apropos, as Southern California becomes a miniaturized globalized economy. In effect, production is "outsourced" at home, with the help of "insourced" immigrant labor.[10] But Southern California is a microcosm of the world in more ways than this, as several of our chapters convey quite clearly.

SOUTHERN CALIFORNIA AS A MICROCOSM OF THE WORLD

The theme of identity restructuring is very prominent in Chapter 5 by Donald E. Miller, Jon Miller, and Grace Dyrness, who argue in "Religious Dimensions of the Immigrant Experience in Southern California" that the notion of a melting pot is becoming less relevant in the "postmodern mood" of Los Angeles. They discuss the role of religion in the role of identity reconstruction, suggesting that the relevant model now is one of "segmented assimilation." Religion plays a range of complementary or even seemingly contradictory roles in this process: a place of refuge, a guardian of traditional values, an incubator for furthering assimilation, and a force for social and political change in the host society.

In many of the societies whose emigrants find their way to Southern California, institutionalized religion is a mainstay of traditional society. This is certainly true of the Roman Catholic Church in Mexico and other regions of Latin America that jointly account for the majority of Southern California immigrants, but also for institutions linked to Christian, Buddhist, Muslim, Hindu, and other immigrant populations arriving from all corners of the world. It is not surprising, therefore, that these same religious institutions (and the religions themselves) should provide systematic reinforcement for and preservation of traditional value systems within their respective immigrant communities[11] and contribute to the status of Southern California as a microcosm of the world's religions.[12] It would be much too simple and simplistic to characterize this assertion of traditional values solely as a retrogressive or reactionary force against more progressive virtues embodied by an idealized Southern California lifestyle, even if one were willing to accept the premise that the latter exists in definable form. Miller, Miller, and Dyrness portray it more as a counterweight to the limitless set of possibilities confronting immigrants as they strive to establish genuine bicultural identities for themselves. This reaffirms once more the central premise of this book: that Southern California is above all a place for becoming.

The impact of immigrant-based religious institutions in Southern California is not confined to the congregations themselves. As Chapter 5 shows, they are also significant forces for social and political change within the region as a whole. An obvious focus for such activity is the overall stance—welcoming or otherwise—of the region's nonimmigrant population to these newcomers. Both Treverton and Miller et al. address specifically the highly contentious and often divisive issues surrounding Proposition 187 in 1994, which sought to limit access to education and other state-funded services to undocumented workers. Antiaffirmative action Proposition 209 in 1996 had a similarly divisive effect on the state's population. Miller et al. describe how Cardinal Mahoney, the ranking figure for the Catholic Church in Southern California, intervened in the debates, admonishing Southern Californians of the biblical injunctive toward "strangers in our midst." Religious institutions were also instrumental in helping to build bridges across ethnic divides after the momentous civil disturbances and violence of 1992—for example, between the African American and Korean American communities in South-Central Los Angeles that were most severely affected. In addition to responding to events within Southern California, religious institutions are also important catalysts for organizing responses from the Southern California community at large to events around the world.

The opening vignette of the Miller et al. chapter is of a scene in Boyle Heights, where a procession in a church parking lot provided direct links to a cathedral in San Salvador, El Salvador.

We have argued here that Southern California's relationship with the rest of the world may be usefully understood in part by examining the ways in which the world writ large is manifested within the region: Southern California as a microcosm of the World. Focusing on a specific facet of this microcosm, Tridib Banerjee and Niraj Verma, in Chapter 6, "The Third World in Los Angeles: A Metaphor Within a Metaphor," apply a method of similarity to probe the extent to which Los Angeles may be understood through the metaphor of a Third World city, in effect: Southern California as a microcosm of the Third World. Acknowledging that this is one of many possible metaphors for Los Angeles,[13] they set out to explore the basis of similarity, or what they term the reference class, for this metaphor as it may be applied to Southern California. They aver that the unstated facets of such metaphors may often be more insightful than those aspects that are articulated explicitly,[14] and argue that this is an advantage that metaphors have over the "partial but imperious view" offered by more formal models of urban places.

Banerjee and Verma's review of the literature on Third World cities leads them to several closely related elements of a reference class by which Los Angeles might be understood: dualism, dependency, culture of poverty, marginality, and the informal sector. The question then becomes whether these characterizations—many of which themselves are often quite contentious even in their original settings—might usefully generate helpful insights into our understanding of aspects of Southern California. There are perhaps several ways to approach this question. On one level, it is clear that many of these characterizations drawn from or originally applied to Third World settings have already been transferred to American settings as well. Indeed, the application of terms such as *culture of poverty* and *dependency* have been introduced quite formally into policy discussions of the inner city in the United States and have been hotly contested, where the issues of contention often parallel those found in the literature and policy debates on Third World development.

On another level, the question may be approached by focusing on the unstated sentiments underlying the metaphor of a Third World city. Banerjee and Verma point to several meanings or interpretations, including a narrative of fear and loss, with underlying constructs of "the Other" and not-so-subtle intimations of invasion by hordes of dark-skinned heathens. It takes little imagination to leap from this narrative to Propositions 187 and 209, as alluded to already in chapters by Treverton and Miller et al. Not all unstated sentiments or meanings of the Third World metaphor need have sinister undertones. For example, Banerjee and Verma point to interpretations of Los Angeles as a capital of the Third World that emphasize Southern California's links as a trading nexus to the Third World.

We have introduced Banerjee and Verma's Third World metaphor here as an aspect of Southern California as a microcosm of the world, but it is also more than that. Metaphors speak to (and are expressed by) symbols and images, constructs of Lefebvre's spaces of representation. As we have noted, these symbols and images are also at the core of the idea of Southern California as it is projected into the rest of the world. Pico Iyer's *Video Night in Kathmandu*,[15] which Banerjee and Verma refer to, calls attention to the sometimes subtle but powerful ways that such imagery can influence recipient cultures. Chapters by Rafael Pizarro, Stanley Rosen, and Robert Cowherd and, Eric J. Heikkila all reinforce this point in different ways. There is a delicious irony, therefore, in the Third World metaphor as applied to Southern California: while Southern California is indeed projected into the (Third) World, the (Third) World projects itself into Southern California, though in different ways.

SOUTHERN CALIFORNIA'S PROJECTION INTO THE WORLD

Much has been written of how Southern California is affected by its global linkages and its polyglot multicultural composition. Of reciprocal interest are the ways in which events and ideas in Southern California affect recipient cultures abroad. The final three chapters focus directly on three respective and illuminating case studies: Quanzhou, China; Bogotá, Colombia; and Jakarta, Indonesia. A common lesson that emerges from these case studies is that the process of cultural hegemony is less one-sided than might first appear to be the case, and that the outcome from cultural interaction depends substantially on the specific local conditions in the recipient culture and the degree to which the recipient culture actively seeks to appropriate Southern California symbols, connections, or wealth to suit their own purposes.

Michael Leaf and Daniel Abramson, in Chapter 7, "Global Networks, Civil Society, and the Transformation of the Urban Core in Quanzhou, China," provide a fascinating account of how global networks and linkages centered on this relatively obscure (for most non-Chinese) city in Southern China's Fujian province helped to shape the course of urban development there. As a major port town along China's southeast coastline since the fourteenth century, Quanzhou has long been a source of out-migration to Southeast Asia, Taiwan, and other overseas destinations, and these extensive networks of overseas Chinese now extend to Southern California as well. These and other immigrant populations often maintain extensive ties to their native lands over great distances and many generations. As mentioned in the context of the Miller et al. chapter, this feat of space-time compression is accomplished with the support of organized religion, family ties, and other forms of institutionalized and enduring linkages from here-in-the-present to there-in-the-past.

In the case of Quanzhou, these networks have had a surprising effect on traditional values in the face of globalization. Conventional wisdom suggests that global linkages would exert steady erosive pressure on traditional values in the face of modernizing influences. However, the specific history and geographic circumstances of Quanzhou wrought global networks that stabilized many informal aspects of the traditional order in the face of the upheavals of the Cultural Revolution and subsequent developments within contemporary China. Ironically, Quanzhou's "exposed" geographic position in relation to Taiwan and other potentially antagonistic influences led the central government in China to limit state investments in the area even during the height of its all-consuming centralized command and control period, and this magnified the importance and leverage of overseas sources of investment. Local officials, who were in many cases linked through family or other social ties to these investors, were therefore careful throughout this tumultuous period to respect the role of private property so as not to alienate a vital source of capital. Because these investors were themselves tied to the area in the form of family and other social ties, the specific form of these investments tended to reinforce these traditional ties in concrete form, both literally and figuratively.

In a narrative that is implicitly evocative of the Miller et al. chapter and in direct contrast with the stultifying effect of the Catholic church in Italy as described by Putnam elsewhere,[16] Leaf and Abramson describe how an extensive network of informal temples in Quanzhou has provided a sustained focus for an active civil society. Many temples were destroyed or ruined by neglect during the tumultuous first half-century of the new China, and only recently have official plans been put under way to prioritize temples for restoration and reconstruction. Ironically, while the informal neighborhood temples have been largely absent from the state-mandated priority lists, they are the ones that are being rebuilt most quickly, due in large measure to support from Quanzhou's overseas networks, and so global links are instrumental to the preservation of traditional local values. Leaf and Abramson conclude that a network view of civil society helps us to get beyond narrow dualistic views that would pit traditional local interests in opposition to the hegemonic forces of globalization.

Rafael Pizarro's Chapter 8, "Exporting the Dream: Hollywood Cinema and Latin American Suburbia," examines the process by which idealized images of American suburbia emanating from Southern California cinema are diffused as material culture to foreign soil, with specific focus on the case of Bogotá, Colombia. He views this process in hegemonic terms, as evidenced by his opening quotation of a haunting passage by Gabriel García Márquez: "Interpretation of our own reality through foreign schemes only contributes to make us every time more unrecognizable to ourselves, every time less free, every time more lonely."

As a counterpoint to the chapters by Clough and by Rosen that examine Hollywood as an industry (i.e., in terms of the direct nexus of their economic linkages to the World), Pizarro focuses on the symbolism and images—Lefebvre's spaces of representation—of an idealized American lifestyle and its impact on material culture abroad. He posits that the development of American-style suburban enclaves outside Bogotá can be understood in part as a reaction to the negative images of the "mean streets" of more urban settings as depicted in film and the recognition that the dystopia of those mean streets is uncomfortably similar to that found in the streets of Bogotá. He argues, further, that the way Latin American viewers interpret these cinematic images differs from that of their American counterparts because the latter are more often able to ground fantasized images of suburbia against their own extensive experience with everyday suburban experience. The Latin American audience has a less extensive experiential basis to balance against the fantasy of an idealized suburbia, and this, he asserts, has led to a misguided attempt to re-create this fantasy in Bogotá, thus evoking the sentiment expressed in the quote from García Márquez above.

Robert Cowherd and Eric J. Heikkila in Chapter 9 share Pizarro's view of suburban development forms as artifacts of material culture. However, they do not see the diffusion process in their case study in the stark hegemonic terms of an active purveyor and a passive recipient culture. Instead, they argue, the act of appropriation in "Orange County, Java: Hybridity, Social Dualism, and an Imagined West" is an active and conscious one, whereby the symbolism and status of Southern California suburban forms are selectively adapted to the unique and complex local circumstances of metropolitan Jakarta. What might appear at first glance to be an invasion of traditional Javanese culture by Southern California suburban forms promulgated by Orange County developers is more apparent than real. Certainly, the real estate links between West Java, Indonesia, and Orange

County, California, are extensive. Not only are the forms of the new Javanese residential developments almost perfect replicas of Orange County originals, the architects and planners are often the same as well, where these Orange County designers are brought in for the express purpose of replicating and authenticating the Javanese *simulacra*.[17]

Closer investigation into the processes at work reveals a mixed set of motivations within a complex economic, historical, and cultural setting, and Cowherd and Heikkila invoke Lefebvre's three aspects or dimensions of space to analyze this phenomenon. The spaces of representation are very much in evidence through the symbolism and exotic imagery implied by the residential developments qua theme parks. The representations of spaces are clearly delineated by the spatially segregated infrastructure and the overall spatial aloofness and demarcations separating these suburban developments from the traditional indigenous housing found in surrounding *kampungs*. These demarcations are reinforced by divisions of religion, ethnicity, and wealth. It is in the realm of material space where the momentum and continuity of life's daily practice most clearly endure, notwithstanding the imposing glamor and internationalization implied by the form of the residential artifact in which these practices are housed. This fact is captured most succinctly in their description of the "Potemkin kitchen," an architectural facade that dutifully serves the purpose of symbolic representation while masking the continuation of traditional culinary practices far removed from Orange County, California.

NOTES

1. See Edward Soja, *Postmodern Geographies* (New York and London: Verso, 1989); and Michael Dear, *The Postmodern Urban Condition* (Oxford: Blackwell, 2000).

2. David Harvey, *The Condition of Postmodernity: An Enquiry into the Origins of Cultural Change* (Oxford: Basil Blackwell; 1989).

3. Martin Heidegger, *Being and Time* (New York: Harper and Row, 1962).

4. Harvey, *The Condition of Postmodernity*.

5. S. Friedman "Beyond White and Other: Relationality and Narratives of Races in Feminist Discourse," *Signs* 21 (1995): 1–49, quoted in ibid.

6. Henri Lefebvre, *La production de l'espace* (Paris: Anthropos, 1974).

7. See also Harvey, *The Condition of Postmodernity* (especially Table 3.1) and Soja, *Postmodern Geographies*.

8. The events of 4 June 1989, attest clearly to this fact. Indeed, many now forget that it was Gorbachev's visit to Beijing in May 1989 that prompted student demonstrations leading to those subsequent fateful and fatal events.

9. Ironically, as discussed already in the context of Michael Clough's chapter, some worry that a Canadian "wolf" is now perched on Hollywood's door.

10. For the record, both coeditors of this volume are themselves "insourced" immigrants.

11. It is fascinating to note, for example, that Miller et al. attest to the existence in Los Angeles and the San Joaquin Valley of no fewer than thirty hometown associations from the Mexican State of Oaxaca alone.

12. In much the same way, we argue that, through different institutional and noninstitutional mechanisms, Southern California has become a truly quintessential microcosm of the world's cultures and peoples.

13. "Edge city," "fortress LA," and "soft city" are cited as other possibilities.

14. Explicit analogies are developed, for example, in David Rieff, *Los Angeles: Capital of the Third World* (New York: Simon & Schuster, 1991).

15. Pico Iyer, *Video Night in Kathmandu* (New York: Vintage, 1988).

16. Robert D. Putnam, *Making Democracy Work: Civic Traditions in Modern Italy* (Princeton, NJ: Princeton University Press, 1993).

17. Cowherd and Heikkila follow Edward Soja and David Harvey in borrowing this term from Baudrillard. See Cowherd and Heikkila's chapter for explanation and bibliographic references.

PART I

SOUTHERN CALIFORNIA AS A NEXUS TO THE WORLD

2

Globalization, Digitalization, and Hollywood

Michael Clough

Southern California has long imagined itself as a region with a grand (and global) destiny. "Here," Carey McWilliams predicted over fifty years ago, "America will build its great city of the Pacific, the most fantastic city in the world."[1] In the mid-1990s, following the Walt Disney Company's historic acquisition of Capital Cities/ABC, many regional boosters believed that McWilliams' prophecy was about to be realized. "With the help of Disney and Warners," writer Joel Kotkin argued, "Burbank now stands to be the media capital of the world. That same opportunity now exists for the region as a whole. With the demise of the traditional networks, Los Angeles enjoys an unprecedented chance to follow Mickey Mouse into the conquest of world markets."[2] This optimism peaked in early 1998 when the *Los Angeles Times* ran a high-profile series declaring "In Local Economy, Hollywood Is Star"[3] and *The New Yorker* published a special "California Issue" that emphasized the role of Hollywood in the state's economic "comeback."[4]

Today, as the new digital-global epoch is beginning to unfold, the future of the regional economy is uncertain. Worrying signs have included reports about "runaway film production,"[5] murmuring that Disney was failing to capitalize on its acquisitions and emerge as a dominant force on the Internet,[6] and the collapse of DreamWorks SKG's plans to build "the digital studio of the future" at Playa Vista.[7] Then in March 2000 came the announcement that the *Los Angeles Times*, which has led the effort to boost the region's role as the megacenter of an emerging cultural-industrial complex, was being sold to the Chicago-based Tribune Company. Reacting to this unexpected blow, one Los Angeles writer warned, "We are a city adrift, and our fate is less in our own hands than it has ever been."[8]

Whether the Southland, which stretches from Ventura to southern Orange County and extends inland to San Bernardino, will regain the momentum and optimism that existed toward the end of the 1990s, or end up looking back on the year 2000 and the sale of the *Los Angeles Times* as the moment that the boosters' dream finally died, will depend in large part on the region's ability to protect its position as the premier filmed entertainment production cluster in the world and on its ability to compete with New York City, the Northern California Bay Area, and other major metropolitan regions for a place at the center of the new economy. The Southland's place in the new order will ultimately depend on its ability to use its comparative advantages in creating popular entertainment and the rich cultural diversity of its population to build a knowledge-based, globally connected, high-tech regional economy.

This chapter examines the challenges and opportunities that are being created for Southern California by two revolutions:

- Globalization is changing the character of (and connections between) America and the rest of the world and widening and altering the market horizons of the newly converging media industry.

- Digitalization, which is changing the ways in which content news, information, and filmed entertainment is produced and distributed, is causing previously distinct segments of the media and entertainment industry to converge into a single medium.

THE HOLLYWOOD CLUSTER

The fortunes of Southern California and the Hollywood filmed entertainment cluster have been intertwined ever since D. W. Griffith encamped there at the beginning of the twentieth century and began to make movies. In the 1920s and 1930s, the motion picture industry was the region's most important industry. As World War II began, however, it was quickly eclipsed by aerospace, and by the late 1960s its weight had declined to the point that it did not even merit a mention in the State of California's annual economic reports. This situation changed dramatically in the late 1980s and early 1990s. As a result of the end of the cold war, the aerospace industry went into decline, and the motion picture industry began to be restructured and revitalized.[9]

A new optimism developed in the mid-1990s largely because the emergence of what film-industry historian Thomas Schatz has called "the new Hollywood studio system"[10] seemed to strengthen Southern California's position in the media and entertainment industry, while at the same time making filmed entertainment a much more valuable product. By the late

1990s, however, the region's prospects had grown more uncertain. To assess the future of the region, it is important to understand the history of the Hollywood filmed entertainment industry cluster.

Over the past decade, scholars working mostly in regional planning, economics, and geography have firmly established that place—the physical location where people interact, corporations do business, and governments govern—matters even in a global economy.[11] Their work has made it clear that there are reasons that particular activities and industries tend to develop and cluster in some places rather than others and that the resulting industry clusters help to strengthen the ability of regions to compete in the global economy. Those reasons include helping to increase the productivity of companies in the cluster, helping to reinforce an area's position as a center of innovation in the industry, and fostering their own expansion by spawning new businesses.[12] The filmed entertainment industry in Hollywood is a textbook example of an industry cluster.

The reasons that the motion picture industry originally came to Hollywood are still a matter of some dispute. One explanation, only partially apocryphal, is that the independent producers who built Hollywood wanted to get as far away from the legal reach of the Edison Trust's patent lawyers as possible, and chose Southern California because they could always make a quick dash across the border into Mexico. More important considerations were that the region's climate and settings made it possible to film many different movies on a year-round basis; and that because Los Angeles was a nonunionized city, wages, and hence production costs, were much lower than in the East (or in San Francisco). But the industry survived and thrived in Southern California largely because of the self-reinforcing quality of economic clusters.

The early concentration of motion picture production in the region made it a magnet for actors, directors, writers, and technicians who made the movies; lawyers and businessmen who handled their contracts and managed the studios' business affairs; and the network of entrepreneurs and workers who specialized in meeting the demand for ancillary goods and services the industry created. Once this cluster was in place, it became self-perpetuating. The fact that just about everybody, every service, and everything that a producer needed to make a movie could be found easily in Southern California created a strong incentive for producers to make pictures there. Conversely, the economic and noneconomic costs of creating an equivalent film production cluster elsewhere were too high for them to consider it. Moreover, the region as a whole began to develop an institutional infrastructure to support and sustain the motion picture industry. Particularly important in this respect was the emergence of film training programs such as those at the University of Southern California, UCLA, the American Film Institute, and Santa Monica Community College, along with the development of industry groups such as the Academy of Motion

Pictures Arts and Sciences, the Motion Picture Association of America, the American Film Marketing Association, and the Directors, Writers, and Producers Guilds.

The collapse of the old studio system's assembly-line model and the shift to a new "flexible production" model in the early years of the post–World War II era made it even more difficult to create a rival cluster. In addition to the costs of duplicating the sound stages and other production facilities that the studios had built, doing so in an age of flexible production would require simultaneous moves by a vast number of independent subcontractors rather than a decision by a single studio.[13] These considerations almost certainly played a major role in the mid-1950s decision of the three original television networks to rely on Hollywood for a steady supply of filmed entertainment rather than to create their own film studios in New York.

Over the long run, the most important determinant of the ability of Southern California to retain its leadership of the filmed entertainment industry will be whether the Hollywood cluster can adapt to globalization, digitalization, and the consequent restructuring of the media and entertainment industry as a whole.

HOLLYWOOD GOES GLOBAL

The New Global Market for Filmed Entertainment

Globalization—the process resulting from the progressive erosion of national and other limits on the worldwide flow of people, ideas, images, information, organisms, capital, and goods—is radically transforming the world.[14] It is creating new connections and relationships between places, groups, markets, and institutions. It is shattering old identities, cultures, interests, and tastes and forging new ones. It is generating new economic, environmental, social, and political threats. And in all of these areas, it is also creating new possibilities. Like the earlier revolution of nationalization that reshaped America in the ninetieth and twentieth centuries, the revolution of globalization is far-reaching and inexorable.[15] And as was the case in that earlier revolution, the media and entertainment industry is fated to play a critical role in pushing it forward and determining its consequences.

The Market Rules

When the Sony Corporation purchased Columbia Pictures and the Matsushita Electric Industry Company of Japan bought Universal Pictures in the late 1980s, it caused a flurry of warnings about the potential danger of a foreign takeover of the American film industry.[16] This worry was part of a broader American fear that "Japan, Inc." was on the verge of buying up America. Today, however, it is clear that this threat was greatly exaggerated. One reason these concerns have faded is that the global clout of Japan has been reduced by the economic and political woes it has experienced over the past decade (and by the tremendous surge in economic growth in the United States). But in the case of entertainment, it is also now clear that foreign ownership has not caused any basic changes in the economic character of the industry.[17] One indicator of the extent to which fears about foreign ownership of Hollywood studios have declined is the lack of a strong reaction to the acquisition of Universal Studios by French conglomerate Vivendi S.A.

The globalization of the media and entertainment industry is being driven by changes in the market, not changes in ownership.[18] Over the past two decades, revolutions in transport and communications and the growing privatization and deregulation of the media industry around the world have created markets for filmed entertainment far larger than ever before imaginable.[19] This process has been greatly accelerated by digitalization. In the words of Time Warner President Richard Parsons, digitalization—the ability to take voice, video, and/or text, reduce it to electronic impulses, send it via wire or satellite to a distant location, then reconstruct it perfectly at the terminus point—"will . . . completely eviscerate the concept of distance as a limiting factor in defining your marketplace. So, in terms of our business—which is really creating, packaging and selling words and images that can then be electronically transmitted—the world has become one, big market. Once you tell me that, then as a businessman I'm going to attempt to market my products throughout my entire marketplace."[20]

In short, regardless of where they are headquartered, global media and entertainment companies have one objective: to distribute the digital content that they create and control to the largest possible market. The result, however, is not simply a single enormous undifferentiated global market.

Over the past decade, the relative importance of domestic revenues and overseas revenues changed. For example, in the 1990s, all of the top-ten worldwide box-office hits earned more overseas than in the United States. In fact, only two of the top twenty-five movies—*Home Alone* and *Mrs. Doubtfire*—did not earn more overseas than at home. In contrast, in the 1980s, only three movies in the top ten—*Indiana Jones and the Last Crusade, Rain Man*, and *Who Framed Roger Rabbit?*—earned more overseas than at home.[21] The same trend is developing in the case of filmed entertainment produced for television. At the most recent annual meeting of the National Association of Television Programming Executives, one entertainment industry official noted that whereas "just a few years ago . . . international distributors . . . were ghettoized into a small pavilion area," in January 2000 the convention floor was "transformed into a true global exhibition."[22]

But these trends actually understate the extent to which the market for filmed entertainment has been globalized. The reason is that at the same time that Hollywood has been earning greater revenues overseas, the character of the domestic market for filmed entertainment in the United States has also become more globalized.

The forces behind the globalization of the domestic market are twofold. First, as the majority of Americans have become better educated, more widely traveled, and, largely as a result of the media, more exposed to other cultures, their tastes have become more cosmopolitan. But even more important, as a result of immigration, the foreign-born share of the population in the United States has increased dramatically.

The impact of these two trends has been accentuated by the growing emphasis on ethnic roots that has been fostered by many communities and schools. This has caused many nonimmigrants to discover and embrace their ties with other parts of the world. Therefore, even if entertainment producers were concerned only about serving the American market, they would now have a much greater incentive to produce globally oriented content.

The Two Global Markets

For these reasons, it is best to think of the new market for filmed entertainment as consisting of two separate components. The biggest prize is the part of the market that is truly global. This is the segment that creates billion-dollar blockbusters such as *Titanic* and *Star Wars*. In seeking to capture this market, the entertainment industry has an interest in emphasizing characters and universal themes that have resonance in all cultures and can be easily translated into many languages.[23] This has, in fact, always been a large part of Hollywood's formula for success. But the difference is that in the past, producers had far fewer reasons to think or worry about how their choice of actors or use of settings might affect their ability to reach the audience.[24] They simply focused on trying to discern which movies would get middle-class America to the box office, confident that if they could succeed in doing that, they would have a financial success. Today, a film with a blockbuster budget that succeeded in attracting only traditional middle-class Americans would be a huge financial disaster.

The other part of the global market is best described as transnational but not global. It consists of audiences that reside in different regions and countries but share a common identity, language, or affinity. Examples include those based on ethnic and racial ties (e.g., Latinos in Latin America, Spain, and the United States) and those based on identification with particular subcultures (such as hip-hop).

In a world of converging media, the potential value of tapping into these transnational subsets of the new global market is much greater than before. In the past, the profits from producing a movie with appeal to a Latino audience were mostly limited to box-office receipts. Today, a movie aimed at a Latino audience can be used to promote sales of related content, including music, videos, and licensed merchandise; to cross-promote other films and content aimed at a Latino audience; and to attract Latino consumers to Web sites that can serve as e-commerce platforms for a wide array of goods and services.[25]

The Future

In the coming decade, the media industry is certain to become even more globalized for three reasons. First, as population and per capita wealth in places such as China continue to increase rapidly, the pull of the global market will become even more irresistible. Second, as television spreads throughout the world and Internet penetration rates in other parts of the world begin to catch up to those in the United States, the ability of the new megamedia giants to reach global audiences and engage them in e-commerce will greatly increase. Finally, barring a major and unlikely reversal of trends toward privatization and deregulation, national barriers to the export of media and entertainment products and services will continue to disappear.

Runaway Production

For nearly a century, despite periodic concerns about the possibility of competition from other metropolitan regions in the United States and the rest of the world, Southern California has maintained its dominant position in the filmed entertainment industry. For example, in 1997 Southern California earned $24.5 billion from the production of motion pictures and videos, which represented nearly 55 percent of the total receipts earned in the United States. Nevertheless, in 1999, when film production in Hollywood seemed to slow and many workers in the industry began to have difficulties finding work, regional leaders began to warn about the dangers of "runaway production."[26] They focused in particular on the threat posed by Canada.[27]

Understanding the Threat

A 1999 study by the Monitor Company, jointly commissioned by the Directors Guild of America and the Screen Actors Guild, found that in 1998 the United States lost 285 "runaway productions" for economic reasons, 232 of which ended up being produced in Canada.[28] Most of the debate over runaway production has centered on cost considerations, including the economic subsidies and incentives offered to film producers by non-U.S. film-producing countries; the strong U.S. dollar, which has made it cheaper to film on location and in studios in weak-currency countries such as Canada; and the differential in labor costs between Hollywood and low-wage, foreign locales.[29] According to the Monitor Company study, the savings gained from producing in Canada rather than the United States can

be as high as 26 percent of the total cost of production.[30] But it also warned
that runaway production could become self-reinforcing by helping to develop the cluster infrastructure necessary for places such as Vancouver and
Toronto to attract even more production later.[31]

Hollywood should take the problem of runaway production seriously.
But it is important to be realistic about the nature of the problem and the
options available for dealing with it. There is very little sympathy in Canada and other film-producing countries for Southern California fears of film
flight. The main reason is that, runaway production notwithstanding, the
United States still dominates the international film and television market—
and is likely to continue to do so for some time. For example, in August
1999 the Irish Film Industry Strategic Review Group reported on the situation in Europe:

U.S. films command some 80% of world market share in theatrical film and some
70% market share in television fiction. . . . American producers dominate European
distribution and screen exhibition and their European sales are incremental to the
more profitable U.S. market, where their dominance is more complete. In spite of
signs of revival and some recent successes, Europe has failed to develop products
with the same international audience appeal as the U.S. product. This has led to a
situation whereby Europe, potentially the largest and most complex market in the
world, is controlled by another market.[32]

In addition, while foreign productions may have reduced the total share
of films and television shows shot in Hollywood, the absolute levels of
production there have increased substantially over the past decade. For
example, according to the Monitor study, the number of U.S. domestic
productions increased from 507 in 1990 to 676 in 1998.[33] Moreover, according to the Entertainment Industry Development Corporation, the number of film-production days in Los Angeles (which includes commercials as
well as theatrical films and television shows) increased from 26,640 in 1993
to 46,410 in 1999.[34] This suggests that the situation is not a zero-sum
game. If, as foreign production increases, the global demand for filmed
entertainment also increases, Hollywood could prosper even if its overall
share of world production decreases. This makes it very important for regional policymakers to have a clear understanding of the forces behind
runaway production.

As the global market for filmed entertainment (and digital content, more
generally) grows, foreign production will increase. This is true for several
reasons. The tremendous growth of the market has greatly increased the
economic gains to be made from developing a competitive filmed entertainment cluster; and the transport/communications revolution has made it
easier for film producers to work in locations outside of Hollywood. In
addition, globalization has had the paradoxical effect of heightening fears
that local cultures will be "Americanized." This has given new impetus to

efforts by France, Canada, and other countries to protect indigenous "cultural industries." Most important, as discussed above, as the importance of the non-U.S. market has grown, producers are now much more concerned about making sure that their product will sell as well in the global market as it does in the domestic market. To do that they need to be close to the market, both to better understand local audience tastes and to ensure that the stories, actors, and settings they choose have the greatest possible local appeal. These considerations are becoming even more important because of the growing relative importance of the foreign television market.

Despite the worldwide popularity of such distinctly American programs as *Dallas* and *Baywatch*, foreign television viewers tend to prefer local fare. Moreover, the interest of other countries in preserving the local character of their television programming is much greater than their interest in de-Americanizing movies. Finally, because of the size of the budgets, cost considerations tend to be especially important in determining where television films are produced. For these reasons, the incentives for Hollywood studios to expand television production in other countries (either by engaging in co-production with foreign companies or building additional facilities abroad) are generally greater than the incentives for them to expand film production in other countries—and they are certain to increase.

Responding Effectively

Whether or not Southern California's interests will be hurt by the growth of foreign film production will depend much less on what the region does to prevent runaway production than on what it does to attract some of the new business that will be created by globalization, and to solidify its comparative advantages in the pre- and postproduction phases of the filmmaking process.

One of the barriers to developing effective regional strategies is the assumption that the filmed entertainment market can be divided into domestic and foreign segments. This assumption underlies the mistaken belief that Southern California's interests lie mainly in protecting the Hollywood cluster's ability to produce films and shows for the U.S. domestic market. In the Monitor Company study, the authors defined "runaway productions" as those that "are developed and are intended for initial release/exhibition or television broadcast in the U.S." but are produced in foreign countries.[35] There are several problems with this definition. It fails to take into account the fact that, even if Americans aren't the primary audience for a film, because of the global reach of U.S. media outlets, there are still powerful marketing reasons to release a film in the United States first. In addition, it fails to recognize the growing importance of the transnational segments of the global market identified above. Segments such as the worldwide Latino audience cannot be usefully broken down into domestic and foreign components. Finally, it implicitly assumes that the norm is for filmed entertainment to be developed and produced in the same country or region. Operating on these assumptions could end up limiting Southern California's ability to gain from the overall growth of global and transnational markets.

Under any circumstances, Hollywood is likely to remain a major filmed entertainment production center for the indefinite future. This is true because of its comparative advantages in workforce size and skills and production infrastructure; and because it is home to so many of the industry's leading producers, directors, and actors. One indicator of the power of these factors to override cost considerations was the decision by the producers of the popular television series *The X-Files* to move production to Hollywood from British Columbia in order to allow star David Duchovny to be closer to home.[36] Therefore, it is important not to exaggerate the threat to Hollywood from runaway production. Moreover, the comparative advantages of the Hollywood cluster in the preproduction/development and postproduction phases of the industry are actually greater than its comparative advantages in the production (filming) phases.

The importance of distinguishing between comparative advantages in production and postproduction was pointed out by UCLA regional planner Michael Storper over a decade ago.[37] In the future, however, the region's advantages in the preproduction phase may become just as important.

The key aspects of the preproduction process are creating story ideas, developing scripts, recruiting creative talent, and acquiring financing. Because of the convergences caused by digitalization, the globalization of the market for filmed entertainment, and the global dispersion of production, these functions are becoming both more important and more complex. For example, producing a film for the Spanish-language market now involves understanding audience sensitivities, production outlets, and potential marketing synergies in Spain, Latin America, and the United States. Southern California, with its combination of unrivaled experience in preproduction and its diverse and globally connected ethnic population, is ideally positioned to dominate this part of the industry in the new digital-global era.

For these reasons, the runaway production debate needs to be recast. Instead of focusing narrowly on efforts to change the economic equation that makes it more profitable to film some productions in places such as Canada and Australia, Southern California needs to pay more attention to preserving and enhancing its existing advantages in the pre- and post phases of the filmed entertainment production process. In this regard, the region's general, long-term interests might, paradoxically, be served best by accepting that some production will run away and by working, instead, to ensure that other regions do not have strong incentives to strengthen their own preproduction/development capabilities.

Ultimately, however, the most serious threat to the Hollywood cluster is likely to be posed by digitalization and the restructuring of the broader media and entertainment industry, not runaway production.

DIGITALIZATION AND THE NEW STRUCTURE OF THE ENTERTAINMENT AND MEDIA INDUSTRY

Mergers of Convergence

Technological change has always been the principal force shaping the evolution of the media and entertainment industry. The cycle though which this occurs has become a familiar one. An invention creates new ways to produce and distribute ideas, images, and information. Then entrepreneurs use the new capabilities to reach existing audiences and markets and create larger ones, often by embracing and promoting new expanded ideas of community. In this way, Johannes Gutenberg's invention of the printing press in the mid-fifteenth century, which made it possible to publish large numbers of printed books, spawned the "print-capitalists," who pushed both the Protestant Reformation and the rise of written national vernacular languages in order to create more profitable markets for their products.[38] The same dynamic occurred following the invention of the telegraph, moving pictures, the radio, the television, and, most recently, the Internet.[39] But the Internet and digital revolution is dramatically different from earlier communications revolutions.

Each of the past revolutions in communications technology created distinct media forms that evolved into their own industries. As new industries emerged, they competed with preexisting industries for audiences and advertising revenues. Sometimes, as in the case of the film industry and television in the 1950s, they became collaborators.[40] But, even when ownership overlapped, newspapers, magazines, radio, television, and movies remained largely separate businesses with their own distinctive markets and cultures. Since the early 1980s, however, the entire media and entertainment industry has been transformed.

Two waves of what are best described as "mergers of convergence" (one of which is still just beginning to break) are merging the old separate and distinct sectors of the industry. A new megaindustry is being forged. Increasingly integrated companies now create multimedia content that can be distributed and cross-promoted to all kinds of audiences, broad and narrow, on platforms—televisions, personal computers, video game players, and the like—that are becoming functionally indistinct.

The First Wave

The first wave of mergers of convergence occurred in the period stretching from 1984 to 1995. During these years, the walls separating broadcasting, publishing, and moviemaking came down. One of the most important aspects of this change was the emergence of what Thomas Schatz has called "the new Hollywood studio system." In this new system, the studios are part of "an increasingly diversified, globalized 'entertainment industry' " that is "geared to produce not simply films but 'franchises,' blockbuster-scale hits which can be systematically reproduced in a range of media forms" including movie sequels and TV series, music videos and soundtrack albums, video games, and theme park rides, graphic novels, and comic books, and an endless array of licensed tie-ins and brand-name consumer products."[41]

By the end of this first wave, in addition to being the film capital of the world, Southern California had become the headquarters of one of the world's two most influential integrated media companies (the Walt Disney Company); and a major center of operations for three of the world's most important non-American media companies (Australia's News Corporation, Japan's Sony Corporation, and Canada's Seagram Corporation). But, even before the first wave was over, a second (and potentially far more powerful) wave was beginning to swell.

The Second Wave

Whereas the first wave was driven largely by marketing synergies, the second wave is being driven by digitalization—the conversion of images, sound, and text into a stream of machine-readable bits—and the rapid growth of the Internet. Together, they are creating four different kinds of convergence.

Converging Content. The translation of written articles, pictures, music, and video into digital formats makes it possible to "repurpose" them quickly and easily for use in different media. Thus, an article written for a newspaper or a television news video can quickly be turned into a digital document that can be uploaded onto a Web site on the Internet. Similarly, a live televised speech can, almost instantaneously, be turned into a text that can be posted on the Internet and printed in a newspaper. As the new digital art form evolves, more and more content will be created in multimedia forms that can be disaggregated and repackaged depending on the desires, needs, and technological capabilities of distributors and consumers. This transformation is obliterating traditional professional distinctions such as those between "print" and "broadcast" journalists. One of the best illustrations of this is the way that Time Warner has used its acquisition of CNN to create a series of television shows and Web sites that feature stories and reporters from its leading magazines such as *Time, Sports Illustrated, Entertainment Weekly, Fortune,* and *People.*

Converging Pipes. The translation of content into digital form is also eliminating differences between the different broadband "pipes" that transmit entertainment and information to consumers. Once a product is digitized it can be transmitted over the air by satellites and cellular networks, sent through hard wires supplied by either phone companies or cable providers, or saved on a compact disc (CD), DVD, or on other portable memory devices. This is radically changing the environment in which both the companies that produce content and those that transmit content must operate. The proliferation of sources of content and transmission options has greatly increased the options available to both sides in this equation, but it has also greatly intensified the pressures on them. In order to reduce uncertainty, content producers have an interest in gaining ensured access to the "pipes" that can give them the fastest and most direct access to their audience; and the "pipe companies" have an interest in ensuring that they have a steady supply of the content that their customers want. As a result, phone companies such as AT&T are becoming media companies, and entertainment and information producers such as Disney are beginning to link up with "pipe" companies such as satellite broadcaster DirectTV.

Converging Platforms. Digitalization is also changing the ways in which consumers and users access entertainment and information. Television sets, personal computers, video game players, and telephones are competing with each other to become the preferred platform for digital content.[42] In this regard, Sony Corporation, which now manufactures a larger and wider range of digital receivers than any other company, has become a twenty-first-century digital analog of the Radio Corporation of America (RCA), a radio manufacturer that played an instrumental role in creating NBC, the first radio broadcasting network. Sony's interest in helping to create digital content is based on its desire to expand its sales of digital receivers. As the Internet revolution accelerates, companies such as the computer giants Dell and Gateway are likely to see themselves forced to join the media game in order to avoid having their products become the equivalents of black-and-white televisions in the age of color.

Converging Commerce. The digital revolution is also causing a fundamental shift in the role of the media in commerce.[43] The Internet now makes it possible for companies to target consumers much more directly than ever before. (In fact, the ability of companies to use the Internet to gather data about individual consumer preferences and buying habits is certain to be one of the major public policy issues of the coming decade.) In addition, the Internet is becoming an extremely convenient and highly efficient way for consumers to shop for and purchase goods and services. In both of these ways, e-commerce is eroding many of the old boundaries between media companies and retailers. For example, CBS no longer has to be satisfied to earn revenues indirectly by selling advertising to Sears and Kmart, it can become Sears and Kmart. Conversely, in order to protect their profits, companies such as Sears and Kmart could find themselves under pressure to develop the kinds of content-rich Web sites that will be required to attract consumers in the Internet Age.[44]

The Future

Recent examples of the industry restructuring caused by these convergences are the pending merger of America Online (AOL) and Time Warner,[45] the acquisition of The Times Mirror Company by the Tribune
Company,[46] AT&T's acquisitions of cable giant TCI[47] and Internet leader
Excite@Home[48] and its pending acquisition of cable provider Media One,
the merger of Viacom and CBS, and the acquisition of the Seagram Company by Vivendi S.A., a French water utility turned telecommunications
and entertainment conglomerate.[49] If approved by the FCC, the new AOL
Time Warner will be a global media behemoth. No other company is currently in a position to match its ability to produce a wide range of different
kinds of content, to ensure an audience for that content, and market goods
and services to that audience on a global scale. Similarly, by purchasing
the Times Mirror Company, the Tribune Company now owns a major
newspaper, a television station, and a regionally oriented Web site in the
three largest metropolitan regions in the United States—New York, Los
Angeles, and Chicago. It has made it clear that it intends to use these
resources to establish itself as a premier local content provider and an e-
commerce platform. By acquiring TCI, Excite@Home and Media One,
AT&T has positioned itself to be a dominant player in the broadband era.
Acquiring Universal Studios in the deal with Seagram will mean that Vivendi chief executive Jean-Marie Messier controls a global media empire
second only to AOL Time Warner in scope and size.

Together, these mergers will place tremendous pressure on other companies in the communications, media, and retailing industries to refashion
themselves to compete in the new economy. And, as evidenced by the May
17, 2000, announcement that Spanish telecommunications giant Terra is
acquiring Lycos, the Internet portal, the competition for control of the new
media industry is going to be truly global.[50] The end result is almost certain
to be a world of huge vertically integrated companies all competing for a
share of the rapidly growing global market for entertainment and information.

The Impact of Digitalization on Hollywood

Digitalization is changing all phases of the process of making and distributing films. Some of the changes will reinforce Hollywood's comparative advantages, but others will threaten them. Some examples of the most
important of these changes include:

• Advances in digital graphics are turning computers into virtual studios that allow
  digital artists and editors to create entire scenes and characters such as the pod

race and Jar Jar Binks in *Star Wars: Episode One*, reducing the need to film live actors on location or in studios.[51]

- The use of digital cameras and the growth in the bandwidth available to transmit video instantaneously is making it much easier for directors, editors, and their collaborators to work together even while being thousands of miles apart.
- The development of digital projection capabilities means that it will soon no longer be necessary to print and distribute physical copies of films. Instead, they will be digitally transmitted to theatres, television stations, or even individual computers via satellites, cable, or broadband phone lines.[52]

Digitalization will benefit Hollywood by enabling it to distribute films much more quickly and inexpensively all around the world. Moreover, as this capability develops, the practical and political ability of countries such as China to limit film imports will decrease. It will also enable Hollywood to disperse production activities to locations and studios around the world while continuing to concentrate postproduction activities in Southern California. Thus, as discussed above, the demand for location shoots and studio time in Los Angeles could decline substantially at the same time that the region's dominance of the postproduction and distribution process increases.

Hollywood is also being forced to adapt rapidly to the spread of the Internet. In the words of film critic Roger Ebert:

Hollywood and the Internet are on a collision course. The Internet will survive, and so will those in Hollywood who understand it. But the day of the unwired mogul is over. The movie industry has the same relationship to the Internet today that it had to talkies in the 1920s: Plug in or quit.[53]

To date, the studios have used the Internet mostly as a promotional medium. But the greatest potential lies in the use of the Internet to distribute entertainment content directly to audiences. After some delays, the studios are moving to seize this opportunity.[54] For example, last fall, DreamWorks SKG joined with Ron Howard's Imagine to back POP.com, which is designed to be a high-quality Web site devoted to providing original content programming.[55] And the Southland's Internet industry is now starting to get a boost from new Hollywood-based venture-capital firms headed by one-time senior executives in entertainment such as former agent Sandy Climan and former Universal Studios head Frank Biondi.[56] Moreover, despite its perceived difficulties, Disney's "Go.com" site is still the most visited kids and family entertainment site on the Web.[57]

There is also a possibility, however, that as the filmed entertainment process moves further into the digital age, the industry's center of gravity could shift northward to the San Francisco Bay Area. This process has already begun. In the late 1970s, after the completion of the original *Star Wars*, George Lucas moved his base of operations and, most important, his special effects company—Industrial Light and Magic (ILM)—to Marin County in the Bay Area. Over the past two decades, the Lucas Empire has grown enormously and spawned new companies, such as Pixar, which has become a leader in animated films as a result of the success of features such as *Toy Story*, *A Bug's Life*, and *Toy Story 2*.

The Lucas stimulus, and the advantages provided by close proximity to Silicon Valley, has led to the creation of a rapidly growing Bay Area digital arts cluster.[58] If, as planned, Lucas moves ILM and his other technology companies to San Francisco's Presidio and builds a new research and training center dedicated to the digital arts, the Bay Area will be positioned to mount a serious challenge to Hollywood's near monopoly in filmed entertainment.[59] Especially important in this regard will be whether digital film artists and producers around the world begin to see the Bay Area rather than Southern California as the place where one must go to "be" at the cutting edge of their industry.[60] But one indicator of the continuing value of being near Hollywood was the recent announcement by Ifilm.com, an Internet film broadcasting site launched last year, that it is moving its headquarters from San Francisco to Southern California.[61] Over the long run, however, the development that could have the greatest positive impact on the Southland's ability to establish itself as a leader in digital filmmaking is the completion of the new Disney digital studio, which was responsible for the production of *Dinosaur*.[62]

The outcome of the developing California rivalry will depend in large part on which region is best able to compensate for its current weaknesses. For the Bay Area, this means developing a greater capacity to create content. For Southern California, it means fostering the emergence of a more technologically oriented culture. But it also needs to be emphasized that this rivalry is not a zero-sum game. In fact, one of the easiest ways for the two regions to strengthen their ability to compete in the filmed entertainment market is to join forces. That is already happening at the level of individual businesses—a prime example being the relationship between Disney and Pixar and, more recently, DreamWorks SKG and Pacific Data Images, a Northern California computer animation and digital effects company that was responsible for the movie *Antz*. There have also been some efforts by industry groups in the two areas to work together. For example, the Entertainment Industry Development Corporation of Los Angeles has partnered with the Bay Area Multimedia Partnership to create SkillsNet, a workforce development consortium that seeks to link industry and educators and provide information and training to job seekers.[63]

The future of Hollywood will also depend on the competition now under way to supplant New York as the media capital of America and the world.

THE REGIONAL COMPETITION FOR LEADERSHIP OF THE NEW GLOBAL MEDIA INDUSTRY

Over the course of the twentieth century, Southern California grew enormously in wealth, stature, and influence. But Greater Los Angeles was never able to challenge the position of Greater New York City as the economic and cultural capital of America—or its claim to be the leader of the international economy. One reason was that Southern California never developed a financial community with the assets and reach of Wall Street. But equally important was the fact that almost all of the nation's most important media companies—including CBS, NBC, ABC, Time Inc., *The New York Times*, and the *Wall Street Journal*—were headquartered in Manhattan. This helped enormously in establishing, preserving, and extending New York's wealth and influence.

The Rise of New York

Four factors contributed to the emergence of New York as the media capital of America—and, eventually, the rest of the world. One of the earliest and most important was the Port of New York.[64] In the pretelegraph era, news traveled with the flow of people and goods; and by the late eighteenth century, more people, goods, and news flowed through New York than through any other city in the United States. As a result, New York media entrepreneurs were much better positioned than their counterparts elsewhere in the United States to both collect and disseminate news, especially from abroad. (The early competition among newspapers for scoops about events in Europe consisted of sending reporters on small boats out into New York harbor to meet arriving trans-Atlantic ships).

New York's early comparative advantage could have disappeared with the development of new modes of long-distance communication following the invention of the telegraph, the telephone, and the radio. It didn't, largely because the individuals responsible for those technological advances and the companies that quickly formed to exploit them concentrated in New York City and its surrounding region.[65] Examples include the Associated Press, AT&T, GE, Westinghouse, RCA, and, of course, the first two major broadcast radio networks: NBC and CBS.

The fact that New York was also the home of Wall Street and the headquarters of a disproportionate share of the nation's largest and most powerful companies and its richest foundations and museums also played a role in making the city the national media capital. Because of their presence, what happened in New York mattered to the rest of the nation much more than what happened in Chicago, or New Orleans, or San Francisco. In fact,

the only city in the country that generated as much "national" news as
New York was Washington, D.C.

A final crucial factor in the development of the region into the world's
leading media center was the leadership role played by key individuals such
as Adolph Ochs, who purchased *The New York Times* in 1896 and began
to turn it into America's most influential newspaper; RCA's David Sarnoff
and CBS's William Paley, who created network broadcasting; and Time-
Life's Henry Luce, who coined the phrase "the American Century" and
used his magazines' resources to promote the vision it represented. Other
cities had their own boosters. For example, Atlanta had Henry Grady, ed-
itor of the *Atlanta Constitution*, who spread the gospel of "a New South";
Los Angeles had General Otis and Harry Chandler, who used their *Los
Angeles Times* to sell the idea that Southern California was a new American
promised land; and "Chicagoland" had Colonel Robert McCormick and
his *Tribune*. But none of them had visions that were as grand or resources
that were as great as their counterparts in Manhattan. Nor did they have
the backing of a local firm that was as rich and powerful, or as cohesive,
as the New York establishment.

The growing influence of the New York media was also strongly self-
reinforcing. For example, by the mid-1800s the city had already developed
into a major publishing center.[66] This caused aspiring writers to flock there.
As they did, the imbalance between the writing talent found in New York
and that found in other cities widened, giving new publishers and magazines even more reason to launch themselves in New York rather than
Philadelphia, Cleveland, or any other major American city. Later, as the
radio and television industries began to develop, the talent pool created by
the attractive power of the publishing industry provided a ready source of
recruits. Another equally important way in which the city's dominant position perpetuated itself involved advertising revenue. As New York established early leads, first in magazine publishing, then in national radio
broadcasting, and finally in television, it drew advertising dollars to the
city. These revenues, in turn, allowed the New York media to make the
investments necessary to maintain and expand their audience—and bring
in even more advertising revenue. In the process, New York also became
the center of the advertising industry.

The concentration of the media industry in New York City also had a
major impact on national opinion. Beginning in the early nineteenth century, opinions expressed in Manhattan had a much greater chance of gaining the attention of the rest of the country than those expressed in other
cities. Moreover, a subtle bias developed whereby the prevailing views of
New York cultural, economic, and political elites were quickly identified
as "national" views, whereas those of their counterparts in the Midwest,
South, and Far West were far more likely to be considered "regional." This
tendency was strengthened by the fact that from the early postindependence

days forward, the leading advocates of "nationalization" were New Yorkers. In fact, of the four political figures that played the greatest role in promoting a national vision of the United States, three—Alexander Hamilton, Theodore Roosevelt, and Franklin Roosevelt—were New Yorkers. The lone exception was Abraham Lincoln.

Challenges to New York

Since the 1970s, New York's control over the media has been seriously challenged. The three most important forces causing this shift have been the enormous demographic growth of the Sunbelt, the fragmentation of the national economy, and the technological revolutions in the media caused by the advent of satellites and, later, digitalization.

Since independence, the American population has steadily flowed westward, but it was not until the 1960s that the demographic balance began to shift decisively in favor of the Sunbelt. This shift is most evident in the enormous change in the relative size of the population of the Northeast and Upper Midwest relative to the population of the South and West. As a result of this shift, audiences and markets in three states in particular— California, Florida, and Texas—have become much more important for the national media.

Income and wealth have also shifted westward. The old highly integrated national industrial economy, which was largely concentrated in a belt stretching from Greater New York to Chicago, has also broken down. It has been replaced by a new, much-more-fragmented economy with multiple centers.[67] These new centers include the metropolitan regions surrounding Atlanta, Charlotte, and Miami in the South; Dallas and Denver in the Southwest; and Los Angeles, Seattle, and San Francisco in the West. Each of these regions has its own economic base and distinctive culture—and each of them is rapidly developing its own worldview and international connections. As a result, it is now much more difficult to cover America from New York.

These demographic and economic shifts put pressure on the national media to change its priorities and broaden its coverage, but it was only after satellites and the Internet created new technological capabilities that a real opportunity to shift control of the media out of New York developed. The impact of cable television on the media landscape was especially evident in the sudden transformation of Atlanta into a major international media center following the meteoric rise of Turner Broadcasting and, especially, CNN. As CNN began to expand its coverage and its reputation, the same kind of effects that had occurred in New York when it became a major media center in the late nineteenth and early twentieth centuries began to manifest themselves. Broadcast journalists began to migrate there. Organizations such as CARE, the world's largest worldwide relief organization, moved their headquarters there. Individuals, organizations, and corporations from Atlanta and the South began to get greater national and international exposure. And Atlanta's baseball team became "America's team."

Southern California's Prospects

Southern California has long seen itself as a potential successor to New York as the capital of America and the world. As the second largest and most diverse region in the country, the Southland had the demographic and economic weight that most of the other emerging metropoles across the country lacked. Moreover, its strategic location on the Pacific Rim made it the natural center of a world economy whose center of gravity seemed to be moving westward. In fact, the connections that began to develop between Los Angeles and Tokyo as the world moved into the global epoch looked very similar to those that had developed between New York and London at the beginning of the national epoch. And, most important, Southern California had the advantage of being the headquarters of the most valuable media assets—the Hollywood studios—that weren't concentrated in New York and the only regional paper in the country, the *Los Angeles Times*, that could realistically imagine itself as a national rival to *The New York Times* and the *Washington Post*.

Southern California's challenge to New York gained credibility as a result of two mergers—the 1985 acquisition of 20th Century Fox by Rupert Murdoch's News Corp. and the 1995 purchase of Capital Cities/ABC by the Walt Disney Company. By the time that Disney purchased ABC, Murdoch's Fox Network had already established itself as a serious rival to the three original networks, whose national ratings were declining sharply. The fact that the Southland now controlled two of the nation's four major networks represented a potentially dramatic shift in the media industry. Five years later, however, the region's transformation into the new global media capital seems to have slowed.

Neither Disney nor News Corp. has seemed interested in using their acquisitions to shift the center of the media industry to Southern California. For example, neither has taken any significant steps to change the fact that the major national news shows are based in New York and Washington, D.C. Moreover, digitalization and the rise of the Internet have dramatically changed the media scene and brought an entirely new set of players into the picture. Control over old-style television networks now matters much less than control over the pipes and portals that will channel the flow of multimedia content to audiences in the future. Thus, who controls companies such as AT&T, AOL, Microsoft, and Yahoo!, and where they are headquartered, is as important as who controls the television networks and where they are located. This reality was dramatically underlined by the recent move by Time Warner to remove ABC Network programming from the offerings on its cable systems because of a dispute with Disney over fees.

Moreover, while Southern California has begun to develop a network of small- and medium-sized high-tech companies, it has not yet emerged as a major player in the new digital economy. The region has several large high-tech companies such as Ingram Micro and Computer Sciences Corporation, but they cannot rival the global technological clout of companies such as Intel, Microsoft, Silicon Graphics, Oracle, and Macromedia. Even in the area of new media, it is still far behind the Bay Area—and, to a lesser extent, New York, Boston, and Seattle. One indicator of this is the regional distribution of the membership of DiMA, the increasingly influential Digital Media Association. One Southland institution that could help to change this equation over the long run is Idealab, a business incubator in Pasadena founded by Bill Gross that has already launched more than thirty "dot-coms."

The high-tech revolution has also radically altered the financial equation in the media ownership game in ways that have not helped the Southland. The astounding rise in the stock valuation of high-tech companies generally and the new dot-com media companies in particular has given them the wherewithal to acquire the old media companies. Five years ago, it would have been considered absurd to suggest that AOL would purchase Time Warner or that Yahoo! would purchase Disney. Today, the first is a reality, and the possibility of the second has been seriously discussed. Even after the recent decline in technology stocks, the market capitalization of companies such as Microsoft and Yahoo! continues to give them enormous potential influence. The region that has gained the most as a result of the surging value of high-tech companies has been the Bay Area. In fact, because of the wealth created by the high-tech industry and its emergence as the capital of the new venture capital industry, the Bay Area is now in a position to exercise the same kind of financial influence over other metropolitan regions that New York and Wall Street have exercised in the past.

Finally, New York City, led by Time Warner, has fought back.[68] The 1989 merger of Time Inc. and Warner Communications created the first company ever to have a dominant position in filmed entertainment, publishing, and cable television. Seven years later, it greatly expanded its position in cable by purchasing Turner Broadcasting. This latter move was particularly significant because it served to ensure that Atlanta and CNN would not continue to evolve into an alternative national news center. Then, at the beginning of the new millennium, Time Warner's Gerald Levin and AOL's Steve Case shocked the media industry by announcing that AOL was acquiring Time Warner. This will create a new megamedia power with the ability to produce a greater and more diverse range of multimedia content than any other company and the capacity to distribute it through all of the most important pipes. An equally important example of the ability of New York institutions to adapt to the new environment is the way *The New York Times* has expanded its coverage of other parts of the country, especially California.

The regional stakes in the struggle for control over the media are extremely large. The probable benefits for the winner will include:

- becoming a magnet for creative talent from around the country and the rest of the world
- becoming a center of the new global, multimedia advertising industry
- gaining a much-heightened ability to shape national and global cultural, economic, and political agendas
- gaining a substantial advantage in the race to profit from the e-commerce revolution

Moreover, the rewards from winning the early rounds in this competition are likely to be self-reinforcing. For these reasons, the long-term future of Southern California's role in the new digital-global world economy will depend in large part on how its civic and corporate leaders choose to respond to the changes now underway in the media and entertainment industry.

A STRATEGY FOR SOUTHERN CALIFORNIA

Southern California's ability to develop a regional strategy to respond to digitalization and globalization is greatly limited by its growing fragmentation and lack of strong institutional leadership. Despite the myth that it didn't exist, "downtown" Los Angeles has been largely responsible for boosting and directing the region's growth. In recent years, however, its role has been weakened by the decline or departure of major corporations that had been headquartered in Los Angeles, the growing push by affluent parts of the city to break away and form their own independent municipalities, and, more recently, the sale of the *Los Angeles Times*. This trend makes the future of Southern California's media and entertainment industry more important than ever.

Throughout most of the twentieth century, a deep cultural chasm separated "Hollywood" from "downtown." While the fate of Los Angeles and its filmed entertainment colony were inextricably intertwined in the public mind, Hollywood executives were never integrated into the informal networks that guided the region in the same way that media executives in Manhattan were integrated into the networks that guided Greater New York City. In the past, this separation wasn't a major cause for concern. Southern California benefited tremendously from the film industry's presence without needing (or necessarily wanting) its participation in regional governance. But that is no longer the case.

The Need for Regional Leadership

As the regional economy has been transformed from one based on aerospace, oil, and traditional manufacturing into one that is increasingly based on entertainment and high-tech, it has become much more urgent that Hollywood assume a leadership role in the region. For better and worse, the ability of the Southland to realize the dream of becoming "Tech Coast"[69] will depend largely on its ability to use the comparative advantages created by its filmed entertainment cluster to compete with Silicon Valley, Greater Seattle, and other metropolitan regions in attracting the individuals and companies who will shape the new digital-global economy. Moreover, the decline of the old downtown networks and visions that guided the region has created a void that can be filled only by the development of networks and visions that include the new Hollywood. As indicated by their efforts to promote the entertainment industry and revitalize Hollywood, Los Angeles Mayor Richard Riordan and other civic leaders clearly recognize the need for a new relationship between Hollywood and downtown—and they are already working hard to create it.

The possibility of a new civic partnership has been greatly enhanced by changes in the character of both the media and entertainment industry and the region's old governing elite. The new Hollywood represented by the Walt Disney Company, News Corp., Sony Entertainment, and Dream-Works SKG is much different from the old Hollywood. Vestiges of the old Hollywood culture described by Carey McWilliams more than fifty years ago remain.[70] But, as a result of the changes in the ownership of the studios and the character of the entertainment industry that occurred as a result of the first wave of mergers of convergence described above, Hollywood now looks, thinks, and acts much more like the old New York media giants. At the same time, the Southern California civic and corporate community has become much more diverse and open. Small indicators of these shifts include the growing civic prominence of Hollywood moguls such as Michael Eisner and David Geffen and the fact that the president of the Los Angeles Dodgers, a team that was closely associated with old downtown interests during the O'Malley era, is Robert Daly, a former head of the Warner Bros. studio.

Over the long run, however, the emergence of a new coalition that includes the region's old downtown establishment, the leaders of its rapidly growing and newly influential ethnic communities, and the new Hollywood will depend on the ability of these groups to coalesce around a new vision of Southern California and its place in the emerging digital-global economy. A good place to begin efforts to develop such a vision would be with a regional dialogue on the future of the filmed entertainment industry and the broader challenges of securing the Southland's emerging position as a global center of the new media industry.

It is beyond the scope of this chapter to recommend a comprehensive strategy to protect Southern California's filmed entertainment industry and promote the region's role as a global media center. The best and ultimately only way to develop an effective strategy and build support for it would be to engage the region as a whole from the start. But it is possible to outline three elements that will need to be a part of any successful effort.

Capitalize on Diversity

Southern California needs to use its ethnic and cultural diversity to strengthen its comparative advantages in the preproduction phases of the filmed entertainment industry and, more broadly, to make the region an even more important influential force in the new global media market.

One of the original sources of Hollywood's ability to understand and capture the hearts and minds of the American audience was the fact that, for most of the twentieth century, Southern California was the national melting pot. From the 1920s until the late 1960s, immigration into America slowed. But in the same period, there was a tremendous migration of people from different parts of the country to Southern California. As a result of this migration, the region's population more closely mirrored the diversity of the rest of the nation than any other place in the country. This made it an ideal place to identify and test the "national" appeal of ideas, images, and themes and hence to create filmed entertainment for the American mass audience. Today, as a result of the immigration over the past three decades from around the world to Southern California, the region is probably the best place in the world to identify and test the "global" appeal of ideas, images, and themes and to create filmed entertainment for the mass audiences of the world. There are, in fact, very few important segments of the new global audience that are not represented in the Southland.

Emphasizing the connection between the cultural and ethnic diversity of Southern California and the ability of media companies based there to reach global markets could help to build regional cohesion in a number of ways. It gives the media and entertainment industry a major economic reason to identify with the region and seek to develop closer relationships with Southland communities. At the same time, it gives ethnic and other globally minded groups in the region a reason to see the industry as an important potential ally in efforts to both create twentieth-first-century jobs for their members and connect with their kith and kin in other parts of the world. The potential in this area is most evident in the way that South Florida has taken advantage of its strong Latin cultural connections to position itself as the media capital of Latin America. The difference in Southern California is that, given its ethnic diversity, it can aspire to be a major media capital of almost every ethnic diaspora in the world. By doing a better job of integrating the region's different ethnic communities (and the global connections and sensitivities they bring with them) into the filmed entertainment cluster, Hollywood could greatly protect itself against potential competition from other metropolitan regions. Similarly, the region's aspiring global television networks and Internet portals would greatly increase their ability to reach into markets abroad by making use of the cultural connections and language abilities of these groups.

Actions that could be taken in this area include:

- Educational institutions such as the School of Cinema-Television at the University of Southern California (USC), the School of Film, Theatre and Television at UCLA, the American Film Institute, and the Academy of Entertainment and Technology at Santa Monica College should work with ethnic and immigrant organizations to develop training programs that prepare students to take advantage of the new opportunities that are being created by the growth of the global market for entertainment and increases in foreign production.
- Regional institutions such as the Norman Lear Center of the Annenberg School of Communication at USC or the Entertainment Industry Development Corporation of Los Angeles should examine the role that ethnic and immigrant communities in Southern California can play in helping to build linkages between the region's media and entertainment industry and their homelands.
- Regional media companies such as the Walt Disney Company and News Corp. should enlist the support of ethnic and immigrant communities to develop content for the global market, and they should consider ways to use their Internet sites as tools to increase connections and communication between those communities and their homelands.

Establish Global Partnerships

One of the most unfortunate effects of the "runaway production" debate is that it serves to create conflict between Southern California and other film-producing regions. This has been especially true with regard to relationships between the Southland and Canada's film centers in British Columbia and Ontario. As argued in previous sections, these conflicts are based on the mistaken assumption that film-producing regions are engaged in a zero-sum competition. Because of its unique advantages in the pre- and postproduction parts of the industry, Hollywood is especially well positioned to benefit from the overall growth in the market for filmed entertainment, even if its share of actual production declines. Conversely, attempts to get the local, state, and national governments to provide economic subsidies for domestic production are unlikely to succeed. And even if they did, it is far from certain that they would significantly reduce runaway production. A better regional strategy would be one that concentrated on helping to expand global demand for filmed entertainment, and developing synergistic relationships with other film-producing regions. Instead of seeking to discourage the development of film industries in other countries, the Southland should seek to carve out a role for itself as the filmed entertainment industry's center of advanced development and innovation, and as a vital partner for other regions seeking to develop their own production capabilities.

Actions that could be taken in this area include:

- City, county, and regional officials responsible for economic development and the Motion Picture Association of America should engage educational institutions, professional groups such as the Directors Guild and the Screen Actors Guild, and local ethnic and immigrant communities in a concerted effort to develop closer cultural, economic, and professional ties with key regions around the world. They should establish programs that would build lasting connections between the Hollywood cluster and the nascent entertainment and media clusters in those countries. (An extremely promising example of this kind of initiative is the new on-line global film school that has been jointly organized by the Australian Film Television and Radio School in Sydney, Australia, the National Film and Television School in London, England, and the UCLA School of Theater Film and Television in Los Angeles.[71])

- The City of Los Angeles could take the lead in creating a global network of film-producing regions that would meet regularly to discuss ways to promote the worldwide growth of demand for filmed entertainment. Such a network could seek to play a leading role in the emerging debates on efforts by companies to deny content producers and distributors access to the broadband pipes that will carry digital content to audiences in the future, on international protection of intellectual property rights, and on other issues that will affect the long-term profitability and growth of the entertainment industry.

Build Bridges to the Bay Area

As argued above, digitalization and the continued concentration of the media industry in New York City represent the greatest potential threat to Southern California's dominant position in the filmed entertainment industry. By changing the production and distribution process, digitalization could reduce the comparative advantages of the Hollywood cluster and make it possible for a region such as the Bay Area with its technological advantages to shift the center of power within the entertainment industry. By exercising control over the distribution and delivery of content, media giants based in New York (or eventually foreign centers such as London, Berlin, or Tokyo) could channel the development of e-commerce and limit the ability of the Southland's entertainment companies to reach global audiences. Both of these possibilities could threaten Southern California's long-term economic interests. There are a number of things that regional actors could do to counter this potential threat. One of the most important is to put even greater effort into developing the technological base of the regional economy.

But the best way for Southern California to protect its interests and ensure that it is prepared to compete in the new global economy would be to work with the Bay Area to develop a coordinated regional strategy. Combining the human resources, economic wealth, global connections, technological advantages, educational resources, and creative capabilities of the Southland and the Bay Area would ensure that California (and the Pacific West more generally) will be the capital of the new digital-global economy. However, creating such a regional axis would not be easy. It would require a concerted effort to overcome long-standing rivalries, deep cultural differences, and the fragmentation of both regions. But the potential rewards from doing so are substantial enough that the effort should be made.

A good place to start to build a new California global partnership would be for state and regional leaders in Southern California and the Bay Area to create a task force bringing together key individuals from government, industry, academia, media, and the independent sector to develop strategies to ensure that the state becomes the headquarters of the new digital media industry.

NOTES

1. Carey McWilliams, *Southern California: An Island on the Land* (Santa Barbara, CA: Gibbs Smith, 1973), 377.

2. Joel Kotkin, "Slow Fade in the Studios," *Los Angeles Times*, 6 August 1995, Sunday Opinion.

3. James Bates, "In Local Economy, Hollywood Is Star," *Los Angeles Times*, 18 January 1998.

4. John Cassidy, "The Comeback," *The New Yorker*. California Issue, 23 February & 2 March 1998.

5. Joel Kotkin, "Runaway Productions Pose Challenge for Hollywood," *Los Angeles Times*, 25 April 1999, Sunday Opinion.

6. Greg Miller and Karen Kaplan, "GO.com Turns from Web Portal Strategy," *Los Angeles Times*, 28 January 2000; and Richard Waters, "Go.com's Losses Climb as Hits Fall," *Financial Times*, 10 February 2000.

7. James Bates, "DreamWorks Kills Studio Plan for Playa Vista," *Los Angeles Times*, 2 July 1999.

8. Michael Ventura, "A City as Envisioned by a Newspaper," *Los Angeles Times*, 19 March 2000, Sunday Opinion; James Sterngold, "In Los Angeles, Tears and a Feeling of Loss," *Los Angeles Times*, 14 March 2000.

9. Jill Leovy, "Show Business Fills the Aerospace Employment Gap in Burbank," *Los Angeles Times*, 18 January 1998; Steve Scott, "The Morphing Econ-

omy," *California Journal*, July 1997. For an attempt to estimate the overall economic impact of the entertainment industry, see Motion Picture Association of America, *State of the Industry: The Economic Impact of the Entertainment Industry on California* (Los Angeles, CA: The Motion Picture Association of America, 1998).

10. Thomas Schatz, "The Return of the Hollywood Studio System," in Eric Barnouw et al., *Conglomerates and the Media* (New York: The New Press, 1997).

11. Michael Porter, "Clusters and the New Economics of Competition," *Harvard Business Review*, November-December 1998; Michael Storper, *The Regional World* (New York: The Guilford Press, 1998); Anna-Lee Saxenian, *Regional Advantage* (Cambridge: Harvard University Press, 1994); and Sir Peter Hall, *Cities in Civilization* (Laguna Niguel: Pantheon, 1998).

12. Porter, "Clusters," p. 80.

13. On the nature and comparative advantages of the Hollywood film production cluster, see Storper, *The Regional World*, Chapter 4; James Bates, "Making Movies and Moving On," *Los Angeles Times*, 19 January 1998; and Anthony Vagnoni, "Escape from New York: Commercial Production Moves West," *The Hollywood Reporter*, 1989, Commercial Production Special Report.

14. The literature on globalization is enormous and growing. For an optimistic account, see Thomas Friedman, *The Lexus and the Olive Tree* (New York: Farrar, Straus, Giroux, 1999). For a pessimistic account see William Greider, *One World: Ready or Not* (New York: Simon & Schuster, 1992).

15. The study of the process of nationalization in America that is most useful in terms of providing a way to understand the current process of globalization is Robert Wiebe, *Search for Order* (New York: Hill and Wang, 1967).

16. On the Sony acquisition of Columbia Pictures, see Paul Farhi and Stuart Auerbach, "Reports of Bid by Sony Raise Questions," *Washington Post*, 27 September 1989.

17. The new corporate and foreign ownership of the global media and entertainment industry does raise some very important political issues. But these issues are beyond the scope of this chapter.

18. For a critical study of the "globalization" of the media and entertainment industry, see Edward Herman and Robert McChesney, *The Global Media: The New Missionaries of Global Capitalism* (New York: Cassell, 1997).

19. Frances Cairncross, *The Death of Distance* (Boston: Harvard Business School Press, 1967).

20. Richard Parsons, President, Time Warner, October 1997.

21. For up-to-date box office statistics see http://www.worldwideboxoffice.com. For current reports on the success of U.S. films overseas see http://www.cinema1.com/intlbox/.

22. See John Dempsey and Chris Pursell, "Int'l Players Singing Soprano in Big Easy," *Variety*, 31 January–6 February 2000.

23. For an argument that the motion picture industry's increased dependence on foreign films is actually killing "the American Film" see David Kirpen, "Planet Hollywood: The Death of the American Film," *World Policy Journal*, Summer 1997.

24. On the history of U.S. film exports, see Martin Dale, *The Movie Game: The Film Business in Britain, Europe and America* (New York: Cassell, 1997); Ian Jarvie, *Hollywood's Overseas Campaign: The North Atlantic Movie Trade, 1920–*

1950 (New York: Cambridge University Press, 1992); and Kristin Thompson, *Exporting Entertainment: America in the World Film Market, 1907–34* (London: BFI Publishing, 1985).

25. Cynthia Littleton, "Webs Play Cross-Lingo Bingo," *Variety*, 15–21 March 1999.

26. On runaway production see Nick Madigan, "H'WOOD FIGHTS THE JITTERS," *Variety*, 1–7 February 1999; Nick Madigan, "Runaway Productions: Looking for Answers," *Filmcrew*, Issue 26, 1999; and Nick Madigan, "Flight or Fight: Industry Gears up to Keep Production in Area," *Variety*, 22–28 November 1999.

27. Jeffrey Gettleman, "Trying to Keep the Movies from Moving," *Los Angeles Times*, 20 January 2000. See also Ryan James, "Action Heats Up in Film Biz War," *The Toronto Sun*, 29 August 1999.

28. Directors Guild of America and the Screen Actors Guild of America, *U.S. Runaway Film and Television Production Study Report*, July 1999, 9. (http://www.sag.org/PDF/runawayALL.pdf).

29. Andrew Pollack, "Rising Costs Pushing Film Production Abroad," *The New York Times*, 25 June 1999.

30. *U.S. Runaway Film and Television Production Study Report*, 23.

31. Ibid., 23–24.

32. Film Industry Strategic Review Group, *The Strategic Development of the Irish Film and Television Industry*, 2000–2010, August 1999 (http://www.iftn.ie/strategyreport/).

33. *U.S. Runaway Film and Television Production Study Report*, 2.

34. Entertainment Industry Development Corporation, *EIDC Annual Report 1998–1999*, 1.

35. *U.S. Runaway Film and Television Production Study Report*, 2.

36. Keith Marder, "THE TRUTH IS OUT HERE; 'THE X-FILES' GROOVIN' AFTER MOVIN' TO L.A.," *The Daily News of Los Angeles*, 8 November 1998.

37. On Hollywood's comparative advantages in postproduction, see Stephanie Argy, " 'Only in L.A' Is Worldwide Post Opinion," *Variety*, 17–23 November 1997. See also Michael Storper and Susan Christopherson, *The Changing Organization and Location of the Motion Picture Industry*, Research Report, Graduate School of Architecture and Urban Planning, UCLA, October 1985.

38. Benedict Anderson, *Imagined Communities*, rev. ed. (New York: Verso, 1991).

39. Brian Winston, *Media Technology and Society: A History from the Telegraph to the Internet* (New York: Routledge, 1998).

40. Christopher Anderson, *HollywoodTV* (Austin: University of Texas, 1994).

41. Schatz, "The Return of the Hollywood Studio System," 73–74.

42. For an insightful assessment of the battle between PCs and TVs, see Joan Van Tassel, "Pandora's Boxes," *The Hollywood Reporter*, 26 November 1997.

43. Carl Shapiro and Hal Varian, *Information Rules* (Boston: Harvard Business School Press, 1999).

44. Miguel Helft, "Clicks-and-Mortar Superstores," *The Industry Standard*, 17 April 2000.

45. On the details of the AOL Time Warner merger, see Steve Lohr, "Media Megadeal: The Behemouth," *The New York Times*, 12 January 2000. On the possible implications of the merger for Southern California and the Pacific West, see

Mike Clough, "AOL Time Warner: A Merger That Puts New York On Top," *Los Angeles Times*, 16 January 2000; Deborah Kong, "California-Based Excite@Home Gets New Competition from AOL," *San Jose Mercury News*, 12 January 2000.

46. On the details of the Tribune's acquisition of Times Mirror, see Sharon Walsh, "Tomorrow's Merger Today," *Washington Post*, 14 March 2000. On the possible implications of the sale for Southern California and the Pacific West, see Michael Clough, "Voice of the West," *San Jose Mercury News*, 19 March 2000, Sunday Perspective.

47. Steve Lohr, "Media Convergence," *The New York Times*, 29 June 1998.

48. Sallie Hofmeister, "Excite@Home Deal Gives AT&T Control," *Los Angeles Times*, 30 March 2000.

49. Peter Goodman, "Europe's New Media Titan," *Washington Post*, 23 June 2000.

50. Hiawatha Bray, "Lycos Acquired in Global Internet Deal," *Boston Globe*, 17 May 2000.

51. See *Cinefex*, Issue 78, July 1999.

52. "Curtains for Celluloid," *The Economist*, 27 March 1999.

53. Roger Ebert, "Sites, Camera, Action," *YAHOO Internet Life*, April 2000.

54. For examples of the ways in which Hollywood is beginning to use the Internet to distribute films, see Andrea Basora and Bilge Ebiri, "The Net Wave," *YAHOO Internet Life*, April 2000.

55. Marc Graser, "Pop Stakes Online Reel Estate," *Variety*, 1–6 November 1999.

56. Robert LaFranco, "Faces of a New Hollywood," *Red Herring*, April 2000. See also Joel Kotkin, "L.A. Joins the Venture-Capital Revolution with a Vengeance," *Los Angeles Times*, 23 January 2000, Sunday Opinion.

57. See http://disney.go.com/pressinfo/dol/releases/200125.html.

58. For an overview of the Lucasfilm Empire and its contributions to the development of the digital arts, see http://www.lucasfilm.com/history_top.html; and http://www.thx.com/history/index.html. On the growing influence of Lucasfilm spin-off Pixar in digital animation see Marc Graser, "Pixar Run by a Focused Group," *Variety*, 20 December–2 January, 2000.

59. On Lucas' plans to establish a digital arts complex at the Presidio, see Mike Clough, "Lucas Strikes Back," *Los Angeles Times*, 11 July 1999, Sunday Opinion. See also http://www.lucasfilm.com/presidio/.

60. For a relatively optimistic assessment of the ability of Southern California to compete in the digital arts, see Allen J. Scott, "Multi-media and Digital Effects: An Emerging Local Labor Market," *Monthly Labor Review*, U.S. Department of Labor, March 1998; and Allen J. Scott, *From Silicon Valley to Hollywood: Growth and Development of the Multimedia Industry in California*. Working Paper No. 13 (UCLA Center for Regional Policy Studies), 1995.

61. Greg Miller, "Internet Movie Firms Shift Focus to L.A." *Los Angeles Times*, 25 January 2000.

62. See David Ansen and Yahlin Chang, "Building a Better Dinosaur," *Newsweek*, 15 May 2000.

63. See http://www.skillsnet.net.

64. Robert Albion, *The Rise of New York Port* (New York: Charles Scribner's Sons, 1939).

65. Menahem Blondheim, *News over the Wire* (Cambridge, MA: Harvard University Press, 1994); Winston, *Media, Technology and Society*.

66. Edwin G. Burrows and Mike Wallace, *Gotham: A History of New York City to 1898* (New York: Oxford University Press, 1999).

67. On the regionalization of the American political economy, see Michael Clough, "Birth of Nations," *Los Angeles Times*, 27 July 1997, Sunday Opinion.

68. On the growth of the Time Warner empire, see David Lieberman, "Levin Deals Himself In, Again," *USA Today*, 17 January, 2000.

69. For an articulation of the "Tech Coast" vision, see "Tech Coast," *Los Angeles Times*: Business, 9 March 1998.

70. McWilliams, *Southern California*, Chapter XVI.

71. See http://www.tft.ucla.edu/filmtv/.

3

The Wolf at the Door: Hollywood and the Film Market in China

Stanley Rosen

"If only 1% of the people go and you only charge one-fiftieth of the admission that you'd charge here, you still get to some pretty big numbers," said Logsdon, who estimated that Hollywood would reap tens of millions of dollars from a more open Chinese market early on.[1]

"Who knows if they will enforce it? The way things work over there, negotiations are incredibly protracted. They could not cooperate with you and you wouldn't even know it." [A studio official at MGM who spoke on condition of anonymity on his reaction to a Chinese ban on cooperation with three Hollywood studios. The ban stemmed from a memo from China's Ministry of Radio, Film and Television that singled out *Seven Years in Tibet* (Columbia Tristar), *Kundun* (Disney) and *Red Corner* (MGM/United Artists) as films that "viciously attack China [and] hurt Chinese people's feelings."][2]

The quotations above neatly encapsulate the hopes, uncertainties, and disappointments of the Hollywood studios in their dealings with China. The market beckons, as always, but the Chinese government's "interference" in the market, often seen as arbitrary if not "inscrutable," continues to prevent Hollywood from "reaping" the profits Logsdon predicted.

INTRODUCTION

By the early 1990s the Chinese film industry was facing a serious crisis. According to one source, attendance at Chinese theaters had dropped from 21 billion in 1982 to just under 4.5 billion in 1991.[3] Compounding the

problem, new entertainment options began to flower following Deng Xi-
aoping's "Southern Tour" in early 1992. Karaoke bars, discos, video parlors, pirated videos, and other previously restricted forms of leisure were
providing intense competition to Chinese cinemas.[4] Desperate for a solution
to the problem, yet unwilling and unable to relax ideological restrictions
forbidding the sure-fire Western formulas of sex and violence, the authorities introduced a series of limited measures in 1992. Zhang Yimou's films
Judou and *Raise the Red Lantern* had their bans lifted. A large-scale film
festival held in Changchun awarded Zhang's new film, *The Story of Qiu
Ju*, its highest award, and leading party officials, to show their support,
arranged a well-publicized preview in the Great Hall of the People.[5]

It was only after the 14th Communist Party Congress in October 1992,
however, that a number of "capitalist-style" reforms aimed at decentralizing the marketing and distribution of films were introduced in an effort
to revive the film industry. Key central documents issued in 1993 (Document No. 3) and 1994 (Document No. 348) are considered the start of the
structural reform of the Chinese film industry. Although the new regulations provided no panacea and many problems still remained, these documents began to break the distribution monopoly of the China Film
Corporation, allowing Chinese film studios to distribute their films through
local units.[6]

As the audience for mainland films was falling dramatically, Hong Kong
videos and laser discs began to flood the market. With inflation running as
high as 20 percent in the major cities in 1992–1993, and state support less
and less forthcoming, China's film professionals were compelled to adopt
new strategies—for example, to look abroad for finance, to attract co-
productions financed through Hong Kong, or to produce and direct television series—in an effort to survive. Indeed, as one informed observer
noted, the larger studios in Beijing and Shanghai were surviving only by
turning themselves into service centers for productions financed from Hong
Kong or Taiwan.[7] In his yearly summary for *Variety* Derek Elley noted that
domestic film production fell in 1993 by 50 percent (in terms of movies
screened); attendances fell by 60 percent; box office grosses fell by 35 percent; and rentals fell by 40 percent.[8] The Chinese film market—from
production to exhibition—was "in desperate need of major long-term investment."[9]

Hollywood's time had finally come. Years of discussions had always met
with firm Chinese resistance to go beyond a willingness to accept a small
number of Hollywood films each year for a flat fee of $30,000–$50,000
per film.[10] In the new, market-driven environment, however, the China Film
Export and Import Corporation, which controls all imports, announced
that China would release ten "excellent" foreign films a year, on a revenue-
sharing basis. Even Xinhua, the official government news agency, gushed

that "an end is in sight to the 40-year-old tradition of buying out-dated and low-grade but cheap foreign movies."[11]

This chapter examines Hollywood's relationship with China from the first imported "megaproduction" (*dapian*—*The Fugitive*—which opened in Beijing on November 12, 1994) until late summer 2000. Over the course of almost six years and forty-six imported American films, the relationship has ebbed and flowed, with alternating periods of optimism and pessimism on each side. In the complex account to follow, however, several conclusions will be documented. First, despite the obvious problems that have marked and continue to affect the relationship, Hollywood and the Chinese film industry will remain locked in an uneasy embrace. By all indications, they appear to need each other. Second, Hollywood was invited in at a time when the Chinese film industry was facing a dire crisis; questions were being raised about its very survival. By summer 2000, with China's imminent entrance to the World Trade Organization on the horizon, the Chinese media were raising similar questions about the survival of the Chinese film industry. One well-known director entitled his article on the future of Chinese film, "To Be or Not to Be?"[12]

Third, the relationship might well be described by the familiar Chinese idiom, *tongchuang yimeng* (same bed, different dreams). Hollywood's long-term aspirations for its initiatives in China are clearly very different from China's expectations. Indeed, one could persuasively argue that Hollywood's dreams are China's fears. But while Hollywood's intentions may be frightening to Chinese authorities, since there is a reasonable possibility that they could succeed, China's intentions—the most important of which is to have a reciprocal relationship under which Chinese films are distributed in significant numbers in the United States—is a clear nonstarter. Fourth, the debate on how to save the Chinese film industry is a fascinating one, contrasting a variety of strategies suggested and implemented by some of China's leading directors and producers. A key issue in this debate is the role of the Chinese government, with some participants arguing that the film industry cannot survive in the absence of government protection, and others suggesting that government intervention in the film industry is precisely the problem.

Related to this, and most fundamentally, the move toward a market economy has confronted the Chinese government with a serious dilemma and a basic contradiction. Moreover, this dilemma has consistently revealed the familiar division between film bureaucrats and film professionals. Since the reforms began there has been an on-going tension between two often-contradictory goals. On the one hand there is the need to "administer" film production to ensure the release of politically desirable films, what the Chinese call "main melody films" (*zhu xuanlu*). On the other hand, there is the need to release films that can succeed in the market.[13] Hollywood films have been successful in China because of their entertainment value. For

Chinese films to compete successfully they will also have to provide an acceptable level of entertainment. Yet, as an important recent circular jointly issued by the State Administration of Radio, Film and Television and the Ministry of Culture made very clear, the "basic task of the film industry" remains building a "socialist spiritual civilization." It must be ensured that "social benefits are given primary consideration" over "economic results."[14] Thus, film professionals are likely to continue to be constrained in their ability to compete for Chinese audiences. Faced with the new specter of WTO, their frustration appears particularly acute.[15]

HOLLYWOOD IN CHINA, THE EARLY YEARS: 1994–1995

The opening of *The Fugitive* (*wangming tianya*, or "Fleeing to the Ends of the Earth" in Chinese) on November 12, 1994, in six Chinese cities was hailed in both the Western and Chinese press as "an event of historic significance" and a great box office success.[16] Equally important for our purposes, many of the problems and contradictions that have plagued the film market in China can be seen in embryo form during the "run" of *The Fugitive*. These include the conflict between economics and ideology, the issue of intellectual piracy, and the struggle among bureaucratic agencies to control the profits of Hollywood productions.

Within a week of the film's opening to packed houses the movie was suddenly withdrawn in Beijing with various official and unofficial explanations offered. The official *China Business Times* reported that the film was withdrawn because some film industry officials believed it would allow foreign distributors to "invade" China's movie market.[17] Other sources reported, more precisely, that the problem stemmed from a struggle between the Beijing Film Distribution Company and the China Film Import and Export Corporation over the rights to proceeds from the film. China Film had booked the movie directly with Beijing theaters, bypassing the local distributor. When the local Beijing distributor lost the battle it took the matter to its parent unit, the city's Cultural Bureau, and to the Central Propaganda Department, claiming that the film violated Chinese political mores, that in fact showing the film was the equivalent of "using socialist money to fatten the capitalist pig."[18] In fact, throughout June and July 1994 the Chinese press debated the impact of the importation of ten blockbuster Hollywood films on the Chinese film industry and on Chinese society more generally, with various film industry professionals suggesting the advantages and disadvantages of this decision.

The more immediate matter of *The Fugitive* was resolved when the Film Bureau within the Ministry of Radio, Television and Broadcasting issued Document No. 348 (mentioned above), to take effect on January 1, 1995, allowing the authorized distributor to deal directly with Chinese cinemas, thereby opening up the distribution market.[19] By mid-January 1995 *The Fugitive* had reopened in Beijing with much fanfare in the local press.[20]

Such blatant ideological appeals in defense of socialism against the encroachment of Western capitalist products were soon to be limited primarily to the remnant leftist media. While a considerable number of American movies were indeed vetoed by China Film—or more often not even submitted by the studios because of the likelihood of a veto—once a film was accepted the main concern became box-office receipts. However, politics has always been a factor in the relationship. The success of the studios in gaining approval for their films and even the assessment of the films in the Chinese media has been dependent on a studio's "sincerity" toward China and, in extraordinary circumstances, on the larger issue of Sino-American relations. The most obvious examples, to be discussed below, are the bans on Columbia Tristar, MGM, and Disney for their *American* films with Chinese themes in 1997, the debate over Disney's *Mulan*, and the total ban on American films following the bombing of the Chinese Embassy in Belgrade in May 1999.

The Fugitive was also plagued by the now-familiar problem of intellectual piracy. Copyright violations of American films and music recordings had been an issue in Sino-American relations even before Warner Bros. had reached an agreement for Chinese cinemas to show *The Fugitive*. According to industry estimates, Chinese theft of copyrighted products such as films and compact discs totaled around $800 million annually. The Motion Picture Association of America (MPA) and the record industry had been pushing the Clinton administration to slap China with a "Special 301" designation, thereby branding it as a blatant intellectual property abuser. Such a designation might then result in quick retaliation against Chinese goods entering the United States. However, as the administration was reviewing the then-annual decision on China's "most-favored-nation" status in 1994, the decision was made to extend the deadline from April 30 to June 30, in an effort to reach a solution with the Chinese government. It was a process that would be repeated often in subsequent years.[21]

Hollywood took heart, however, in June when U.S. trade representative Mickey Kantor put China on the Super 301 watch list of countries suspected of tolerating theft of intellectual property, effectively giving it six months to enforce copyright. This was followed by a landmark decision by a Chinese court in favor of a copyright infringement suit filed by the Walt Disney Company against a publisher of children's books. The publisher was found guilty of illegally publishing and distributing books based on Disney animated films featuring such characters as Mickey Mouse, Cinderella, Peter Pan, and Snow White.[22]

The Chinese government, however, ironically soon found itself identifying with Dr. Richard Kimble, the protagonist of *The Fugitive*, when it was accused of permitting at least three state-run cable television stations in southern China to broadcast the film. In addition, it was clear that the pirated videos being shown derived from one of twenty-nine Chinese factories known to be producing illegal copies of American products, ranging

from cornflakes to blockbuster films. China Film denied authorizing duplication, distribution, or broadcast rights of *The Fugitive* to any company
or individual. Suggesting that intellectual property rights were new to
China and some cable operators may not have been aware they were breaking the law, China Film—the state import monopoly—issued a notice in
Renmin ribao calling for tough action against the Chinese bootleggers.[23]
But the damage had been done. As successful as it was, pulling in 25.8
million yuan at the box office, *The Fugitive* was far less successful than it
would have been had it not been withdrawn from Beijing theaters in November and had it not been widely pirated and shown on Chinese cable
television. It remained for the second American film, *True Lies*, starring
Arnold Schwarzenegger, to fulfill the promise in 1995 suggested by *The
Fugitive*.

By November 1994 Hong Kong's Golden Harvest Entertainment had
signed a deal to release the first Hong Kong film in China, also on a
revenue-sharing basis. Jackie Chan's *Drunken Master II* was chosen with
a release date set for December 10. Equally significant, Golden Harvest
announced that Jackie Chan's *Rumble in the Bronx* would be released simultaneously in mainland China, Hong Kong, and Taiwan during the
Spring Festival (Chinese New Year) 1995, in an effort to minimize piracy
and maximize the box office.[24] The stage was set for Hong Kong and Hollywood to compete for the potentially lucrative China market.

Having learned the lessons of *The Fugitive*, Chinese authorities went to
great efforts to support those first two imported megaproductions of 1995.
Each was overwhelmingly successful and thus contributed greatly to a revival of the Chinese film market. The success of these films also triggered
a renewed debate in the film industry about protecting national cinema,
one that continues today as China prepares to join the WTO. The impact
of *Rumble in the Bronx*, particularly in Guangzhou (Canton), can hardly
be overestimated. This was the first time that Jackie Chan fans—and they
are legion in China—could see their favorite hero on the big screen rather
than on the blurred monitors of video parlors. Box-office receipts during
the two-week run in Guangzhou amounted to 3 million yuan, far surpass-
ing those gained from the rampantly pirated *Fugitive*, and breaking all box-
office records up to that time. In Beijing as well, now seemingly free of
bureaucratic squabbles, a new and carefully planned marketing strategy
was employed and *Rumble in the Bronx* brought in 5.16 million yuan
during the Spring Festival.[25]

True Lies followed quickly, opening in Beijing on April 20, and eventually bringing in 102 million yuan nationally, a total succeeded in subsequent years only by the massive success of *Titanic* in 1998. Although
Forrest Gump, the third American import in 1995, was a relative failure,
almost all the Hollywood imports in 1995 and 1996 were successful at the
box office, as can be seen in Table 3.1.[26] It was clear that imported films

Table 3.1

Box Office Receipts for American "Megafilms" (Dapian) in China

FILM TITLE	PRODUCTION COMPANY/ DISTRIBUTOR	Renminbi (millionyuan)* (BOX OFFICE IN CHINA)
1994		
1 The Fugitive	Warner Bros.	25.8
1995		
2 True Lies	United International Pictures (UIP)**	102.0
3 Forrest Gump	UIP	19.6
4 The Lion King	Disney	41.3
5 Speed	20th Century Fox	37.8
6 Bad Boys	Columbia Tristar	32.8
7 Die Hard 3	Edko	47.0
1996		
8 Outbreak	Warner Bros.	32.6
9 A Walk in the Clouds	Fox	20.5
10 The Bridges of Madison County	Warner Bros.	39.5
11 (Broken Arrow)	Fox	50.5
12 Waterworld	UIP	34.0
13 Toy Story	Disney	31.8
14 Jumanji	Columbia Tristar	47.7
15 Twister	UIP	54.5
16 The Rock	Disney	47.7
17 Mission Impossible	UIP	45.1
1997		
18 Sabrina	UIP	20.0
19 Eraser	Warner	45.8
20 Courage Under Fire	Fox	25.0
21 Space Jam	Warner	24.1
22 Dante's Peak	UIP	47.6
23 Jurassic Park: The Lost World	UIP	72.1
24 Speed 2	Fox	30.4
1998		
25 Batman and Robin	Warner	20.0
26 Volcano	Fox	17.8
27 Titanic	Fox	359.5

Table 3.1 (continued)

28 Daylight	UIP	15.9
29 Home Alone 3	Fox	40.2
30 Deep Impact	Dreamworks/CJ	51.3
31 Saving Private Ryan	UIP	82.3
1999		
32 Rush Hour	New Line	25.0
33 Mulan	Disney	11.0
34 Enemy of the State	Disney	22.0
35 Star Wars, Episode 1: The Phantom Menace	Fox	33.0
36 Tarzan	Disney	11.0
37 Entrapment	Fox	29.0
2000		
38 The Matrix	Warner Brothers	17.0
39 Stuart Little	Sony	20.8
40 Double Jeopardy	UIP	15.0
41 The General's Daughter	UIP	21.0
42 Mickey Blue Eyes	Polygram	6.0
43 U571	Canal+/Summit***	
44 Dinosaur	Disney	
45 Gladiator	UIP	
46 Mission Impossible II	UIP	

* One U.S. dollar is equivalent to around 8.2 Chinese yuan (RMB).
** UIP distributes films for Universal, Paramount, and MGM.
*** U-571 was released by Universal in the United States but was distributed abroad by Canal+/Summit.

Source: Interviews conducted in China.

had become essential to the survival of the Chinese film industry. Already by 1994, imports had brought China Film 60 percent of its $12 million revenue. Total box office receipts in the first half of 1995 jumped 50 percent over the same period a year earlier, and summer attendance at theaters in Beijing had increased by 70 percent. Moreover, the success of the imports carried over to domestic releases; the crowds were beginning to return to Chinese cinemas.[27]

THE MARKET "MATURES": HIGHS (*TITANIC*) AND LOWS (BANS AND LOW PROFITS) AMID CONTINUING UNCERTAINTIES

Hollywood's Successes

Despite a variety of administrative measures aimed at controlling unbridled market forces, imported films have taken a majority share of the Chinese market. One well-placed interviewee in the Chinese film bureaucracy suggested that the ten imported revenue-sharing films occupied 70 percent of the market, leaving the remaining 30 percent for the 100 or more domestic films. The problem the Chinese government faces stems, in large part, from the contradictions noted in the introduction to this chapter. The Chinese film industry cannot survive unless filmgoers in relatively large numbers can be enticed to pay their own way into a theater to watch domestic films. Yet the film industry in China represents far more than a means for entertaining the public. Film, as Lenin pointed out long ago, is essential for building support for the government and properly socializing Chinese citizens. Politics and commerce therefore have often collided in the 1990s. Unless the government has taken draconian measures—for example, the outright bans on American films and/or film studios discussed below that left no recourse—film industry professionals have generally been able to skirt official regulations that interfered with market forces. When market forces have not been impeded, Hollywood films have been most successful. When administrative regulations have been most forcefully implemented, Hollywood films have been denied market share.

One important example of the government's efforts to control the market is the "Regulations on the Management of Films," issued as Document No. 200 by the State Council on 29 May 1996, after it had become clear that Chinese films could not compete with imported films without governmental support. Article 45 of the Regulations mandates that at least two-thirds of the total time given to exhibiting films in theaters must be reserved for domestic films. Theater operators, however, have routinely violated this regulation.[28]

Hollywood's domination of the market is of course a recent phenomenon. Before the opening of China's film market to imported megaproductions the public's knowledge of foreign films came primarily from old movies seen on television and on video, as well as from stories in newspapers and magazines. The explosion in knowledge about the outside world since 1995, particularly in the area of popular culture, has been remarkable. A good example of this can be seen in the changing popularity of film stars in China over the past five years. Tables 3.2, 3.3, and 3.4 provide survey data on the most popular foreign and domestic film stars. Table 3.2 comes from a survey conducted by Horizon Survey Company and *Beijing Youth Daily* in May 1995. The survey was entitled "The World in the Eyes of the Chinese" and asked 1,050 respondents in five major cities to compare foreign countries with China on a range of measures.

One question asked participants to list their favorite foreign movie star. Although 74 actors were listed, the largest number of respondents—44.8 percent of the sample—gave no response. Of the top ten names on the list, seven were American or foreign actors who had become world famous as a result of their American films, showing Hollywood's influence even before the large influx of imported theatrical films. There were also two Japanese and one Frenchman on the list. Looking more closely one is struck by how

Table 3.2
Most Popular Foreign Film Stars in China (Five Major Cities, May 1995,
N=1,050)

FILM STAR	PERCENTAGE
Sylvester Stallone (U.S.)	7.7
Alain Delon (France)	7.0
Marilyn Monroe (U.S.)	4.7
Charlie Chaplin (U.S.)	4.0
Ingrid Bergman (Sweden-U.S.)	2.7
Yamaguchi Momoe (Japan)	2.3
Shirley Temple (U.S.)	2.0
Arnold Schwarzenegger (U.S.)	1.5
Vivien Leigh (U.K.-U.S.)	1.3
Takakura Ken (Japan)	1.3

Source: "Zhongguo ren yanzhong de shijie," in Horizon Research Company and State Statistical Bureau, eds., *Guancha Zhongguo* (Observing China), (Beijing: Gongshang chubanshe, 1997), p. 39.

many of the actors were no longer working, or in some cases even living. Although Sylvester Stallone came at the top and Arnold Schwarzenegger came in eighth—*True Lies* had opened shortly before this poll—virtually all the other names on the list, including the non-Americans, had been popular in previous decades.

Tables 3.3 and 3.4 come from a more recent survey of junior and senior high students in five coastal cities, conducted from July to October 1999. Table 3.3 asked the students to list their favorite international film star. Hong Kong and Hollywood dominate the list. Hong Kong superstar Jackie Chan is the clear favorite of the students. However, since *Rumble in the Bronx* was reedited for the American market in 1996, he has become widely known in North America as well. Indeed, recent films such as *Rush Hour* and *Shanghai Noon*, both widely seen in China, have made him a Hollywood star in his own right. Of the top fifteen names on the list, five are Hong Kong actors and eight are Hollywood actors. Chow Yun-fat and Jet Li, of course, have also made the move to Hollywood.

Table 3.4 is from the same survey and lists the most popular domestic movie stars of the high school students. The results are of interest for several reasons. First, the number of students who had a favorite domestic film star is far lower than the number who had a favorite international star. The fifteen names on the list of international stars total 71.4 percent of the student responses; the fifteen names on the list of domestic stars total only 26.1 percent. This strongly suggests that the large majority of the students

Table 3.3
Favorite Foreign Movie Stars of High School Students (Junior and Senior High, Five Coastal Cities, July–October 1999, N=1,589)

FILM STAR	PERCENTAGE
Jackie Chan (H.K.)	18.6
Arnold Schwarzenegger (U.S.)	8.1
Sylvester Stallone (U.S.)	7.0
Leonardo Dicaprio (U.S.)	6.3
Chow Yun-Fat (H.K.)	6.2
Tom Cruise (U.S.)	5.2
Maggie Cheung (H.K.)	4.4
Steven Chiau (H.K.)	3.4
Vivian Leigh (U.S.)	2.6
Jet Li (H.K.)	2.2
Alain Delon (France)	2.0
Kashiwabara Takashi (Japan)	1.6
Kate Winslet (U.S.)	1.4
Tom Hanks (U.S.)	1.2
Gene Kelly (U.S.)	1.2

Source: *Xun Cool Yidai* (Looking for the Cool Generation), *Horizon Research Report*, Beijing, December 15, 1999, p. 57.

surveyed do not have a favorite domestic film star, and that they greatly prefer films made outside China to those made on the mainland.

A closer look at the list in Table 3.4 reveals even more strikingly the serious problems faced by China's film industry. Of the top five names on the list—representing almost half of all student votes for "domestic" (*guonei*) film stars—three are from Hong Kong (Gu Tianle, Steven Chiau, and Jackie Chan) and one is from Taiwan (Yu Xiaofan). Moreover, even the one bona fide mainland star on the list—Zhao Wei—made her reputation as the star of an enormously popular television series called *Huanju gege* rather than as a film actress. Indeed, several other names on the list—for example, Taiwan actress Lin Xinru and Taiwan actors Su Youpeng and Chen Zhipeng—also became well known as a result of this television series (although Su and Chen had also been popular as part of a singing group). The series itself, a fanciful tale that takes place in the Qing emperor's household, was written by Taiwan writer Qiong Yao and has been criticized on the mainland for distorting Chinese history. It is only in sixth and seventh place on the list—at 1.6 percent of the votes—that one finds certifiable

Table 3.4
Favorite Chinese Movie Stars of High School Students (Junior and Senior High,
Five Coastal Cities, July–October 1999 (N=1,589)

FILM STAR	PERCENTAGE
Zhao Wei (Mainland)	4.5
Gu Tianle (H.K.)	2.3
Yu Xiaofan (Taiwan)	2.2
Steven Chiau (H.K.)	2.0
Jackie Chan (H.K.)	1.9
Ge You (Mainland)	1.6
Gong Li (Mainland)	1.6
Wang Yan	1.5
Liu Pei (Mainland)	1.5
Lin Xinru (Taiwan)	1.4
Chen Zhipeng (Taiwan)	1.2
Shu Qi (H.K.)	1.1
Su Youpeng (Taiwan)	0.9
Jet Li (H.K.)	0.8
Zhang Fengyi (Mainland)	0.8
Zheng Yijian (H.K.)	0.8

Source: *Xun Cool Yidai* (Looking for the Cool Generation), *Horizon Research Report*, Beijing,
   December 15, 1999, p. 57.

mainland film stars Ge You and Gong Li. The Chinese press has frequently
noted the inability of mainland stars to compete, even in China, with their
Hollywood and "Greater China" counterparts. One report noted that
China's "box office superstars are pitifully few in number," suggesting that
"Gong Li stands alone, as her screen lovers are invariably unhandsome,
'ugly,' or 'jokester' stars." The report concludes, somberly, that another
famous Chinese actress, Ning Jing, "also stands in lonely isolation, because
she does not have a male partner who is a young and skilled actor; many
of her screen lovers are handsome 'foreign devils' "[29]
   Hollywood's influence and success can also be seen in the vast changes
in the availability of popular literature about American films and film
publications more generally. High-gloss film magazines with far better production values than their American counterparts now introduce the latest
Hollywood films and movie stars each month, selling out quickly on news-
stands. *Dianying shijie* (English title: *The Movies Show*) and *Kan dianying*

zuopin (English title: *Movie View*), published in Changchun, Jilin province and Chengdu, Sichuan province respectively, are widely considered the best of these new publications. Each issue comes with a full-color poster of a recent American film and is filled with enticing visuals, statistical data, and the latest information (and gossip) on Hollywood personalities. It would be difficult to publish such an opulent film magazine in the United States because of the prohibitively high production costs. These more recent publications, selling for 10 yuan (less than $1.25), have taken over a substantial part of the market from more traditional film magazines, such as the venerable *Dazhong dianying* (*Popular Cinema*), now struggling to reinvent itself and expand its coverage of Hollywood product in order to compete.

Popular Cinema was first issued on 16 June 1950 and has long been one of the best-selling periodicals in China. Although it was closed down from 1966 to 1979, as were virtually all "reader-friendly" magazines because of the "Cultural Revolution," by 1981 the circulation for each issue was again in the millions. In some places, local post offices had to impose a quota system to limit the number of subscribers.[30] *Popular Cinema* was also well known for sponsoring the annual "One Hundred Flowers Film Awards." Started in 1962, this award gave movie fans all over the country the opportunity to vote for their favorite films and film stars. At its height the issue that carried the ballots for the award had a circulation of 9.6 million copies. As late as 1989, a record high 2.3 million ballots were collected.

The fate of *Popular Cinema* is a good indication of the fate of Chinese cinema more generally. Only about 30,000 ballots were reportedly collected for the "22nd One Hundred Flowers Film Awards" in 1999, including both the printed and Web-based voting outlets.[31] Indeed, one Chinese source reported that only 20,000 ballots were cast in 1996.[32] Circulation for an average issue as of 1998 was 308,333, still making it one of China's leading periodicals, but this is a far cry from its previous prominence.[33] Indeed, according to interviewees, its relatively low cost, large institutional subscription base, and name recognition have kept it afloat, albeit under increasing pressure to adjust to new market conditions.

Undoubtedly Hollywood's greatest success in China, as it was virtually everywhere, was the performance of *Titanic* at the box office. As Table 3.1 makes clear, the success of *Titanic* has dwarfed all other films in China, imported or domestic. Its box office of 359.5 million yuan was more than triple the second most successful film, *True Lies*, which brought in 102 million yuan. This success has been reflected in surveys on audience preferences. One survey, for example, asked 1,500 residents eighteen years old and older in Beijing, Shanghai, and Guangzhou to list their favorite imported film. *Titanic* was chosen by 35 percent; *True Lies* came in second, albeit with only 1.6 percent. No other imported film scored higher than 0.7 percent. Indeed, when respondents were asked in the survey to choose their favorite domestic film, none reached the level of 6 percent.[34] The success of *Titanic* and its potential lessons for Chinese films was also a frequent topic for discussion in Chinese film journals.[35]

Hollywood's Continuing Frustrations

The roots of Hollywood's current disappointment with the film market in China can be found in the (recent) past, the present, and the (imagined) future. There is frustration with the gap between what executives feel *could be* and what is; with the continuing uncertainties of doing business in an environment in which the rule of law is still in its early stages, and law (including the "law" of the market) is often superseded by political and cultural considerations; and by unhappy experiences in which American films have been banned or in other heavy-handed ways prevented from succeeding in the marketplace. Some of the constraints have been based on general administrative regulations or bureaucratic infighting, as was noted above in discussing the fate of *The Fugitive*; others have stemmed from specific political decisions related to the larger issue of Sino-American relations. While Hollywood has understandably devoted its efforts to persuading China to alter its restrictive regulations—often indirectly by lobbying the U.S. government to include its demands in trade packages— the Chinese government has demonstrated forcefully, on several occasions, that Chairman Mao's familiar dictum that "politics takes command" (*zhengzhi guashuai*) still remains relevant on selective occasions.

We will begin with the formal and informal administrative constraints that mark China's policy toward the film industry and Hollywood's efforts to ease such constraints. Following that we will turn to specific examples of governmental intervention in the film market for imported films. The most important cases have been the ban on three leading American studios in 1997 after each released an "anti-China" film, and the ban on the showing of any American films following the bombing of the Chinese Embassy in Belgrade in May 1999. But perhaps the most revealing case concerns Disney's *Mulan*, which the studio felt was ideal for the Chinese market. The reception of *Mulan* in China is worthy of more detailed discussion, since its lack of success at the box office and later vilification in the press are closely related to the themes addressed in this chapter. Among other problems, *Mulan* offers an example of the importance of timing; the film fell victim to both the 1997 ban and the outrage that accompanied the 1999 bombing. However, a full discussion of the *Mulan* case is a separate issue.

Administrative Constraints

The importance of the China market to the American film industry was clearly demonstrated during the congressional debate over granting China

Permanent Normal Trade Relations (PNTR). As that debate was reaching a climax in the first half of 2000, the film industry brought out its biggest guns. A new lobbying group called the China Trade Relations Committee was established and included the top executives from the seven major American film studios. Coordinated by MPA CEO Jack Valenti—who had traveled to China numerous times in an effort to pry open the market—the committee included CEOs and other top officials from Disney (Michael Eisner), MGM (Alex Yemenidjian), Sony (John Calley), Universal (Edgar Bronfman, Lew Wasserman, and Ron Meyer), Warner Bros. (Gerald Levin and Barry Meyer), Viacom/Paramount (Sumner Redstone), and 20th Century Fox (Rupert Murdoch).[36]

What was most striking, however, was the massive effort undertaken for a market that annually accounts for about $20 million, roughly the size of the return from Peru, and less than a studio might take in on one modest film in the United States. To further put this figure into perspective, MPA statistics reveal that the total foreign box office for American films in 1998 was close to $7 billion. In addition, U.S. government figures suggest that film revenues from China are among the smallest in Asia, less than in Singapore, Malaysia, Thailand, or the Philippines.[37]

The explanation for such seemingly puzzling behavior, of course, can be found in the often-repeated mantra that China is the largest, potentially most lucrative market in the world, and normalizing trade relations is critical to developing it. As one prominent China specialist put it, in supporting Hollywood's effort, "It's a necessary step, a historical step along a protracted, tortuous path that will have many setbacks. But it's better to be on this path than not be on it."[38]

What, then, is Hollywood's plan for developing this market and how has the recent PNTR/WTO trade agreement furthered these aspirations? Before addressing these questions, it is useful to list some of the market entry barriers that Hollywood feels has restricted its success. Among the most important are the following: (1) the monopoly over imported films exercised by the China Film Corporation; (2) the prohibition Hollywood studios face in distributing their films directly; (3) restrictions on foreign investment in the film industry; (4) the informal quota that limits the number of imported films each year; (5) the structure of the taxation/import duty regulations that imposes a variety of fees and taxes on imported films; and (6) censorship.[39]

Some of these obstacles are more easily negotiable than others and the trade agreement has provided the studios some limited success in several areas, particularly with regard to quotas and investment. First, Hollywood has sought to increase the informal quota on imported films from the current ten per year to as many as the market will bear. As Table 3.1 revealed, the largest number of imported Hollywood films in any year thus far has been nine, although that number will likely be exceeded by the end of 2000.

Second, Hollywood would like to invest millions of dollars in cinema construction, particularly the building of modern multiplexes.[40] Perhaps the
most important Chinese concession is an increase in the number of films
China will allow under the current revenue-sharing agreement from ten to
twenty. Again, to put this figure into some perspective, it should be noted
that this number includes movies from all countries outside China, including Hong Kong, and that the number of films released into theaters each
year in the United States by studios and independent film companies is
around 500. In the initial negotiations Hollywood had sought a quota
closer to forty films a year. A second concession allows foreign companies
to own 49 percent of Chinese cinemas. This was an important issue for
Hollywood executives, since it is believed that the construction of additional cinemas will eventually create pressure on China to let in more foreign films. Currently there is one movie theater for every 122,000 Chinese,
compared with one for every 8,600 Americans. However, even assuming
that such expectations are met, American investors will still be subject to
decisions made by the majority partner, a government agency. And, as was
noted above, economic results are still considered subordinate to social
effect, and the basic task of the film industry remains the building of a
socialist spiritual civilization.

Perhaps equally important, given current ticket prices, it is simply not
possible for many Chinese families to afford an evening at the movies when
an imported American film is showing. The cost of a ticket to see *Saving
Private Ryan* in Beijing, to take one example, ranged from 30 to 60 yuan.
Such a family outing can easily cost more than 10 percent of a family's
monthly income. Given the alternative of pirated video compact discs
(VCDs) costing no more than eight yuan—albeit of admittedly far inferior
quality—many families simply watched the film at home. This problem has
affected attendance for Chinese films as well. Surveys have shown that the
major reason for the decline in film attendance may well stem from the
economics of the market. When four VCDs can easily be purchased on the
street for 10 yuan, one can watch between five and twenty films at home
for the same amount it costs to see one movie in a theater, and afterward
one can exchange the discs with other people. Indeed, by the summer of
2000 the situation had become even more serious for American films. Not
only were many films not available theatrically—such as *American
Beauty*—easily available on VCD, but the most popular American films
distributed theatrically in China had all become easily available on DVD
as well, with far better quality than the VCDs. Even older films unavailable
on DVD in the United States—such as the *The Godfather* and *Star Wars*
series—can be purchased in this format in China.

This issue is likely to remain contentious for the foreseeable future. Indeed, after the Emei Film Corporation in Sichuan Province announced on
3 November 2000 that it was lowering ticket prices to 5 yuan for both

domestic and imported films in the 15 cinemas it controlled in Chengdu—beginning with the American blockbuster *The Perfect Storm* (*Wanmei fengbao*)—long lines began to form outside these theaters. While theaters in Shanghai and Beijing generally found this strategy foolhardy, many supporters thought it contained the seeds of the solution to China's post-WTO problems. The debate continues to rage and has been widely reported in the Chinese press.[41]

Other key issues that prevent Hollywood from realizing its China dreams were not addressed in the agreement. For example, the revenue-sharing agreement allows the foreign studios, after payment of taxes, fees and duties, only about 13 percent of the box office. Thus, even a massive hit like *Titanic*, which took in around $44 million at the box office, generated well below $10 million for 20th Century Fox. Nor has China Film been willing to abandon its monopoly over distribution, although a leading official at the China Film Corporation conceded in an interview that it will be difficult to maintain the monopoly indefinitely and that Hollywood might be able to forge an agreement in another five years that would allow for more direct distribution of their films.[42] In addition, a variety of administrative regulations, including blackout dates for foreign films during key holiday periods such as Chinese New Year, continue to hinder films such as *Mulan*, which was not released in China until after students had returned to schools and viewers who were most enthusiastic had already seen it on pirated video compact discs. Censorship, not surprisingly, is also nonnegotiable. Indeed, even in pre-1949 China, when 90 percent of the films shown were of American origin, government censors not infrequently banned American movies considered "offensive" to Chinese culture.[43]

Specific Political Interventions

In 1997 Chinese authorities strongly objected to three American releases because of their alleged "anti-China bias." Although the three films—MGM's *Red Corner*, Sony/Columbia/Tristar's *Seven Years in Tibet*, and Touchstone/Disney's *Kundun*—were never intended for distribution in China, the release of these films in the United States and other world markets was enough to produce a ban on the importation of any films from these studios. Bai Ling, the lead actress in *Red Corner*, a film starring Richard Gere as an American businessman framed for a murder in China and then subjected to the draconian Chinese legal system, came in for particular vilification in the Chinese press. Shanghai's *Wenhui bao* accused Bai Ling, a graduate of the Xian Film Studio, of betraying China "in order to get into A-rated films."[44]

To get these bans rescinded, the studios had to convince the Chinese government of their "sincerity," often requiring, among other things, a high-level trip to China by a delegation headed by the company's CEO, as in the case of MGM, which finally had its ban rescinded late in 2000. The other two studios, much more heavily invested in the China market, were successful in getting their bans lifted much earlier. Disney in particular, with its plans for China including theme parks and other large-scale ventures, and with *Mulan* released in 1998, undertook extensive damage-control efforts to get the ban rescinded.

On the eve of the release of Martin Scorsese's *Kundun,* a film about the early years of the Dalai Lama, Disney hired Henry Kissinger to help explain the company's rather awkward position to his Chinese friends. Disney's position was awkward in part because both Warner Bros. and Universal, also with substantial interests in developing the China market had, despite Scorsese's reputation as perhaps the leading American film director, rejected the film.[45] Disney's efforts to return to China's good graces culminated in a trip to Beijing in October 1997 by CEO Michael Eisner in which he met with senior Chinese officials, including propaganda chief Ding Guan'gen. China has long criticized Hollywood for sending American cultural products to China while—at least in the view of Chinese officials—refusing to distribute and promote Chinese cultural products in the United States. Eisner pleased his hosts by agreeing to distribute two Chinese films in the United States and sponsoring a Chinese acrobatic troupe in Europe. In a letter to Disney shareholders on 8 December, Eisner described how impressed he was with the success of the ubiquitous McDonald's in the China market, noting that he was "completely confident that the Chinese people love Mickey no less than Big Mac."[46] Despite these efforts, the ban on Disney films was not lifted until February 1999, at which point *Mulan* was finally released in China.

Far more serious was the ban on the showing of any American films from May to October 1999. This proved devastating to Chinese theaters, already having a very poor year even before the embassy bombing. Many were reported on the verge of bankruptcy. Overall, the film market declined 50 percent compared to 1998.[47] A number of film critics also used these results to refute those who argued that audiences would not see Chinese movies as long as American imports were showing. Even in the absence of the American films, audiences were simply not interested in going to see Chinese films.[48] But the Chinese government once again showed that commercial considerations were secondary to political imperatives.

What was particularly interesting in the aftermath of the embassy bombing was the change in press coverage of American films, with the vilification in print lasting for around four months. *Beijing Youth Daily (Beijing qingnian bao),* for example, indicted the American film industry for its complicity in paving the way, culturally, for American hegemonic interests. The most successful movies in the Chinese market—including *Titanic, Saving Private Ryan,* and *Star Wars Episode I: The Phantom Menace*—were all seen as so-called main melody films (*zhu xuan lu*), a term often used for Chinese films that further the government's propaganda mission. These

movies were sent abroad for the purposes of cultural and economic imperialism, presenting a worldview supportive of the United States and dominating commercial markets, thereby driving out domestic films. At the
same time, the *Beijing Youth Daily* went on, in the United States movies
like *Red Corner* would aid American authorities in creating an anti-China
tide within their own market.[49] This theme was repeated in other
publications as well. The leading trade journal for the film industry—*China
Film Market* (*Zhongguo dianying shichang*)—published an article entitled
"Drawing Aside Hollywood's Veil" in which the author laments the fact
that American films have become so crucial to the survival of the Chinese
theaters. Attacking virtually every genre of American film, including science
fiction, gangster, war, and romance, the author concludes that it is necessary to "expose and conduct . . . class repudiation of the hypocritical hu-
manism of such films, which make people who watch a few of them
prostrate themselves before American society."[50]

The themes of hypocrisy and the hidden agenda deeply embedded in
American cultural products were common ones at this time. One critic,
adopting the title of the second most successful American film in China,
wrote of "the vivid language of hegemony" (*huoyu baquan*) as a "true lie"
that characterized American films and the "American spirit." The American
hero always must represent the "will" of mankind, including freedom, justice, and equality. American films shown in China, such as *Speed*, *Water-
world*, and *True Lies*, were cited as examples, although *Independence Day*,
too patriotic for the Chinese censors to approve as a theatrical release but
available nevertheless in China's thriving marketplace and discussed in detail in film magazines, came in for particular censure. The author concluded
that Hollywood films were like opium. Once entering the imaginary world
of the film the viewer underwent a form of hypnotherapy and was no
longer capable of rational judgment.[51]

Another critic saw an "invisible hand" (*kanbujian de shou*) behind the
"dreamland" *(menghuan)* presented by Hollywood. He lumped Hollywood
films with such other American icons as Coca-Cola and McDonald's as
links in a chain carrying American cultural imperialism throughout the
world, eventually taking over the minds of the target audiences. In Hollywood's formulation every region of the world has its special characteristics.
Africa is presented as a barbarian land with many wild animals, while Asia
is a land of spies and opium smokers. The only paradise is the United States
itself, the land where beautiful dreams really do come true.[52]

Not surprisingly, critics also went after the easiest target, reinterpreting
Mulan, which before the bombing had received generally good reviews.
Writing in *Popular Cinema* one critic indignantly complained about "the
Americans' disfigurement of Chinese history, their lack of understanding of
the Chinese environment, their eternal inability to understand Chinese cul-
ture, and their skewed comprehension of the Chinese people."[53] The

scatter-shot attack on the film ranged from the "scandalous" (Mulan jumps on the emperor, hugs him, and swings him around) to the bizarre (Mulan is said to look "Vietnamese" but it is also claimed that no characters in the film look "normal"). Finally, the author concluded that the film's disrespect for Chinese cultural traditions is "unforgivable, as was the bombing of our embassy in Yugoslavia, no matter what highfalutin diplomatic excuses they cook up."[54]

CONCLUSION

Hollywood films entered the China market at a time when the Chinese film industry was desperate for an immediate stimulus and long-term investment in a market that had been on a steady decline. After almost ten years it is still too early to offer a prognosis. Has Hollywood saved the Chinese film industry or further damaged it? With WTO entrance now close at hand, these issues are currently under intense debate in the Chinese press. In particular, industry professionals are examining various strategies to compete with the Hollywood product. While a detailed analysis of these strategies must be left for another time, it is useful to conclude by examining in brief the current state of the Chinese domestic film industry and some of the competing proposals being presented.

First, everyone acknowledges that the large majority of films produced in China lose money. Indeed, 70 percent of Chinese-made films each year fail to recover their copyright and printing costs. Perhaps as many as 15 percent are able to show some profit, although even this figure is questioned by some Chinese interviewees.[55] Table 3.5, which reports on the box office figures for Chinese films from 1997 to 1999, is indicative of the difficulties most films have in finding an audience. In all three years, the majority of Chinese films brought in less than 1 million yuan (about $120,000) at the box office, in most cases much less. In 1997 and 1998 only a few films were able to reach the 10 million yuan mark, and some of those were clearly "main melody films" subsidized by the organized purchase of group tickets by state organs. Of most interest for our purposes are the results for 1999. The average production cost of each domestic film that year was 3 million yuan, although many high-profile films were of course much more expensive to produce. On average each film earned 600,000 yuan, although if one factors out the four most successful films, the average take for the remaining films that year was 300,000 yuan.[56] Still, as many as eight films that year attained box-office results of at least 10 million yuan. Among the most successful films we can find in microcosm the main competing strategies of Chinese filmmakers.

The number-one film for 1999 was Feng Xiaogang's *Bujian busan* (*Be There or Be Square*). Feng has been completely unabashed in his desire to beat Hollywood at its own game, to make only commercial films that au-

Table 3.5
Box Office Figures for the Top 40 Chinese Films in 1997, 1998, and 1999

1999

Top 2 films: Exceeds 30 million Renminbi (RMB)
Number 3: Exceeds 20 million RMB
Numbers 4-8: Around 10 million yuan
Numbers 9-13: Around 5 million yuan
Numbers 14-20: Just above 1 million yuan
Numbers 21-40: Below 500,000 RMB

1998

Top 3 films: Around 10 million RMB
Numbers 4-10: Exceed 5 million RMB
Numbers 11-13: Exceed 3 million RMB
Numbers 14-16: Exceed 1 million RMB
Numbers 24-40: Below 400,000 RMB

1997

Top 5 films: Exceed 10 million RMB
Numbers 6-7: Exceed 3 million RMB
Numbers 8-14: Exceed 1 million RMB
Numbers 25-40: Below 200,000 RMB

Table 3.5 (continued)

Notes:
1. No figures were provided for numbers 17–23 in 1998 and numbers 15–24 in 1997.
2. One U.S. Dollar is equivalent to approximately 8.2 RMB.
3. The top 2 films in 1999 were Feng Xiaogang's *Bujian Busan* (Be There Or Be Square) and Zhang Yimou's *Yige Dou Buneng Shao* (Not One Less).
4. The top 3 films for 1998 were Fu Hongxing's documentary *Zhou Enlai Waijiao Fengyun* (Zhou Enlai's Diplomatic Troubles), Feng Xiaogang's *Jiafang Yifang* (Party A, Party B), and Ye Ying's *Hongse Lianren* (A Time To Remember).
5. The top 5 films in 1997 were Xie Jin's *Yapian Zhanzheng* (The Opium War), Feng Xiao-ning's *Hong Hegu* (Red River Valley), Wei Lian's *Da Zhuanzhe* (The Turning Point), Zhang Yimou's *Youhua, Hao Hao Shuo* (Keep Cool), and Lei Xianhe and Kang Ning's *Likai Leifeng De Rizi* (The Days Without a Hero).

Source: For 1999, see *Dianying Yishu* (Film Art) no. 3, 2000, pp. 4–5; for 1998, see *dianying yishu* (Film Art) no. 3, 1999, pp. 4–5; for 1997, see *Dianying Yishu* (Film Art) no. 3, 1998, pp. 4–5.

diences will pay their own money to see. He has thus far made three highly successful films and, despite some critical vilification in the Chinese press regarding the "vulgarity" of his aesthetic, Feng's strategy has thus far been the most successful at the box office.[57] One difficulty Feng has faced is the regional appeal of his films, marked as they are by the extensive use of Beijing slang. They have been much less successful outside the north, for example in Shanghai or Guangzhou.

The second most successful film in 1999 was Zhang Yimou's *Yige dou buneng shao* (*Not One Less*). Zhang of course is the leading "Fifth Generation" filmmaker. His films often win prestigious international awards but have faced outright bans (for example *To Live*) or critical displeasure at home. While *Not One Less* was chosen best film at the Venice International Film Festival—after being snubbed at Cannes because of its allegedly progovernment propaganda—it represents a departure for Zhang. He is unlikely to continue making films on similar themes (an uplifting tale of a temporary teacher at a poor village school who will go to any lengths to prevent even a single dropout). Moreover, given Zhang's international reputation, and his previous problems with government censors, his financing normally is obtained abroad. *Not One Less*, as with many recent Zhang Yimou and Chen Kaige films, was supported by Columbia/Tristar. As with Feng Xiaogang, Zhang has been a frequent contributor to the Chinese press, offering suggestions for post-WTO strategy. Each of these leading directors has been forthright in criticizing the other's approach.

The third most successful film in 1999 was *Bao lian deng* (*The Lotus Lantern*), an expensive animated film that China hopes will be able to compete internationally with Japanese anime and the best of Disney animation. Leading Chinese actors, including Jiang Wen and Ning Jing, voiced the major characters. Moreover, voices were dubbed in Japanese and English at considerable expense in an effort to tap into these major overseas markets. The story is based on Chinese mythology and resonated well with local audiences, but the film is unlikely to be successful beyond China's borders.

Finally, the fourth most successful film in 1999 was *Guoge* (*National Anthem*), a good example of a "main melody film" that glorifies wartime patriotism, self-sacrifice, and other sterling virtues. *Guoge* represents the type of film the state would like to promote, both domestically and internationally (it was one of five films chosen by the government to show as part of an exhibition of Chinese films in the United States in 1999). Putting aside the fact that box-office receipts were inflated by subsidized ticket purchases, the film still brought in only 15 million yuan, despite winning major national awards. According to Kang Jianmin, the head of the Xiaoxiang Film Studio that produced the film, *Guoge* cost 20 million yuan. Indeed, the studio produced three films that won major national awards in 1999 at a cost of 24 million yuan, but received only 5 million yuan as their share of the total box office. The loss for the studio from their three most "successful" films totaled over 18 million yuan. Although a number of factors were cited for this outcome, the most fundamental problem was that people simply were not interested in seeing these films. As Kang put it, "we emphasized ideology and art and did not pay attention to the entertainment factor."[58]

This issue of art versus politics versus commerce is likely to remain the biggest obstacle to the development of a commercial market that can compete with Hollywood films. Much of the debate and criticism regarding the failure of domestic films to find an audience starts from this premise. Perhaps the most extreme example of this problem—and one pointed to by frustrated film professionals—concerns the movie *Kong Fansen*, a film depicting the life of a deceased Han cadre who devoted many years to improving conditions in Tibet and the betterment of Sino-Tibetan relations. It proved to be the biggest box office success in 1996, pulling in 30 million yuan. An analysis of the box office from twenty regions suggests, however, how misleading box-office figures can be. Nationally, only 5 percent paid their own way into theaters; in Beijing the figure was 0.5 percent; in Sichuan it was 0.2 percent.

As the number of Hollywood films entering China increases to twenty, thirty, or forty per year, will domestic films maintain a reasonable share of the market? The results from other markets are of some interest. In Taiwan, a formerly thriving film industry has been completely decimated. Despite having some of the world's most honored directors, including Hou Hsiaohsien and Edward Yang, Taiwan films simply have provided no competition to Hollywood in their domestic market. In Hong Kong, one of the world's great film markets and a major exporter of films to other Asian markets, the results appear to have been a bit better, since the top two box-

Table 3.6
Domestic Film Share of Market in Selected Film-Producing Countries

COUNTRY	1988	1994	1998
France	38.97%	35%	28%
Italy	20% (1989)	15%	n/a
Germany	16.7%	10.35%	9.5%
Japan	21%	16.7%	36%

Source: Zheng Dongtian, "Shengcun, haishi huimie: jinru WTO yihou de zhongguo dianying"
   (To Be or Not to Be?: Chinese Film after Entrance to the WTO), *Beijing guancha* (Beijing
   Observation) No. 4, April 2000, p. 51.

office hits in 1998 were made in Hong Kong (*The Storm Riders* and *Who
Am I?*), but only three of the top ten were not from Hollywood. Moreover,
as everyone knows, many of the leading Hong Kong filmmakers, including
John Woo, Jackie Chan, Chow Yun-fat, and Jet Li, have moved their professional careers to Hollywood.[59]

   Zheng Dongtian, one of China's leading directors and a professor at the
Beijing Film Academy, has suggested that the issue facing the Chinese film
industry can be simply stated: "To Be or Not to Be?"[60] As Table 3.6, from
a recent article of Zheng's reveals, the domestic market for European films
has been declining between 1988 and 1998 under the onslaught from Hollywood. Only Japan has been able to increase its domestic market in the
last five years. Even there, however, only three of the top ten films in 1998
were not from Hollywood. Zheng's solution is to make films Hollywood
is not able to make, noting that even after American films were allowed
back into China after the six-month ban in 1999, the five films released in
a two-month period earned much less than expected at the box office. By
contrast, Feng Xiaogang's *Meiwan, meiliao* (Sorry, Baby) was a megahit
during the New Year holiday. Thus, despite much critical distaste, Feng
may be the only answer China has.

NOTES

   1. Entertainment analyst Jeffrey Logsdon of Seidler Cos. in Los Angeles, in Alan
Citron and Claudia Eller, "Hollywood Moves to Colonize China," *Los Angeles
Times*, 26 April 1994, sec. D, p. 4.

2. Sharon Waxman, "China Bans Work with Film Studios," *Washington Post*, 1 November 1997, sec. C, p. 1.

3. Dierdre L. Nickerson and Todd Lappin, "Frustration in Peking: Chinese Directors Win Acclaim Abroad But Not At Home," *Far Eastern Economic Review*, 12 August 1993, 57, citing *China Film*. It should be noted, however, that box-office statistics for Chinese films are highly inconsistent. One well-informed interviewee in Beijing in July 2000 actually warned me not to believe what I read about this in the Chinese press, that official publications overreported attendance. For example, Seth Faison reported in *The New York Times*, 21 November, 1995, sec. C, p. 1, that attendance had declined from a peak of 14 billion in 1992, while William Brent reported in *The China Business Review* (September–October 1994, 38) that only 1.2 billion tickets were sold in 1993. An authoritative Chinese source noted that the total audience had dropped by 50 percent from 1979 (29.3 billion) to 1991 (14.4 billion). See Ni Zhen, ed., *Gaige yu zhongguo dianying* (*Reform and Chinese Film*) (Beijing: Dianying chubanshe, 1994), 50. There were many reasons for the decline ranging from poor distribution, the low quality of government-approved films, and the growing popularity of other forms of entertainment. In the late 1980s, just prior to the Tiananmen military crackdown of June 1989, Chinese studios increasingly relied on pure entertainment films in an effort to increase the box office. Communist Party officials were not at all pleased that more than 60 percent of Chinese films in 1988 were kung fu films, thrillers, and musicals. See *Renmin ribao* (*People's Daily*), 31 January 1989, cited in *Xinhua*, in English, reprinted in *Foreign Broadcast Information Service* (*FBIS*), *China*, 89–021, 2 February 1989, 30.

4. At the beginning of the reforms there was only one "cabaret" in China, at the Dongfang Hotel in Guangzhou. By 1994, according to *Renmin ribao*, there were hundreds of cabarets, at least 200,000 karaoke bars, and 60,000 "video viewing rooms." See *Los Angeles Times*, 29 November 1994, sec. F, p. 9.

5. *Hong Kong Standard*, 18 September 1992, 11, reprinted in *FBIS China*, 92–182, 18 September 1992, 22.

6. For Document No. 3 (issued by the Ministry of Radio, Film and Television on 5 January 1993), see China Film Corporation, ed., *Dianying zhengce fagui zhongyao wenjian huibian* (*A Collection of Important Regulations on Film Policy*) (Beijing: Dizhi chubanshe, 1997), 12–15. For Document No. 348 (issued by the same agency on August 1, 1994) see ibid., 16.

7. Tony Rayns in *The Independent* (London), 26 September 1993, 48. Also see Kyoto News Agency, 16 November 1992, reprinted in *FBIS China*, 92–221, 16 November 1992, 27–28; and Derek Elley, "China," in Peter Cowie, ed., *Variety International Film Guide 1994* (Hollywood: Samuel French Trade, 1993), 122.

8. Derek Elley, "China," in Peter Cowie, ed., *Variety International Film Guide 1995* (Hollywood: Samuel French Trade, 1994), 136. It should be noted that some major centers, such as Beijing, Shanghai, and Jiangsu province, were doing better because of a few popular titles.

9. Ibid.

10. Twelve Hollywood films had been imported in 1992 for this flat fee. See *Daily Variety*, 21 March 1994, 1.

11. *Xinhua* in English, 14 July 1994, reprinted in *FBIS China*, 94–135, 14 July 1994, 25–26.

12. Zheng Dongtian, "To Be or Not to Be? Jinru WTO yihou de zhongguo

dianying shengcun beijing fenxi" (To Be or Not to Be? Background and Analysis on the Existence of Chinese Film after Entrance to WTO), *Dianying yishu (Film Art)* no. 2 (2000): 4–8. To ensure greater circulation for his views, this article was published, with a slightly different title, in *Beijing guancha (Beijing Observation)* no. 2 (April 2000), 50–55. In both articles "To Be or Not to Be?" is written in English.

13. For translations of articles on different sides of this ideological divide, see Stanley Rosen, ed., "Hollywood Films and Chinese Domestic Films in China (Part I)," *Chinese Sociology and Anthropology* 32, no. 1, particularly 12–22. For a discussion of "main melody film," see Linda Jaivin, "Guns and Butter: A Survey of Recent Chinese Cinema," *China News Analysis* no. 1466, 15 August 1992, 2. As Jaivin cites from *Renmin ribao*, 30 August 1991, 5, main melody films are supposed to help people to "find their way and strengthen their belief in the face of the extremely complicated political disturbances in China and abroad at this time."

14. "More Reform Urged for PRC's Film Industry," *Xinhua* in Chinese, 7 July 2000, translated in *FBIS China*, 7 July 2000 (Internet). This circular has been extensively reported in the Chinese press. For example, see "Deepen the Reform of the Film Industry, Foreign Capital is Permitted for Investment," *Beijing wanbao*, 8 July 2000, 14.

15. For a recent critique of the burdens of producing main melody films by film professionals, see Yin Hong, "1999 zhongguo dianying beiwang" (A Memorandum on Chinese Film in 1999), *Dangdai dianying (Contemporary Film)* no. 1, 2000, 10–15.

16. Chang Bin, "Megaproductions: The Seven Year Itch," *Xiju dianying bao (Movie and Drama Weekly)*, 5 May 2000, 3. This article provides a useful year-by-year summary of Hollywood films shown in China and includes the opening date for each film, box office figures for Beijing's Capital Cinema, and other useful data. Also see Rone Tempest, "How Do You Say Boffo in Chinese? The Fugitive," *Los Angeles Times*, 29 November 1994, sec. F, pp. 1, 9.

17. Cited in the *Associated Press*, 19 November 1994.

18. Tempest, *Los Angeles Times*, 29 November 1994, op. cit.

19. *Daily Variety*, 28 November–4 December 1994, 48. The decision to import *The Fugitive* and the impact of Hollywood blockbusters into the China market more generally was discussed in a variety of Chinese sources at the time, including such industry publications as *Xiju dianying bao (Film and Theater News)*, *Zhongguo dianying zhoubao (China Film Weekly)*, *Zhongguo dianying shichang (China Film Market)*, *Wenhui dianying shibao (Wenhui Film Times)*, and *Zhongguo wenhua bao (Chinese Cultural News)* One of the most detailed accounts, summarizing not only the dispute and its chronology, but also the process by which *The Fugitive* was brought to China, can be found in Zi Shan, "The Western Galaxy Is Moving East and the Path Has Not Been Smooth: A True Account of the Storm Over 'The Fugitive' in Beijing," *Zhongguo dianying shichang (China Film Market)* no. 1, January 1995, 15–17.

20. For a discussion of the return of *The Fugitive* to Beijing theaters, see Gao Feng, "The Autumn Leaves Pass Through the Winter and Welcome the Spring: 'The Fugitive' Returns to Beijing Screens" in *Zhongguo dianying shichang (China Film Market)* no. 3, March 1995, 10–11. Because of this dispute, the box office figures for *The Fugitive* in Beijing in 1994 were less than one-sixth the figures for Shanghai.

21. *Daily Variety*, 3 May 1994, 4.

22. *Daily Variety*, 5 August 1994, 5.

23. *Maclean's*, 20 February 1995, 18; *Financial Times* (London), 8 February 1995, 4.

24. *Daily Variety*, 29 November 1994, 4.

25. See Fan Jianghua, Mao Yu, and Yang Yuan, "Tour of the 1995 Film Market," *Zhongguo dianying shichang* (*China Film Market*) no. 1, January 1996, 4–7, translated in Stanley Rosen, ed., "The Film Market in China," *Chinese Education and Society* Vol. 32, no. 2, March–April 1999, 37–50.

26. *Forrest Gump* opened on 9 June in Beijing and 16 June in Shanghai, but only 35 percent of the seats were sold. Among various problems were the poor dubbing done by the August 1 Film Studio, the fact that most Chinese were not familiar enough with American history, and the general lack of excitement and entertainment value provided by the film, particularly in comparison with *The Fugitive* and *True Lies*. After the initial buzz created by the film's success at the Academy Awards, Chinese audiences stayed away and theaters lowered their ticket prices from 20 to 10 yuan. See *United Press International*, 20 June 1995.

27. *Los Angeles Times*, 17 October 1995, sec. D, pp. 1, 7, and 3 November 1995, sec. D, p. 4. For a detailed account of the revival of the film market in China that was spurred by the imports, see Lao Mei, "Chinese Domestic Films: First Light and Shadows," *Dianying yishu* (*Film Art*) no. 2, 1996, 43–48.

28. Document 200 is reprinted in China Film Corporation, ed., *Dianying zhengce fagui zhongyao wenjian huibian* (Compendium of the Important Official Documents on Film Policies and Regulations) (Beijing: Dizhi chubanshe, 1997), 1–11, at 8. On the violation of this regulation, see *Wang Gengnian, Zhongguo dianying bao* (*China Film News*), 17 February 2000, 1.

29. Zhan Shibang, "Who Are the Stars of Today's Box Office?" in *Nanfang zhoumo* (*Southern Weekend*), 4 December 1998, 9. Chinese readers would also be aware that Ning Jing married her foreign costar from *Red River Valley* (*Hong hegu*), suggesting that she was unable to find a suitable mate among Chinese males.

30. Yingjin Zhang and Zhiwei Xiao, *Encyclopedia of Chinese Film* (London and New York: Routledge, 1998), 272. Because of a typographical error the annual figure for *Popular Cinema*'s circulation is listed in the *Encyclopedia* as 960 million copies (instead of 9.6 million for the special issue that had the "Hundred Flowers" award ballot) [personal communication from Zhiwei Xiao]. Academic publications on film have also declined in recent years. The two most important, also discussed in the *Encyclopedia*, are *Dianying yishu* (*Film Art*), first published in 1959, and *Dangdai dianying* (*Contemporary Cinema*), first published in 1984. Indeed, one leading film professional told me that *Film Art* might be forced to close down because of financial difficulties (Interview, Beijing, July 2000).

31. "China's Highest Film Awards Face New Set of Challenges," in http://filmbazaar.com, 3 April 2000.

32. Yi Xudong, "When Will China's Restless, Impetuous Cinema Become Calm?" *Xin Shiji* (*New Times*) no. 7, July 1997, 66.

33. Circulation figures can be found in *Zhongguo xinwen chuban tongji ziliao huibian 1998* (*A Compendium of Statistical Data on Chinese Journalism and Publications*) (Beijing: Zhongguo tongji chubanshe, 1998), 170.

34. See *Di yi shou* (*First Hand*) no. 36, 1 September 1998, 3, published by Horizon Research.

35. For examples, see *Mao Qiang*, "Analysis of the 1998 Nationwide Market for American Shared-Profit Films"; He Wenjin, "Thoughts Elicited by Charts Showing 'Titanic' Box Office Trends"; and Weng Li, "Insights from the Market Phenomenon of 'Titanic'," all translated in Stanley Rosen, ed., "Hollywood Films and Chinese Domestic Films in China (Part I)," *Chinese Sociology and Anthropology*, Fall 1999, 33–37, 47–54, and 58–69.

36. *National Journal's Congress Daily*, 10 February 2000 (online version); *Variety*, 14–20 February 2000, 22; and *Los Angeles Times*, 23 May 2000, sec. A, pp. 1, 14.

37. *Los Angeles Times*, 31 October 1999, sec. C, pp. 1, 8.

38. Michel Oksenberg, quoted in *Los Angeles Times*, 30 May 2000, sec. C, p. 1.

39. For a discussion of these restrictions and the China film market more generally, see Lora Chen, "Personal Notes on Changes in the Chinese Film Industry: Globalization and the Market Economy" (unpublished paper).

40. For an excellent discussion of the obstacles to Hollywood's dreams of a vast China market, see James Bates, "China Deal Won't Be a Quick Hit for Hollywood," *Los Angeles Times*, 30 May 2000, sec. C, pp. 1, 4.

41. There are many articles on this debate in newspapers and magazines. See, inter alia, Xu Lijing, and Lan Xiding, "Wuyuan piaojia: nengfou xianqi yingjie (*Wanmei fengbao*: A Five Yuan Ticket: Will It Set Off 'The Perfect Storm' in Film Circles?), *Jingji ribao* (*Economic Daily*), 23 November 2000, 9; and Mao Guo, "Wuyuan piaojia: Rang shichang shuohua" (A Five Yuan Ticket: Let the Market Decide), *Zhongguo dianying bao* (China Film News), 23 November 2000, 3. On this issue more generally, see Zhang Yan, "Are Cinema Prices Really Too High?" *Beijing qingnian bao*, 5 December 1999, 14, translated in Stanley Rosen, ed., "Hollywood Films and Chinese Domestic Films in China (I)," *Chinese Sociology and Anthropology*, Vol. 32, no. 1, Fall 1999, 43–46; and Tang Jiqun, "The ABC's of Shanghai's Film Market: A Survey Report of Yangpu District Cultural Bureau (Part Two)," *Zhongguo dianying shichang* no. 8, August 1999, 32–33, translated in Rosen, "Hollywood Films and Chinese Domestic Films in China (II)," *Chinese Sociology and Anthropology*, Vol. 32, no. 2 (Winter 1999–2000), 82–88. The information on the availability and quality of VCDs and DVDs is based on my observations in Beijing in July 2000.

42. Rosen interview with Jin Zhongqiang, Beijing, 12 December 1999.

43. The best work on censorship in pre-1949 China has been done by Xiao Zhiwei. See "Anti-Imperialism and Film Censorship during the Nanjing Decade, 1927–1937," in Sheldon Lu, ed., *Transnational Chinese Cinemas: Identity, Nationhood, Gender* (Honolulu: University of Hawaii Press, 1997), 35–57.

44. *Asiaweek*, 10 April 1998, 35. Also see *South China Morning Post*, 24 September 1997 (Internet edition) and 9 December 1997 (Internet edition).

45. *The New York Times*, 10 October 1997, sec. B, p. 7. After Disney had signed a deal with Scorsese they really had no choice except to proceed with *Kundun*. Not to do so would have subjected the studio to charges of censorship and damaged their reputation within the artistic community in Hollywood.

46. *Washington Post*, 8 February 1999, sec. A, p. 1. It was clear that Disney was placating Chinese sensibilities rather than seriously planning the distribution of the two films in the United States. One film—*A Time to Remember* (*Hongse*

lianren)—is a patriotic love story set during the Communist revolution and would have little interest for U.S. audiences.

47. Chang Bin, "Dapian qinian zhiyang" (Seven Years of Megafilms), *Xiju dianying bao* (*Movie and Drama Weekly*), 5 May 2000, 3.

48. Wang Tong, "WTO yu Zhongguo dianying" (WTO and Chinese Film), *Xiju dianying bao* (*Movie and Drama Weekly*), 19 May 2000, 7. This was part of a "great debate" in the Chinese film industry over how to survive in the wake of WTO entrance.

49. En Na, "Killer: Chongxin renshi Meiguo dapian" (Killer: Understanding American Megafilms in a New Light), *Beijing qingnian bao*, 19 May 1999, 3.

50. Zeng Yabo, "Jiekai haolaiwu de miansha" (Drawing Aside Hollywood's Veil), *Zhongguo dianying shichang* (*Chinese Film Market*) no. 7, July 1999, 10.

51. Chen Xiaoyun, " 'Zhenshi huangyan': Meiguo dianying de huoyu baquan" ("True Lies": The Vivid Language of Hegemony of American Films), *Zhongguo dianying bao* (*China Film News*), 12 August 1999, 2.

52. Du Zhongjie, "Menghuan bei hou you zhi kanbujian de shou" (There Is an Invisible Hand Behind the Dreamland), *Zhongguo dianying bao* (*China Film News*), 12 August 1999, 2.

53. Zhang Rejie, "Mulan ci—kan donghuapian Hua Mulan" (Ode to Mulan—Seeing the Animated Film Mulan), *Dazhong dianying* (*Popular Cinema*) no. 8, August 1998, 15.

54. Ibid.

55. Wang Yongzhi and Ren Yi, "Yinjin da pian yinchu de ganga" (The Embarrassment Caused by Importing Major Films), *Banyuetan neibuban* (Internally circulated edition of bimonthly forum) no. 7, July 1999, 40–41. One leading film authority in China warned me never to believe box-office figures officially released. On his many visits to Chinese theaters to see films not subsidized by group ticket purchases, he finds very few others in the audience.

56. Liu Hong, "Jiaru WTO: Zhongguo dianyingye jiyu yu tiaozhan bingcun" (Entering WTO: The Chinese Film Industry Faces Both Opportunities and Challenges), unpublished research report from the Guangxi Film Studio.

57. On some of these competing strategies, also see Shaoyi Sun, "Under the Shadow of Commercialization: The Changing Landscape of Chinese Cinema" (unpublished paper).

58. Kang Jianmin, "Zhendui wenti, xunzhao tupo" (Seeking a Breakthrough by Finding the Problems), *Dianying yishu* (*Film Art*) no. 3, 5 May 1999, 13–15.

59. On box-office figures around the world, see Peter Cowie, ed., *Variety International Film Guide 2000* (Los Angeles: Silman-James Press, 1999), 62–72.

60. Zheng Dongtian, "Shengcun, haishi huimie" (To Be or Not to Be?), *Beijing guancha* (*Beijing Observation*) no. 4, April 2000, 50–55.

4

Making the Most of Southern California's Global Engagement

Gregory F. Treverton

The premise of this chapter is that Southern California's role in what has come to be called, infelicitously and somewhat misleadingly (because the process is so uneven across the globe), "globalization" was not well understood. This chapter "maps" the dimensions of globalization's impact on Southern California, and it asks what policies might better enable the region to draw the benefits of its engagement in the global economy while mitigating the downsides.[1] Those "policies" are scarcely the province of governments alone; rather, they include actions that might be taken by private citizens, alone and in cooperation with governments at various levels.

Two interrelated dynamics are driving the global economy. One is the technology revolution, particularly in information, that is making distance less relevant; transactions occur with dizzying speed across long distances. The other is the triumph of the market, which does not compel nations to follow particular economic policies but surely penalizes them if they don't; nations can be rich or autarkic but not both.

The two transformations together are both shrinking and changing the role of the state. Technology permits a plethora of actors—from bankers and businesspeople to criminals and drug traffickers—to operate around and through the apparatus of the state. Markets impel governments to desist from some economic activities, and market forces given form in international financial institutions compel them to pursue particular economic policies. It is not the rise of the "virtual state," in Richard Rosecrance's phrase; rather it is the rise of the "market state."[2]

Globalization is not, however, entirely "deterritorializing." Rather, some economic activities are clustering.[3] Some services, like finance in New York or entertainment in Southern California, benefit from the proximity to one another of different specialists; speed replaces weight as the reason for clustering. The same factors may account for high-tech clustering in Silicon Valley. And it may be simply that creative teams work better face to face; anyone who has ever done business by video or teleconference knows that something is lost in the process, and what is lost may be precisely the intangibles of interaction on which creativity turns.

SOUTHERN CALIFORNIA'S ECONOMIC INSERTION

Measuring and assessing Southern California's insertion in the global economy is no easy task, for the most widely used Commerce Department data on customs districts measure the dollar value of flows through the region's ports and airports, without regard to whether those flows were produced and consumed in the region, or were simply transshipped from or to somewhere else.[4] Transshipment creates employment in warehousing, finance, port facilities, and other logistical services, but the jobs created are far fewer than if goods for export were produced in the region. The point is important because at issue is whether Southern California is an export "underachiever" in terms of goods produced locally.

To be sure, those flows are impressive. By 1996, imports through the Los Angeles customs district had taken over first place in the country from New York. Los Angeles also led in exports, having grown by over 60 percent after 1993, or three times as fast as New York. San Francisco ranked fourth in exports (after Detroit) but had doubled in those three years. Based on the best data, about half of total Los Angeles exports ($74 billion in 1997) was produced in the region.[5] Japan took about a quarter of those exports, Canada slightly more than a tenth, and Mexico slightly less than a tenth. Asian countries figured more and more prominently in the list of top export markets, but the list was diverse enough to limit the impact on exports of Asia's financial crisis of the late 1990s, except in a few specific sectors.

The region's manufactured exports are also diversified in product lines. Transportation equipment (air and spacecraft, auto parts) ranks first, accounting for about a quarter of the total, followed by industrial machinery, computers, and electronic equipment (17 percent), scientific and measuring instruments (15 percent), chemicals, food and apparel (13 percent). Within the region, exporters are spreading; Los Angeles County still accounts for more than two-thirds of exports, but that share is shrinking.

It has become common wisdom that services will be the key to the future global economy, and to Southern California's place in it, but calibrating service exports is no mean feat. The region, like most of the country, is "deindustrializing," with manufacturing being supplanted by services; for

Southern California, this trend was exacerbated by the defense cuts that began in the mid-1980s and began to bite by the 1990s. Yet no direct data on state or regional service exports exist, so the best that can be done is to use national export data, allocating regional exports according to the region's share in national production. By that method, Southern California exported about $10 billion in services in 1996, travel and tourism accounting for half, and freight and port services over a quarter.

These numbers are, however, as impressive for what they don't include as what they do. They do not include entertainment—film and music royalties and fees. The motion picture industry estimated its international box-office receipts at over $3 billion in 1997, making foreign markets more important than the domestic one. Roughly half of those international receipts are earned by companies based in the region—Disney, Sony, and Fox. Using standard multipliers, the region's manufactured exports created about a half-million jobs and its service exports added about 135,000 more—making about one in nine of total jobs in the region (6 million) export-related. For reasons including transshipment, this number is probably conservative.

Interviews with senior executives in the region's apparel, fabricated metal, printing, entertainment, health, and business services industries provide texture to the bare numbers.[6] Unsurprisingly, the executives expressed ambivalence about globalization. On the positive side, labor is more fluid, trade barriers are lower, and easier communications and transport facilitate meeting demands abroad. On the negative side, competition is intense; not all trade is equally fair—they cited East Asia in particular—and they become hostage to unpredictable fluctuations in foreign markets.

The executives were generally positive about the region's place in the globalizing economy—but with concerns about the future. Geographic proximity to Mexico and the Pacific Rim nations is an advantage, notwithstanding faster global flows of information and goods. Critically, while the executives cited both an abundance of skilled labor and a pool of low-cost, largely immigrant workers—"one of the region's understated strengths" (Interview conducted for the Pacific Council's Making the Most of Southern California's Global Engagement Project)—they worried about sustaining the skilled pool as immigrants become a larger and larger share of the region's labor force.

Each industry in the region had its own story to tell, its own calculations of the benefits and costs of globalization. For apparel, the story is one of moving production abroad in response to competitive pressures, the North American Free Trade Agreement in particular, and, perhaps, to union efforts to increase local wages. Outsourcing abroad has created new jobs in the region, in design, logistics, and monitoring foreign operations, but it has put special pressure on the region's small firms.

For entertainment, globalization's balance sheet is, in money terms at least, almost entirely positive. There are, to be sure, pressures to cater more

directly to foreign markets, coupled with incentives to move television production abroad, to Canada in particular. Yet while foreign markets together are bigger than the domestic one, no single market comes close. Even
the industry's extraordinary degree of unionization is an advantage, for
union benefits help retain workers in the region through the business' no-
torious cycles.

Fabricated metal producing, a diverse cluster of firms, has been in decline
because of aerospace cuts. Some firms have been successful in shifting from
military specifications to civilian production, including exporting or shifting
production abroad, but the challenge of meeting international standards
has been costly for many smaller companies. For all of the technological
change in printing, the industry remains one of small firms, mostly independent, including many that have been in business for a half-century. It
also, interestingly, remains committed to clients that mostly are close at
hand.

Business and health services are the two largest service industries in the
region. Both are growing fast. And while, in principle, technology ought to
permit both to reach well beyond the region, niches in foreign markets have
been elusive. One entrepreneur of substance-abuse programs cited myriad
problems marketing in Canada, from strange bureaucracies to unaccus-
tomed delays, to handicaps marketing to French-Canadians.

WINNERS AND LOSERS

Globalization *is* replacing manufacturing with services in Southern California. This is true across the United States; it is more of a change for
other places, like New York, where manufacturing bulked larger in the
regional economy. Still, its first effect is the same for this region: if the
image of engineers being reduced to hamburger flippers at the local
McDonald's is not quite right, the manufacturing jobs that are lost often
are better paying than the service ones that are created. The income distribution can be worsened.

While globalization can be good for the region as a whole, it is important
to ask, more specifically, "for whom?" Globalization is a fact, here to stay,
and, in general, international competition improves efficiency and so makes
for higher *aggregate* incomes. Yet the distributional effects of trade are
perhaps adverse, and its benefits long-term; Latinos may benefit, but African Americans and blue-collar whites may lose. For Southern California,
globalization is creating a multicultural middle class that is oblivious to
race, but that fact could make the plight of globalization's "losers" all the
worse.

There is broad agreement that U.S. industry has been hollowed out and
that incomes of less-skilled laborers have declined. The question is why?
Sorting out the cause is knotty. Most U.S. trade in manufactured goods is

with other high-wage countries, so globalization in the sense of competition with low-wage countries is hard to pin down as the culprit for the hollowing out of U.S. industry. Rather, it appears that technological advances have increased the reward for skilled labor, while putting downward pressure on the wages of those who are less skilled. That said, technological advances cannot be readily separated from the global competition that drives their adoption.[7] More trade makes it easier to substitute an import for a domestic good, and thus makes domestic manufacturers less willing to raise prices. Labor's bargaining power is reduced, especially so when capital is very mobile.

Regions can embody a kind of "social capital."[8] In this sense, again, location matters; location is a kind of externality not usually captured in economic analysis. Jobs in Seattle, for instance, are not much threatened by cheap products from low-wage Beijing. Given skilled labor and infrastructure, the aircraft industry will stay. And the high-skill sector will drive up wages in the nontrade service sector (office workers and the like)—jobs that are often occupied by less-educated labor.

Putting these pieces together suggests two apparently contradictory propositions. On the one hand, regions grow faster, and perhaps do better in international trade, if they are initially more equitable. On the other hand, trade itself is associated with widening inequality. Trade winners do, it turns out, tend to be characterized by lower levels of poverty and inequality, and while trade losers face the fastest worsening of inequality, trade winners are not far behind. Yet regional protectionism is no answer: regions that are the least affected by imports initially do experience the least worsening in inequality as trade increases, but they were the most unequal to begin with.

This abstract point is made vivid by the experience of the Alameda Corridor project. This $2 billion dollar project will connect the region's San Pedro bay ports with key transcontinental railyards near downtown Los Angeles. Its construction will produce at least 10,000 jobs and perhaps seven times that many in international trade by 2010. Yet a number of cities along the corridor filed suit against the project in 1995. Why? It turned out that all the cities along the corridor that sued were trade losers. More generally, using data on neighborhoods of about 150,000, the trade winners in Los Angeles County were generally white and richer, while the losers were poorer and more populated by minority groups.[9]

PHYSICAL CAPITAL: INFRASTRUCTURE

As Southern California engages the globe, it does so with infrastructure— both physical and, to some extent, human—that is the legacy of choices made more than a generation ago. It is living off what one participant called the "Eisenhower-Brown inheritance," referring to federal largesse for highways in the 1950s and to the spending on education associated with former governor Edmund ("Pat") Brown that made California the envy of other states (if not always the favorite of its local politicians).

A distinct example of that aging is the region's transportation infrastructure. Southern California has only one fully international airport—in contrast to the Bay Area, which has three—and demands on it, now nearing capacity, are projected to nearly double by 2015. By the same token, truck traffic in the region is expected to grow by nearly half over the next twenty years, and, with the shift in the 1990s from building freeways to managing traffic, Southern California built only one freeway in the last decade of the twentieth century.[10]

The "big three" projects—port improvements for Long Beach and Los Angeles, the Alameda Corridor, and the Los Angeles airport (LAX) master plan—are critical to the region's trade future. Together, these represent the nation's largest trade infrastructure program. They also raise a clutch of puzzles around the issue of dispersed benefits but concentrated costs, of which the Alameda Corridor is a stark example. While the project unquestionably will promote trade and create jobs, citizens in the poor communities along the project ask, with good reason, jobs where and for whom? If most of the jobs will be created elsewhere in the region, not to mention in Texas or New York, those citizens may well judge the immediate costs—noise, pollution, and disrupted traffic during construction— not worth the long-term benefits.

This is why the question of whether the region is a trade "underachiever" is important. Is the region a trade center or merely a transshipment hub, a kind of West Coast New Orleans capturing few of the benefits of trade in the region? If the latter, then the costs and benefits of infrastructure projects will be judged accordingly. Both Los Angeles and Long Beach have, for instance, been tempted to deprive the ports of investment capital by diverting port revenues to general municipal coffers. Half of the region's "international trade" in 1995 was indeed transshipment from other states. To frame a better answer to the underachiever question, export earnings can be compared with total income to measure success at selling to foreigners. By that measure, Southern California does better than the nation and New York but only about half as well as San Jose, Detroit, and Seattle, whose exports are high-value computer electronics, automobiles, and aircraft, respectively.

In these circumstances, citing airports is a Catch-22: "In order to have demand, you have to have population density. And when you have population density, you have conflict." The airline industry would like a massive expansion of LAX and the creation of big new airport at the old Marine facility in Orange County, El Toro. But both have run into local opposition. Already, as one participant put it, the citizens of Los Angeles' Westchester neighborhood have as much say over LAX as they do over their local streets. While nearly 40 percent of LAX's direct jobs, mostly in air cargo, are within ten miles of the airport, local residents still worry that expansion will create more noise, congestion, and pollution, and reduce property values.

HUMAN CAPITAL: PEOPLE FLOWS

Immigration is reshaping the human capital of Southern California, not utterly but more than any other region of the United States. An immigrant diaspora of more than 100,000 people in the region hail from eight countries, and they tend to live in enclaves separated from each other and from natives. The Mexican diaspora, 4 million people, half of them born in Mexico, dwarfs all the others.

The debate over immigration sometimes ignores the basic fact that emigrating is uncomfortable, and so it takes more than economic promise to lure migrants. It takes some family or community at the other end. In Southern California's case, the roots of Mexican immigration go back to the World War II *bracero* program. What was intended as an interim substitute for farm workers in short supply lasted twenty years, and so the region's Mexican immigrants do not reflect Mexico as a whole but rather still come from the slice of west coast Mexican states from whence the *braceros* were recruited.

The region's wave of immigration from abroad is new, and thus the controversy about it is unsurprising. A scant generation ago, Southern California looked much like the rest of the nation; now it is a third Latino. More immigrants arrived in the 1970s, 1.8 million, than in all earlier decades combined, and that number doubled again in the 1980s. Indeed, one-third of all immigrants coming to the United States come to California, and about two-thirds of those settle in Southern California. Moreover, immigrants are highly concentrated in Los Angeles County: about half the state's immigrants live there. The very diversity of Southern California can be a factor of strength, in reaching entertainment markets abroad, for instance; yet there remains concern that the diversity of the region will become a source of political, if not social, tension.

The immigration issue, which can be incandescent in its own right, runs through most other aspects of the region's global engagement. The debate over which Americans, or which Californians, benefit will continue. Employers benefit from cheaper labor, low-skilled native workers suffer from competition, and consumers benefit from cheaper services and goods. Whether immigrants are a net tax burden or benefit depends on whether they are low-skilled, like most Mexicans and Central Americans, or higher skilled. There is now, moreover, concern that if migration has so far been an economic plus to the region, it might turn negative, especially as waves of less-educated migrants cause the region to lose its once-vaunted educational lead over the rest of the country. In 1970, Los Angeles County's labor force had a ten-month advantage over the rest of the nation, but by 1990 that had become a six-month deficit.

Immigration has boosted job growth in the region because immigrants are paid less than natives but are, at any level of education, at least as productive—a conclusion that came through the interviews with business leaders. Employers report that if they seek low-skilled workers, they need only circulate word among their existing Latino workers. The downside of this advantage is that immigrants push down the wages and employment of low-skilled natives, African Americans in particular, though by how much is hotly debated.[11]

On measures like learning English, becoming American citizens, and participating in politics, recent immigrants seem to resemble older ones. By the third generation, for example, the vast majority of immigrants either speak only English at home or are bilingual. The question at issue is whether the Latino diaspora, especially the Mexican, will be an exception to older patterns. For it, low education and large enclaves might trap many Mexicans in a cycle of poverty and separateness. These children run the risk of growing up with greater expectations than their parents but not much chance of realizing them. That, in turn, might make for ethnic politics more akin to that of African Americans than of older, mostly European, immigrant groups. For those older groups, ethnicity was soon overshadowed by class and education as determinants of political behavior.[12]

IMPROVING THE INFRASTRUCTURE: HIGHER EDUCATION

Southern California engages the world by continuing to be a magnet for foreign students. The entire state takes more than 12 percent of the 450,000 international students in the United States. In nine very different Southern California institutions of higher education, the percentage of international students ranged from 5 to 15, the latter at the University of Southern California, which amounted to the third largest number among research universities nationwide. For all nine institutions, international students pumped some $200 million into the local economy.

To be sure, international students are only one aspect of the region's globalization in higher education. Another is the presence of foreign scholars; there, the Berkeley, Los Angeles, and San Diego branches of the University of California trail only Harvard in total numbers. Those scholars are predominantly researchers, not teachers, they hail from Asia (43 percent) more than Europe (38 percent) and Latin America (6 percent), and, like the international students, they are heavily engaged in mathematics and engineering and the physical and life sciences.

Yet globalization requires not just the presence of international students and scholars in the region; it also requires wider perspectives to cope with, let alone take advantage of the internationalization of the region. Schools of business have long taught international finance and the like; what is new is the recognition that doing business in today's global economy requires not just technical skills but also appreciation of the cultural context of the places where business is done: hence, courses in cross-cultural understanding have blossomed in the region.

For the region's education schools, the challenge is to cope not with the presence of students from abroad but with the internationalization that is going on at home. It has become commonplace to observe that in aggregate students in Southern California's schools speak 150 languages at home. By 1990, for instance, a third of Los Angeles County was foreign-born, and half the immigrants spoke a language other than English at home. And so schools of education have moved well beyond the challenges of teaching English and of bilingualism to efforts to understand the effects of culture on cognition, measurement and the like; indeed, teacher training becomes the domestic equivalent of study abroad programs.

In framing a broader assessment of higher education's role in the region's global engagement, it is worth asking the provocative question: If higher educators could replace all existing foreign students with tuition payers from Nebraska, would they? Should they?

HOLLYWOOD AND SOUTHERN CALIFORNIA

There is no gainsaying that the world is more and more important to the cluster of music, film, and entertainment industries labeled in shorthand "Hollywood." Foreign showings now account for 60 percent of film earnings; for television the number is 20 percent and rising fast. For many abroad, the preeminent image of the region, and of America, is that purveyed by Hollywood, as is attested to by several other chapters in this book, Michael Clough's in particular.[13]

Yet the question remains, what connection does Hollywood have to the region? If Hollywood and Southern California are inseparable in the minds of most Americans, in fact until recently Hollywood was less important to the region's economy than real estate, oil, automobiles, and aerospace. And the separation between the region's traditional "downtown" establishment, predominantly Anglo, and the Hollywood elite, heavily Jewish, was almost complete.

For the future, the crucial question is one that cannot be answered definitively: will Hollywood will become the region's driving leader? Or will it "deregionalize" as it globalizes, suspended in air, in but not much of the region? In the past, Southern California chased New York for mastery of the media battleground. In the future, under the twin challenges of globalization and digitalization, will Hollywood continue to have the preeminence it has achieved rather lately? Northern California might emerge as a real competitor if Yahoo!, WebTV, and their kin turn out to be real alternatives to existing media.

The seeds of today's media conglomerates were sown, paradoxically, in the 1950s, when the big studios suffered the twin blows of television and antitrust judgments that divested them of their monopoly over film exhibition in theaters. In 1954, Disney agreed to produce a weekly show for ABC, and the next year Warner Bros. also decided to produce prime-time television. This "television era" lasted a generation, until the 1970s, when it was undone by, above all, the rise of cable.

The 1980s saw the consolidation of the big four entertainment companies—Disney, Fox, Sony, and Time Warner—whose reach extended in the next decade to sports networks and teams and to news outlets like CNN. This consolidation coincided with the decline of the nation-state, and thus of the national authority of Washington and New York, and was accompanied by the "reregionalization" and increasing diversity of the United States. This increasing diversity might confer advantages on Southern California: Earlier, it was the melting pot of immigrants from within the United States and so the ideal place from which to reach a more homogenous America; now, its internationalism makes it a place from which to reach a very diverse global market.

There are those who seek to loosen the region's hold on Hollywood, as other cities and nations, Canada in particular, try to lure production away. Technological advances are making it easier to disperse production and so let other regions compete for pieces of the industry. Yet there is no other market anywhere near the scale of that in the United States; the other markets are just that, plural. Trying to locate production near all of them would be prohibitive, and so Hollywood is not likely to migrate abroad to the same extent as other industries.

If, however, globalization does not affect *where* entertainment is produced, it will affect *what* is produced. Already, witty American comedy, hard to translate and appeal across cultures, is losing out to action movies that are nearly dialogue-free or to teenage romance, which can be carried with not much more language. And Hollywood will feel the hot breath of those who govern its foreign markets, as it did when China tried to discourage Disney from releasing films that Beijing perceived as favoring the independence of Tibet.

In 1998 the *Los Angeles Times* ran a major series, "In Local Economy, Hollywood Is Star." Is that true? Will entertainment become the apex of the regional economy, serving as a magnet for talent, a spur to ancillary industries, the shaper of a regional identity and a builder of social capital? Perhaps, but the question of Hollywood's regional connection remains. Times have changed, but the Hollywood crowd is still an elite apart, more likely to contribute to presidential campaigns or to saving endangered species than to local parks. And while the fact that non-Americans own Fox and Sony may have little economic impact on the region, it does seem likely that those owners will not see themselves as regional leaders.

POLICY IMPLICATIONS

Globalization *is* here to stay, so the task for the region is to make the most of it. That will require not just new ideas but new forms of action—by governments, by private groups, and by the two in varying combinations. There are a number of policy ideas suggested by the mapping of Southern California's engagement in the global economy.

Trading Better

Mundane but important, better data, especially on services, would help the region better frame policy. As the region's trade grows, Los Angeles airport and ports become even more important as regional assets. That is true just as competition for trade business intensifies—from other West Coast or Gulf Coast ports, from Denver and Phoenix airports. Tourism benefits the region and could be still larger if steps were taken to mitigate Southern California's image as a difficult place in which to get around.

The region has been perhaps too focused on Asia in recent years. Given Asia's uncertainty, future trade growth will depend on other markets, especially Mexico and especially high-tech. With the spur of NAFTA, total cross-border trade in precision instruments almost doubled between 1993 and 1997, from $2.95 billion to $5.20 billion. Demand will grow apace with aging populations and increased health-care spending.

Another set of agenda items is also implicit in the interviews with businesspeople discussed earlier. Not only do the region's leaders need to do a better job of communicating globalization's benefits, they need to become more engaged in areas that at first blush seem tangential to trade—for instance, finding, and eventually training, workers for the export sector. Quality industrial space is in short supply in the region. Much of the potential space is in South-Central Los Angeles; recycling that space not only would be attractive, given proximity to the airport and ports, it could also help local African American and Latino communities that risk being left behind by globalization.

Dealing with Globalization's Strugglers

Globalization is here to stay. The genie cannot be put back in the bottle, nor, given the benefits, should the region want to try. Temptations by community leaders to turn inward, away from global trade, are to be resisted.

The challenge is not to stand against the tide of international change, but rather to try to ensure that it raises as many boats as possible.

The counterpart, though, is the realization that those who would promote globalization in the region's interest need to pay attention to who struggles in the process. If they do not, they risk, at a minimum, that those strugglers will undermine support for openness, thus leading the region to cut off its nose to spite its face. And for a region that has suffered both urban riots and threats of suburban secession, the risk is hardly one to be dismissed.

There is no shortage of ideas if the political will is there. "Industrial policy" has a bad name, partly justified, but as the region looks to which international trade business "clusters" to promote, it could look beyond the overall benefits to whether poorer citizens might be employed. So, too, the community development corporations (CDCs), a key vehicle for poor communities, might train local people for jobs in international trade. It is easy to say that education is vital in making the region more competitive, but that education will need to take many forms, much of it not in school but rather on the job.

In the end, though, much of what can be done will boil down to participation, to finding ways to engage low-income residents in thinking about the regional economy. For instance, after its early missteps, the Alameda Corridor Authority established a Business Outreach Committee focused on temporary jobs that will be created during construction. That committee might be made permanent as a means of helping local businesses better connect to international opportunities the project will produce.

Keeping Immigration a Plus

Continuing immigration is making the region less and less like the rest of the state and the rest of the nation. Given the dominating size of the Mexican diaspora, immigration is also underscoring the connections between Southern California and Mexico, its north in particular. At one level, integration of the immigrant diasporas into Southern California's civil society is proceeding at least as rapidly as was the case for earlier immigrants.

Yet, given a constant stream of new immigrants, this integration may well seem too slow, both to natives and to the immigrants themselves. In the end, the risk that the region's politics might veer toward conflict along ethnic lines is due less to ethnicity itself than to increasing income disparities. The majority of children in the region's schools are Latino, and they are graduating from high school and going to college at rates well below those of other students. They enter a labor market that is less and less hospitable to high school drop-outs or even to those who have only a high school diploma. During the decade of the 1980s, 850,000 new jobs were created in Los Angeles County but only 32,000 of these new jobs were filled by someone with a high school education or less. Changes in immigration policies that would over time decrease the share of ill-educated immigrants who settle in the region would also help, though they would make a difference only slowly. All citizens of the region have a powerful interest in seeing that the children of the Mexican diaspora are not left behind in education and income.[14]

The concentration of immigrants in Los Angeles County, and especially the City of Los Angeles, raises issues of governance similar to those entailed in other local effects of globalization. On one hand, the various immigrant groups are very different, so local communities are best positioned to tend to their needs. Yet those local governments may not have the resources to do so. Some sharing of burdens across the region would make sense, all the more so if the region is to recognize its common stake in speeding the integration of immigrants into local society and in taking advantage of the target of opportunity those immigrants present to increase trade with their home countries.

Immigrants, especially Mexican ones, will make their voices heard on matters of policy. That is already happening, though the group's area of interest is understandably limited mostly to educational and economic opportunities in the region. Over time, the interests of Mexican Americans will broaden. The group is not, however, likely to be of one voice nor, having voted with its feet, will it automatically be supportive of Mexico's policies. It will continue to focus on bread-and-butter issues here and on minimizing friction between the United States and Mexico, on developing the border region, and, more generally, on supporting economic and democratic advance in Mexico itself.

Targeting Education

The concern that the region is living off inherited educational infrastructure is real but must be decomposed. At the end of the 1980s, Southern California's economy was in recession, and its leaders would have echoed other Americans in fearing that without better education the United States would not be able to compete with Japan or Germany. By 2000, national unemployment was below 4 percent, and Southern California's only slightly above. Schools could not have improved so dramatically in the interim, and, indeed, the same bemoaning of schools is heard now in a booming America as was heard in an America in the doldrums.

That suggests caution in drawing too clear a line between education and growth. Aggregate education levels in Los Angeles County have fallen, but there is no evidence that productivity has—at least not yet. The immediate concern about education fixes on those, often immigrants, with the least skills. Without some special attention, they risk being left behind, their dreams frustrated, and their fellow citizens made worse off both by their absence as productive fellow workers and their presence as drains on public resources. Thus, the greatest challenge for the region is a tall order—framing policies that will move more Latinos through high school and into college.

Profiting from Entertainment

Entertainment can become much more than a regional employer—indeed its job total will be less than manufacturing, services, and other sectors—it will be the key to whether Southern California becomes a dominant new media center. In Chapter 2, Clough bets that the new media giants will be more connected to the region than the old film industry, and so will be more likely to take a lead in formulating a long-run strategy for the region. The social divide between "downtown" and "Hollywood" is diminishing. As Clough attests in his chapter, the executives who run Disney, Fox, and Sony are not nearly as different from their counterparts in other corporate sectors as the old movie moguls were from the managers who ran the region's banks, factories, and local governments in the golden age of the old studio system.

A number of concrete steps could enhance the global competitiveness of the region's entertainment industry and use the presence of that industry to expand the region's global connections. The first aim would indicate, for instance, a concerted effort to turn the region's ethnic diversity into a global asset. Employing more Asian Americans, African Americans, or Latinos in the industry is not affirmative action; rather, it helps Hollywood appeal to diverse global markets. Making it easier for foreign talent to work here would serve the same goal, as would cooperative arrangements and training programs that gave foreign countries where Hollywood bulks large more of a stake in the prosperity of the industry in this region.

Beginning to develop a strategy to take advantage of Hollywood's global reach would go beyond including entertainment industry representatives in foreign trade missions, though that is a good idea. It would mean identifying countries and regions that are of strategic importance to Southern California, and then searching for ways the entertainment industry's presence and connections can be used to build collaboration.

CHALLENGES TO GOVERNANCE, PUBLIC AND PRIVATE

Globalization's benefits are dispersed, but its costs often are concentrated. That is as true of projects, like airports, as it is of "fast track" authority for the president to negotiate freer trade. Consumers who benefit from cheaper goods, imported from abroad or made here under the pressure of foreign competition, don't organize. Nor are there lobbyists for jobs that globalization will create in the future. By contrast, workers who lose jobs to foreign competition or citizens who live in the shadow of new infrastructure projects do organize and are vocal.

This theme was most visible in infrastructure projects like the Alameda Corridor, for them "paying" had a very specific meaning—noise and congestion from construction or lost sales or jobs because streets were disrupted. The ports or airports are a regional, even a national asset, but the costs of building or living with them are concentrated in the neighborhoods where they are located. The dispersion of benefits may be less for airports than ports to the extent that the jobs created cluster near the airport, but the basic mismatch remains. NIMBY ("not in my backyard") is everywhere. In principle, almost everyone agrees that a bigger airport in Orange County would make sense. Yet whether it should be an expansion of John Wayne in northern Orange County or of El Toro in the south becomes an emotional NIMBY issue.

In another sense, the question of whether the region is a export underachiever is also an issue of how dispersed are the benefits of globalization. Jobs created in transshipment are nice, but if the Port of Los Angeles transships goods made in Texas or even New York, people in this region might wish the roles could be reversed, with them having the manufacturing jobs and someone else the traffic and pollution of the port.

The broader form of the same issue is who benefits and who pays. People along the Alameda Corridor had reason to feel they were losers in two senses. Already poor, they were losing out on globalization's benefits for the region. Then, they worried that they would also suffer the costs of construction along the corridor without much sharing in even the jobs that construction brought.

Immigrants benefit from their move (else they would return home); so do those who employ them (more cheaply than they could hire natives). Who may pay are the African Americans or blue-collar whites who either will lose jobs to immigrants or, more likely, suffer downward pressure on their wages due to the constant stream of lower-paid arrivers from abroad.

In a longer view, there is the concern that if immigration turned from a plus to a minus for the region, those costs would be both concentrated and dispersed. They would fall most heavily on the immigrants who fell further and further behind both their expectations and their fellow citizens. But the region would also suffer if education levels declined, taking productivity with it, and making the region less attractive for the economic activity it seeks; still worse if the vicious cycle increased claims on public institutions and money or risked civil strife. For a long time, though, those costs might be dispersed enough not to rally political support to do much of anything about them.

The days are gone, and doubtless unlamented, when a cohesive local business elite made major decisions, both public and private, in a Los Angeles downtown men's club. Perhaps that past is misremembered, and the

Committee of Twenty-Five may not have dominated civic affairs to the extent that is thought.[15] Still, the image is accurate of a strong business community but political structures inherited from the Progressive era, ones that were designed to be weak, overlapping, with confusing jurisdictions so that no one would abuse power. That business dominance broke down for a number of reasons, but not in the least that industry structure changed. Home-grown CEOs whose businesses were entangled with the region were replaced by leaders of multinational companies who neither understood the region nor were primarily responsible to it.

Now, what is striking is the fragmentation of leadership. Downtown, Hollywood, and Latino leaders still often do not speak the same language, sometimes literally. That state of affairs may be changing, but this mapping leaves it an open question of how much. On one hand, the downtown elite are gone, but Hollywood leaders are as likely to be more connected to the region than the old movie moguls. On the other hand, those leaders also now run global corporations, many of which just happen to be in Southern California. As one person active in philanthropy put it: "it's still easier to raise money in Hollywood to save rain forests in the Amazon than local parks."

Politics can compound the puzzle of dispersed benefits but with concentrated costs. While the logic of trade would argue for much more integrated regionwide planning, political currents seem to be flowing in the opposite direction. Charter reform was in the 1990s atop the City of Los Angeles' agenda, driven there by the interest in forestalling secession by the San Fernando Valley. That interest argued for more decentralization, for neighborhood councils with real power. Yet existing governing authorities already tended, for instance, to give the citizens of Los Angeles' Westchester neighborhood as much say over Los Angeles airport as they had about local streets. The stimulus of Valley secession and the response of charter reform were a reminder that while Los Angeles may be weakly governed, that governance is not decentralized.

There is nothing new about this mismatch in American governance: efficiency often argues for larger units, while accountability indicates smaller ones, closer to citizens. If the tension is sharper now, it is because its effects cut across existing jurisdictions much more than in the past. There is no way, for instance, for the Southern California region to act on its regional interest in, for instance, education, or, still less, immigration.

The anti-immigration proposition 187 in 1994 and anti-affirmative action proposition 209 in 1996 did propel Latinos, in particular, toward political participation. The question is, what will be the vehicles for that participation and to what effect? The reformist impulse gave California weak political parties and spared it party machines on the model of the big eastern cities. Absent these parties, though, immigrants to the region will be left to fend for themselves and find their own ways into the system.

Some may neither need nor desire politics. Others may be too absorbed with the immediate well-being of their families to have much energy for politics; Mexican American participation rates have remained low probably for just that reason. The 1992 Los Angeles riots were graphic testimony to the hard edges of ethnic relations in the region. Without mediating institutions, will immigrants turn to a politics rooted in ethnicity?

Beyond parties, it is at least in question whether existing regional institutions are adequate to frame a regional perspective. Regional special-purpose districts, such as for ports or airports, have a long history, one that is controversial. They can become very powerful, perhaps too powerful, by comparison to elected leaders, but they can act to frame a broader perspective and in so doing act as a counterweight to concentrated costs and concentrated responsibilities.

Existing regional authorities, such as they are, link *governments*. Yet it seems ever clearer that approaches to the local challenges entailed in the global economy will emerge as much from private initiatives and from private-public partnerships as from traditional government action. Flush state (and federal) revenue coffers are promising but do not fully negate that point. Rising tax revenues offer some chance that California as a whole might move toward the position it once occupied near the top of state investment in public education. But that broad rising tide will still leave some boats, especially those of newly arrived Latin immigrants, far below those of other students. If there are to be initiatives targeted on that disparity, those will have to emerge from the private sector, both nonprofit and for-profit.

For Southern California, the appropriate modes of action may give pride of place to private initiative over public action, to less-intrusive rather than more arrangements, to incremental rather than dramatic changes, and to consensus gradually developed rather than decisions starkly imposed. The point can be overstated, and often is to the point of caricature, but in the West still more than in the rest of the United States, the individual is of paramount value. Perhaps it is precisely the looseness of governance and the primacy of the individual in Southern California that have permitted the stark political contrasts to coexist: very conservative Orange County exists cheek-by-jowl with liberal Los Angeles. For these reasons and others, not least the ease of drawing in the private sector, informal cooperative arrangements may be preferable to more formal ones. In that regard, organizations like the Pacific Council on International Policy, networks that are informal but real, can perhaps play a useful role.

NOTES

1. This chapter is the product of a Pacific Council on International Policy project, "Southern California's Global Engagement." The project was sponsored by

the John Randolph and Dora Haynes Foundation, to which I am grateful. An expanded version of this chapter will also be published by the Pacific Council. I thank the other authors in the project, whose work will be cited in these notes.

2. This discussion owes much to my conversations with Philip Bobbitt, and the term "market state" is his. See his *The Shield of Achilles* (New York: Knopf, 2001). Richard Rosecrance speaks of the "virtual state," and Jessica Mathews also writes of technology breaking government monopolies on collecting and managing information. See Richard Rosecrance, "The Rise of the Virtual State," *Foreign Affairs* (July/August 1996), 45–61; and Jessica T. Mathews, "Power Shift," *Foreign Affairs* (January/February 1997), 50–66.

3. See, for instance, work by Michael Porter, at http://www.dor.hbs.edu/fi_redirect.jhtml? facInfo=pub&facEmId=mporter.

4. How to define "the region" is an issue. Given Southern California's spread, focusing on the City of Los Angeles or even Los Angeles County would have been too narrow. Given San Diego's links to Los Angeles, especially in transport, there is an argument for defining the region to include San Diego (and Tijuana, in Mexico). In the end, to keep the focus manageable, the region was defined as the five-county area—Los Angeles, Orange, Ventura, San Bernardino, and Riverside. It also includes Las Vegas, Nevada, in the customs district of Los Angeles.

5. These data are from the Bureau of the Census Exporter Location (EL) series, and were provided by Ken Ackbarali and Jack Kyser of the Los Angeles Economic Development Corporation.

6. Demetra Constantinou conducted these interviews for the Pacific Council project cited above.

7. See Dani Rodrik, *Has Globalization Gone Too Far?* (Washington, DC: Institute for International Economics, 1997), pp. 16ff.

8. See Manuel Pastor, J. *Widening the Winners' Circle from Global Trade in Southern California* (Los Angeles: Pacific Council on International Policy, Aug. 2001).

9. See ibid.

10. For an overview of California's movement of goods, see California Department of Transportation and San Diego Association of Governments, *California Trade and Goods Movement Study* (June 1996), pp. 51ff.

11. See, for instance, Kevin F. McCarthy and Georges Vernez, *Immigration in a Changing Economy: California's Experience* (Santa Monica: RAND, 1997); and National Research Council, *The New Americans: Economic, Demographic and Fiscal Effects of Immigration* (Washington, DC: National Academy Press, 1997).

12. See McCarthy and Vernez, cited in ibid., and Louis DeSipio, *Counting on the Latino Vote: Latinos as a New Electorate* (Charlottesville: University of Virginia Press, 1996).

13. Another version of Clough's chapter was published by the Pacific Council on International Policy as *Can Hollywood Remain the Capital of the Global Entertainment Industry?* (Los Angeles: Pacific Council on International Policy, September 2000).

14. See, for instance, Dowell Myers, *The Changing Immigrants of Southern California* (Los Angeles: University of Southern California, 1995).

15. The Committee of Twenty-Five was an informal group of leading citizens,

including the heads of major businesses with headquarters in Los Angeles. Meeting in a downtown men's club, the group is commonly believed to have been movers and shakers behind the scenes in the region until the middle of the twentieth century. It was powerful networking before the team came into use.

PART II

SOUTHERN CALIFORNIA AS A MICROCOSM OF THE WORLD

5

Religious Dimensions of the Immigrant Experience in Southern California

Donald E. Miller, Jon Miller, and Grace Dyrness

In recent years, Los Angeles, leading California as a whole, has experienced a dramatic shift in population[1], due in large part to the waves of immigration that followed the change in immigration law in 1965. Today, nearly one person in three in the county is foreign born. The demographic, economic, and fiscal effects of these changes have been extensively documented and sometimes vigorously debated and, according to recent research[2] and a prominent *Los Angeles Times* article[3], estimates and projections from the 2000 census can only fuel further debate about the (apparently moderating) rate of immigration and the (apparently improving) economic status of immigrant groups in Los Angeles and California.

Our research focuses on the part that religion plays in the experiences of immigrants and, on the other side of the equation, we are documenting the impact that immigration has had on the religious mosaic of the Los Angeles region. Three recent religious events—one in a Catholic mission in East Los Angeles, another in a Buddhist temple in Long Beach, and the third in an Armenian Apostolic church in Pasadena—dramatically capture the variety of these experiences.

On July 28, 2000, a six-foot replicate image of the Divine Savior of the World, "El Salvador," completed a ten-day journey from the cathedral in San Salvador, El Salvador, to Los Angeles. Hundreds of people were gathered in the parking lot at Dolores Mission, a church in Boyle Heights that over the years has given refuge to thousands of immigrants. The emotion in the air was palpable. The news media was out in full force, with their microwave towers raised to the sky. When the red pickup truck carrying the figure rounded the corner and headed toward the Mission, people crowded into the street, wiping away tears and beaming smiles as this transnational symbol of hope and peace came toward them. After a few short speeches, a mariachi band stepped to the front of the procession and the crowd sang and prayed its way through the housing projects in the neighborhood surrounding the church. A week later, thousands of Salvadorans gathered in front of Precious Blood Catholic Church in Pico-Union and witnessed the transfiguration of this same "El Salvador" as he descended down into a huge world globe they had constructed and minutes later reappeared in a white robe. But perhaps the most compelling stories deal with what happened at the start of the figure's pilgrimage from El Salvador to California, when Salvadoran mothers, who had bid farewell to sons and daughters migrating northward a decade earlier, kissed and touched the image which they viewed as connecting them with their loved ones, some of whom, we must suppose, now joined the figure's procession around the streets of Los Angeles.

Several months earlier and twenty miles south of the scene in Boyle Heights, a less dramatic but equally important event occurred in a Cambodian Buddhist monastery in Long Beach. Nearly a thousand people crowded into Temple Khemara Bhuddhikarm, bearing food and gifts, to pay homage to their departed relatives. As Rev. Kong Chhean burned slips of paper with the deceased ones' names, his fellow priests chanted, and family units sat together on the floor unpacking their canisters of food, remembering together the events that had brought them to this strange land. There was a young woman in the group who, as a child, had walked through the "killing fields" over dead bodies as she and her family made their escape. And there was a woman, now middle aged, whose two children had died from dysentery on the same day in the early 1970s. There are 150 documented cases of psychosomatic blindness among women in Long Beach who witnessed the torture of their husbands, the rape of their daughters, and the obliteration of their villages. Rev. Chhean, who has training in psychology, refers his members to a local clinic for medication and treatment when they are amenable to Western styles of intervention, and otherwise he performs magical incantations to help them cope with the trauma of their past.

A few weeks later in the San Gabriel foothills an age-old ritual was repeated in the City of Pasadena where some 10,000 Armenians have settled. Resident here are the sons, daughters, and grandchildren of survivors of the genocide in Turkey which claimed the lives of 1.5 million Armenians. It is Saturday, and Tavit (David) is being baptized at Saint Gregory Armenian Apostolic Church. The young child cries as he is held naked in the baptismal font and Father Vazken pours water on him, following the most ancient rite of Christendom, because it was 1,700 years ago that Armenia became the first nation to convert to Christianity (see Figure 5.1 for an example of a baptism). After the baptism, Father Vazken tells a visiting

Figure 5.1. Baptism at Saint Gregory the Illuminator Armenian Apostolic Church, Pasadena, California. Photograph by Jerry Berndt, courtesy of the USC Center for Religion and Civic Culture.

journalist that Armenians can never accept the Turkish denial of the genocide, but, on the other hand, he has chosen this day and every April 24 (see Figure 5.2) to have a blood drive at the church in which the blood of Armenians is available to all—perhaps, as he said, even to a Turk who is in need.

RELIGION, IMMIGRATION, AND THE CHANGING FACE OF LOS ANGELES

Latinos currently constitute 44 percent of the population of Los Angeles County, and Asians, at 12 percent, have surpassed African Americans (10 percent) who are gradually declining as a proportion of LA County's residents.[4] But these are not the only immigrant groups in Los Angeles. There are more immigrants from the Middle East in Los Angeles than in any other region of the country. Armenians, for example, are the second largest group of limited-English-speaking students in the Los Angeles Unified School District. There are also immigrants from Africa, as well as a continuing trickle from Europe. In 1990, Los Angeles was home to 3.9 million immigrants, 400,000 more than New York.[5] Approximately one-third of all the zip codes in Los Angeles County do not have a single ethnic group that constitutes a majority. Los Angeles leads the way in redefining the

Figure 5.2. Armenian Martyrs Day ceremony led by Father Vazken Movsesian, Montebello, California. Photograph by Jerry Bernot, courtesy of the USC Center for Religion and Civic Culture.

State of California which, according to preliminary findings from the 2000 census, is now just 49.9 percent "Anglo."[6]

How the demography of immigration affects the city as a whole, including the lives of nonimmigrants, is plain to see. But equally important is the question, Who is helping the immigrants to become incorporated into American life? Who helps them find housing and employment, assists them with understanding a new legal system, connects them to medical care in an emergency, negotiates the inevitable problems that arise between first-generation immigrants and their children, helps them find their way in a complex mix of contrasting and competing ethnic identities, and offers a helping hand if they run out of cash or have a brush with the law? Many public and private, religious and secular institutions share these responsibilities, of course, but historically, religious groups have always played a central role in settling new immigrants in this country. Now is no exception, judging from our interviews and field studies carried out in congregations representing twelve ethnic and national categories. Immigrants bring elements of their religious institutions with them, of course, but resident congregations, including churches, temples, synagogues, and mosques—and interfaith coalitions of these—have viewed it as their duty to welcome the newcomers, providing sources of assistance that are often amplified by the timely informal assistance offered by individual members of those congregations. In many cases new kinds of interplay between religion and the public sector are evident. To take just one example, the U.S. government worked closely with the U.S. Catholic Conference, Lutheran Social Services, and various other religious groups such as the Mennonites in settling refugees from Vietnam and Cambodia during the 1970s and 1980s. In response to the needs of newcomers, various faith-based advocacy groups, such as the Interfaith Coalition for Immigrant Rights and the Jesuit Refugee Services, have stepped forward to mediate contacts between immigrants and employers and between immigrants and various agencies of government, including the Immigration and Naturalization Service (INS). Many local congregations have developed extensive programs to minister to the needs of immigrants in their immediate neighborhoods, sometimes with infusions of money from public agencies and government programs.

The traditional sociological view of religion's role for immigrants stressed the function of assimilation (see works by Herberg, Gordon, Gans, and Portes and Rumbaut).[7] This view fit reasonably well the reality prior to the 1960s, when most newcomers were from Europe and who, in a generation or two, were thoroughly incorporated into American life, barely distinguishable from the rest of the population. However, with the Immigration Act of 1965 the pattern of immigration changed radically and unexpectedly, enabling large numbers of individuals from Asia, Africa, and Latin America to emigrate much more easily. In 1998, for example, the Immigration and Naturalization Service reported that the top ten countries with immigration to the United States (in order) were Mexico (131,575), China (36,884), India (36,482), Philippines (34,466), Dominican Republic (20,387), Vietnam (17,649), Cuba (17,375), Jamaica (15,146), El Salvador (14,590), and Korea (14,268). Each year, close to a million new immigrants come to the United States, roughly 700,000 of them legally and approximately 300,000 illegally.[8]

While many of America's new immigrants are assimilating in much the same way as did European immigrants of earlier years, there are nevertheless some important differences. For one thing, many of the new immigrants are Asian, Latin American, or African, and, hence, even after English has become their primary language they still are distinguishable from the typical Anglo American. Furthermore, many new immigrants do not share the Judeo-Christian background of earlier generations of immigrants. They are Buddhists, Hindus, Muslims, Sikhs, and various indigenous religions, including, for example, Mayan. Hence, the old argument, that regardless of one's ancestry one could be a "true American" so long as one was a Protestant, Catholic, or Jew, is simply no longer accurate.

In the construction of a new paradigm to address these realities, it must be acknowledged that religion may aid in incorporation to the United States, but it also functions to preserve identification with the home country. It helps immigrants maintain their national identity as Guatemalans, Armenians, or Koreans. To be sure, some members of the second generation join "American churches" and shed their connection with the homeland. But it is equally likely that many of these immigrant congregations will continue into the second and third generation—if not longer—precisely because they provide occasions and places where ethnic groups can enjoy the company of individuals with similar roots. If there is a melting pot facilitated by religion, it is around broad identification as Latino Catholics, Asian Protestants, or Muslims from the Middle East and Asia. For example, Latinos from Mexico, Puerto Rico, Guatemala, and El Salvador search out points of commonality as they worship together in their Catholic or, increasingly, Pentecostal churches. Alternatively, Muslims from Iran, Egypt, and Lebanon, as well as the Indian subcontinent, find common connections as they pray together in their local mosques, even if they were possibly antagonistic toward each other in their home countries. And some second-generation Korean churches in our study seek to become "*Asian* enclaves" (as contrasted with "*Korean* enclaves") hoping to attract Filipinos and Chinese to their services in addition to immigrants from Korea.

For all of these reasons, many researchers agree that, rather than a linear and uniform process of absorption and upward mobility, a more appropriate, though more complex, model for today's immigration may be that of "segmented assimilation"[9] in which preservation of immigrants' own values and promotion of national solidarity with the homeland are compatible with assimilation to American culture.[10] Under this model, religion has two social roles, not one, and they are not contradictory in an era of global connectedness. At a time when (or to the extent that) the United States was a place where people lost their language within a generation and sought to blend with the dominant culture as quickly as possible, religion could function as an unofficial instrument of the state, helping people to assimilate, adapt, "fit in"—even if many first-generation immigrants continued to gather nostalgically in church basements to speak their native language, eat their ethnic food, and celebrate some of the customs from the homeland.[11]

This assimilation or incorporation function is still a major social role of religion in the United States. But since the mid-1960s the churches, temples, mosques, and synagogues have expanded their role as they have mediated between the country of origin and the country of present residence for many immigrants and their offspring, serving as one of the most important points of reference as individuals create multicultural identities. Indeed, compilations of research on the new immigrants by Warner and Wittner and Ebaugh and Chafetz indicate that the immigrant congregation is unrivaled as the place where homeland values are maintained, celebrated, and passed on to the next generation. In performing this function, religion is permanently changing the culture of Southern California.[12]

Figure 5.3. Worship on Easter Sunday at St. Philomena Catholic Church, Carson, California. Photograph by Jerry Berndt, courtesy of USC Center for Religion and Civic Culture.

IMMIGRANT RELIGION AND SOCIAL CHANGE IN SOUTHERN CALIFORNIA

In the contemporary metaphor, the arrival of immigrants in large numbers has changed the religious "marketplace" of Los Angeles and religious institutions, as providers, have responded in visible ways. Church marquees and other announcements of the times and subjects of religious services are not in one language but often two, three, or four. According to information provided by the office of the Catholic archdiocese, more than 60 percent of its 4 million members are Latino, and there are Spanish-language masses in 187 of 287 churches. There are Catholic churches where more Filipinos than Anglos worship (see Figure 5.3). Similarly, there are Catholic churches with niche congregations of Vietnamese and other Asian populations. Clearly the Catholic hierarchy is scrambling to meet the demands of these new immigrants to Los Angeles, and learning Spanish is a requirement for all seminarians. Given the shortage of clergy in the United States, the church relies increasingly on priests trained in Mexico and elsewhere in Latin America who, being themselves immigrants, are in this respect closer to their parishioners in Los Angeles but who, because of their conservative theological training, are sometimes at odds with many of the things the church is doing to accommodate its changing membership base.

This is one of many topics we will examine more closely as our research proceeds. But Catholics are not the only group responding to changing demographics. All over Los Angeles County there are Protestant churches with multiple congregations. In Glendale there is a Presbyterian church with Arabic-, Spanish-, Armenian-, and English-speaking congregations all meeting on the same campus. A Nazarene church in downtown Los Angeles (indeed, the "mother church" of that historically Anglo denomination) has set up separate governance structures for its Filipino, Spanish, Korean, and English congregations, with each having proportional representation in church decisions. In Pasadena, an evangelical "megachurch" has given over to a Spanish-speaking congregation the sanctuary that the Anglo congregation outgrew and has hired a staff to minister to the growing Latino population in the immediate neighborhood of the church. On Broadway in downtown Los Angeles, several ornate former "movie palaces" have been turned into churches, and one of the largest congregations among the many to be found there is the Universal Church, an import from Brazil.

Predominantly Anglo churches (should we still call them the "mainstream"?) are also seeking to symbolize their solidarity with the changing demographics of Los Angeles. For example, at All Saints Episcopal Church in Pasadena, songs in Spanish are often incorporated into the liturgy, even though very few Latinos attend this upper-middle-class church. Thanks to the efforts of the custodial staff, All Saints has formed a partnership with Agua Verde, a village in Mexico where the joint effort has helped to construct a library and launch other social projects. In some Protestant churches, such as Immanuel Presbyterian in the Wilshire district, there has been a dramatic blending of Protestant and Catholic elements in their worship. A person who attended the Good Friday "Stations of the Cross" procession through the streets adjoining this cathedral-style church might think it is a Catholic service as the crowd stops to pray and listen to short homilies before home-made altars and shrines that have been placed on the sidewalk. Mainline Protestant churches that are not embracing the culture of their neighborhood residents are dying, and consequently there is great interest by Methodists, Baptists, and others to figure out strategies for ministering to the new residents in their neighborhoods.

The religious "marketplace" changes in response to "consumer" demand, and consequently some of the fastest-growing churches in Los Angeles are Pentecostal and charismatic, because these are among the most vital congregations in the members' homelands. Guatemala, for example, is according to some reports 30 percent Pentecostal and growing, much to the dismay of Catholic clergy who sometimes accuse their Protestant colleagues of "sheep stealing."[13] On the other hand, Catholic churches such as St. Thomas the Apostle in Pico-Union (an area near downtown Los Angeles that is populated predominantly by Central American immigrants) have embraced a charismatic movement of lay members who, every Friday

Figure 5.4. Healing Prayer at El Sembrador charismatic service, Friday evening at St. Thomas the Apostle Catholic Church, Los Angeles, California. Photograph by Jerry Berndt, courtesy of USC Center for Religion and Civic Culture.

night, lead the congregation in enthusiastic praise choruses and hand clapping, followed by a period of healing and laying on of hands (see Figure 5.4). Furthermore, Catholics are accommodating their members' desires for concrete symbols in their lives, such as the Virgin of Guadeloupe, a replica of whose image was brought to Los Angeles and became the focus of a commemoration mass in the Los Angeles Coliseum that drew tens of thousands of enthusiasts. It was clear that this image of the Virgin had been elevated to the status of transnational symbol of immigrant hope as people carried flags from the many nations represented in the Catholic archdiocese's multiethnic membership (see Figure 5.5).

As immigrants are attracted to Los Angeles from many parts of the world, they are building impressive houses of worship as expressions of their commitment and in doing so are changing the landscape of religious and community architecture. The Hsi Lai Temple in Hacienda Heights is the largest Buddhist Temple in the Western Hemisphere and is an architectural monument as well as a functional monastery and place where people, particularly Chinese from Taiwan, come to connect with their cultural and spiritual roots (see Figure 5.6). The Hindu Temple in Malibu is also an architectural gem, and the Swaminarayan Hindu sect, with headquarters in Whittier, has been attempting to buy a substantial parcel in Southern California in order to build a temple that will reflect the affluence of their

Figure 5.5. Palm Sunday at St. Thomas the Apostle Catholic Church, Los Angeles, California. Photograph by Jerry Berndt, courtesy of USC Center for Religion and Civic Culture.

Figure 5.6. Walking meditation at Hsi Lai Temple, Hacienda Heights, California. Photo by Jerry Berndt, courtesy of USC Center for Religion and Civic Culture.

congregation from India. One must also include in the list of architectural statements the King Fahd Mosque in Culver City, which is just one of 68 mosques in Southern California. Indeed, consistent with speculation that Muslims will outnumber Jews in the United States within the next decade, Los Angeles has the third largest number of mosques in the United States, after Chicago and New York.

Although the evidence is not usually architectural, it is Koreans who are by some measures the most obviously religiously committed group of immigrants in the Southern California basin. Church attendance is pegged at 80 percent or more, and two of the largest congregations (Young Nak Presbyterian Church, just east of downtown Los Angeles, and the Oriental Mission in Koreatown) welcome more than 5,000 worshippers each Sunday. When one of our graduate researchers wanted to look at Korean Christian student groups at UCLA, she found herself dealing with over a dozen recognized organizations. Some estimates suggest that there are as many as 600 immigrant and second-generation Korean churches in the Los Angeles area. Many of these are small congregations that offer leadership opportunities to immigrants who feel shut out from mainstream society and/or from long established and culturally conservative Korean churches. The influx of Korean Christians has been important to the financial health of Protestant seminaries and colleges in Southern California, with Fuller Seminary, Claremont School of Theology, and Biola University all having high percentages of Korean and Korean American students. As is true with many immigrant groups, Korean churches are deeply committed to missionary work in various parts of the world, and from their base in Los Angeles they are sending missionaries to Mexico and elsewhere in Latin America, as well as to countries in the former Soviet Union.

Armenians, who are also well represented in Los Angeles County, have large immigrant populations in Glendale, Hollywood, and Pasadena. The ancient Apostolic Church has two different branches, but there are also dozens of evangelical Armenian churches that are competing for the flock, and from all appearances, rather successfully. Like many immigrant groups, these churches have private day schools as well as Saturday schools where children and youth come to learn the language and something about the customs and history of the homeland. Armenian churches also play a major role in diaspora politics, with their members supporting political candidates who are advocates for the homeland; additionally, hundreds of thousands of dollars are funneled by the church and its ancillary organizations back to the homeland for various relief and development projects.

WHAT DO IMMIGRANTS OFFER LOS ANGELES?

While there is no doubt that immigrants are reshaping Los Angeles in various ways, especially demographically, what else can we say about their impact on and contributions to this "City of the Angels"? The answers are complex and sometimes subject to debate. That the evolving mix of nationalities forever alters the rhythm of "race and ethnic relations" in Los Angeles hardly needs to be pointed out. Although the balance of fiscal and economic consequences of immigration remains subject to debate, some investigators (for example, McCarthy and Vernez and Smith and Edmonston) note that the relatively robust economy of Southern California owes much of its resiliency to immigrant workers, whether they are in the garment industry, where sweatshop conditions often prevail, or in the high-tech sector that relies increasingly on foreign-trained professionals.[14] Occupancy rates of high-rise office buildings and the continuing attraction of tourist venues, restaurants, and hotels depend directly upon a reliable and growing service sector, again largely immigrant-based. Middle-class lifestyles, occupational opportunities, and two-earner incomes are predicated upon the availability of affordable child care and household labor, again provided almost entirely by immigrant workers. The rapid aging of the U.S. population creates a growing demand for health care, and thus elder care professionals, and increasingly this demand is met by immigrant workers performing valuable functions on both the higher (physicians and nurses) and lower (attendant care) rungs of the employment ladder. Perhaps most dramatically, the dynamics of electoral politics have shifted in response to recent spikes in applications for citizenship and increasing rates of political participation in immigrant communities.

Closer to our own area of study, however, there is an equally important contribution that immigrants are making to Los Angeles, and this is one of moral renewal. Immigrant groups consistently place an emphasis on values associated with family, children, and community. If one of the problems of modern society is the breakdown of primary institutions such as the family, fueled by a rugged individualism that puts self and consumerism above all other values,[15] then we have something to learn from our immigrant populations. Indeed, a common concern that immigrants express about raising their children in this society is that it is difficult to maintain a focus on shared communal values in a society so dominated by consumerism and self-interest. Their efforts in this regard are visible in the parks in our urban neighborhoods, filled with families picnicking and playing soccer. Indeed, it is often extended families at these gatherings, and children are typically taught to respect their elders as much as they do their mothers and fathers.

Many immigrants believe that they can juggle the best of both worlds—the advantages of life in the United States and the values of their home country—so long as their children can associate with a strong religious community. As one member of the Swaminarayan Hindu Temple said, echoing what many others told us, "We are giving [our children] opportunities of being in the United States and everything that comes along with it, but at the same time we are teaching them that [there are] things that are not good for you." The importance of having a protective alternative community was stressed by another individual from the same temple who said "Even if the Swaminaryan religion cannot stop everything [that threatens our children], it minimizes the chances of going astray or succumbing to temptation or peer pressure. So, religion does help. . . . Oh, yes, religion does make a difference." In essence, religion provides an alternative community and peer group that articulates through rite, ritual, and communal activities the values associated with the homeland.

Indeed, religion and homeland values are inseparable for all of these immigrant groups. Their cultures are integrally tied to their religious practices, and it is in feast days, festivals, and other celebrations—many of which are connected to the religious calendar of the country—that these values are renewed as well as enacted. A Mayan from Guatemala said that in his community he was taught that even one glass of water needs to be shared by all members of the community, which sharply contrasts with the pervasive individualism that competes with the spirit of community in the United States. In *Bowling Alone*, Robert Putnam expresses a deep concern among academics that our "social capital," by which he means collective effort and shared commitments, is decreasing in American society. He captures this sentiment in the metaphor of solitary bowling: more people than ever bowl, but they are bowling alone, not in leagues. He also notes in the same vein the decline in people volunteering to oversee Scout troops or joining such traditional collective organizations as the PTA and the League of Women Voters.[16]

But there is another reality at work, which Putnam and other cultural pessimists should note. Within Los Angeles there are hundreds of "hometown associations," a name given to groups of people from cities and villages in Mexico and Central America who now live in Los Angeles and who have come together to maintain their common culture and at the same time find ways to fund projects back in their village or city. These associations are often closely related to churches, and their resources sometimes go into the restoration of a church or church activities at home; at other times the objective may be building a road, digging a well, or buying books for the school library. These hometown associations raise money by putting on dances, beauty pageants, and dinners. In some cases, they partner with the government back home on matching funds. These are sophisticated organizations, oftentimes legally incorporated, or, if not, they are affiliated with not-for-profit federations. From the Mexican state of Oaxaca alone, we have found at least thirty hometown associations in Los Angeles and the San Joaquin Valley, and the Mexican Consulate in Los Angeles has registered 170 hometown associations within the Los Angeles Metropolitan area.

Another sign of moral engagement is that each year immigrants living in

Los Angeles send hundreds of millions of dollars back to their families. Based on anecdotal evidence, many immigrants wire $200 to $300 home each month, and this is from people who may be earning a minimum wage or who are working as day laborers or in sweatshops for even less than minimum wage. This type of heroic moral commitment has to be considered whenever the media highlights an immigrant gang or criminal activity by an immigrant. Indeed, many immigrants come to this country, not for their own personal economic advancement, but so they can support a family back home, pay for medical treatment for a relative, or send someone to school. A woman from El Salvador told us that she came to Los Angeles when she was only twenty because her son, born prematurely, needed an operation to correct a heart condition. The only way she could finance this expensive surgery was to come to the United States, leaving her baby behind her.

WHAT DO IMMIGRANTS NEED?

It is good to be cautious in generalizing about immigrants, because there are substantial differences from one group to another and from one generation to another. It is always important to ask, "Which immigrants?" and "What generation?" The Immigration and Naturalization Service recognizes three broad groups: (1) refugees and asylees, a category that in 1997 accounted for 14 percent of all foreigners admitted to the United States and included, for example, refugees from the former Soviet Union and Bosnia; (2) individuals and their families who are admitted for economic or employment reasons, including people of "extraordinary" ability in the arts or sciences, as well as multinational executives and people with professional or advanced degrees; and (3) immigrants who are children, parents, or spouses of individuals already living in the United States.[17] In addition, there are several hundred thousand unauthorized or undocumented migrants who come to the United States without valid visas. About 60 percent of these individuals cross the Mexico-U.S. border without being apprehended, and the remaining 40 percent enter the United States legally, often as tourists, and then decide to stay without seeking proper registration.[18]

From a religious point of view, a different but overlapping set of concerns or categories is important for the congregations, advocacy groups, and nonprofit organizations that respond to the needs of immigrants. The "presenting needs" of immigrants vary widely depending on their socioeconomic status, and in Los Angeles there are two distinct groups that are easily separated by education. For example, Mexicans constitute almost half of all new immigrants in Los Angeles, and they average only seven years of education. Included in this group are campesinos who may be illiterate and whose primary vocational skill is picking fruit or doing manual labor. Salvadorans and Guatemalans together constitute another 10 percent, and they average eight years of education. In contrast, Asians on the average, with the exception of some groups such as Cambodians, are highly educated. Chinese immigrants to Los Angeles average sixteen years of education, Filipinos fifteen years, and Koreans thirteen years. Obviously there are well educated and poorly educated individuals in any group, but the generalization stands that among immigrants, those from Mexico and Central America tend to be employed in low-level jobs in Los Angeles, while those from Asia are much more likely to be represented in professional and managerial positions.

A second cluster of concerns is that some immigrants come here to escape highly traumatizing backgrounds, and these individuals are not necessarily those the INS classifies as refugees. The refugee designation is often complicated by political variables that bear little relationship to the circumstances people have actually faced. Many immigrants from Guatemala and El Salvador, for example, though not legally refugees, have witnessed the killing, rape, and torture of family members and friends by government forces that were supported by the U.S. military. Refugees from Vietnam and Cambodia have similarly experienced violent bloodshed, including the annihilation of entire villages. There are also the pastoral demands put on clergy who confront the dilemma of men and women who remarried, thinking that their spouses had been killed, only to meet them once again in the United States. Pastoral care needs differ from one immigrant group to another. An Armenian cleric, to take one case in point, said that for many immigrants from the (formerly Soviet) Republic of Armenia, cheating the government was a way of life—it was how one survived. Hence, he went on, there is a need to "resocialize" these individuals, in order to displace the expectations engrained by seventy years of communist rule.

Legal documentation is a marker for another dimension of need. Undocumented immigrants often come to a church or temple because they see it as a place of refuge and hope. Included in this category are men and women who have left children behind with grandparents and other family members, seeking higher wages in order to enhance the prospects of the children they are not able to bring with them. Most often these are women who become "transnational parents" (they could also be called "dual parents"), working as domestics taking care of the children of well-to-do people (often at wages well below the legal minimum and without any benefits) at the same time that they are preoccupied with the welfare of their own children at home. Often men, too, have the same preoccupations with the children they left at home but who continue to be the primary focus in their lives. One Latino pastor we interviewed said that his task is to give hope to people caught in such situations, urging them to have dreams and telling them that they can have a better life. "We treat people right," he said when we asked him about the methodology in his ministry—"We treat them with dignity." The numbers that are attracted to congregations such as his would seem to bear out his choice of methods.

Finally, quite simply, many immigrants in all categories arrive in this country feeling isolated and fearful, faced by language barriers as well as cultural challenges. If they are separated from their families, they keenly feel the lack of a supportive network—a safety net if they get sick or cannot find a job immediately. Many immigrants living in Los Angeles who were scientists, doctors, and professionals in their home country are working in what for them are menial jobs because of licensing regulations or language deficiencies. Or perhaps they emigrated because their children preceded them and they wanted to live near their grandchildren. With a variety of causes, then, loneliness and lack of self-esteem are issues that religious communities help to mitigate for the immigrants they serve.

While many Americans simply see immigrants as a problem—always thinking first of someone who has unlawfully entered their country—there is always a story of hope behind every individual who has circumvented the law in coming to the United States. The task of the religious community is clearly not to apprehend these individuals; that is the responsibility of the INS and federal authorities. Rather, it is to hear their stories, care for them in times of need, and offer them hope that something better is in store for them. This is the viewpoint that we heard again and again from the clergy we interviewed, regardless of their religious tradition.

RELIGIOUS PRACTICE AND LIVING IN LOS ANGELES

That there is considerable freedom and many options from which to choose is for many part of the cultural shock of living in Los Angeles. There is no longer the certainty of one assumed religious identity. In this area of life alone, people face literally dozens of options. Moreover, even for a person surrounded by a kinship group, the cultural restraints on making choices are rarely as limiting as they were in the home country. Although immigrants interviewed for this project often remarked on the dangers of such pluralism, they also tended to like the freedom they experienced. They felt that they could "be themselves" in this new homeland. With some frequency, immigrants from Hindu and Muslim countries said that they felt they could live "more honestly" in America, by which they meant they were free from bribes, corruption, and other practices that sometimes are a way of life in their home country. Having said this, however, they also indicated there were temptations in Los Angeles that they did not face at home—especially temptations associated with drugs, alcohol, and promiscuous sex. Women sometimes commented with approval that here, they could practice their religion in public ways that were proscribed in the homeland, where they had to confine their worship to the home. Finally, those we interviewed rarely mentioned religious discrimination once they moved to Los Angeles. In fact, some individuals, especially college students, said that being an "ethnic" practicing an "exotic" religion brought them a certain envious regard among their peers.

Indeed, a Hindu we interviewed said "In India it was much easier to preserve and practice Hinduism because it is all over the place," whereas here, she said, it takes a conscious effort to drive "all the way to Malibu to keep track of auspicious days and festivals." But on the other side of the balance, it was not at all uncommon among those who shared their experiences with us to say that their faith had grown stronger since moving to the United States. They offered several explanations for this increased commitment and energy. Some said that at home their religion was taken for granted. Several times a year they might go to the temple to offer oblations, but religion was so pervasive and so unquestioned that it never felt like a conscious choice. Even prayer, some said (including Muslims who pray five times a day), was something done routinely, without thinking.

On this same theme, in the American context and particularly in Los Angeles, immigrants often see a stark contrast between the values they have been raised with and the values of American mainstream culture. Hence, they find themselves faced with a clear if sometimes painful choice. Those we interviewed often *elected* to embrace their religion more firmly—now making a clear, conscious *choice*—rather than to float along with what they perceived to be the permissive values of American culture. A Muslim from Lebanon, asked whether his faith had changed upon coming to the United States, replied, "Actually, it has improved, to be frank with you. I think we devote more time to the religion [here] even though it should have been more over there, back home." And several second-generation Sikh boys told us that, at first, they wanted to abandon the turban worn by their fathers, but now see it as an important element of their Sikh identity. In spite of adolescent peer pressure to conform (backward baseball caps?), they have chosen to be different (see Figure 5.7).

Finally, for many immigrants religion continues to exercise a strong attraction because it provides a setting and a reason to be in contact with their fellow immigrants. Religion, in other words, is a source of community, a place to speak one's native tongue, eat one's native food, and, not unimportantly, find a husband or wife who shares one's cultural background. A group of Hindu women told us that they didn't mind doing the cooking for the temple's activities on the weekends because it provided a welcome time for them to see their friends and talk in Gujarati. And young people in the same temple, one of our research assistants noted, seemed to quite enjoy being at the temple, wearing *gaghras* and saris and the latest chic Indian fashions, especially for important religious occasions.

But a complete picture requires us to note that there are also negative factors related to religious practice and life in Los Angeles. Immigrants often mentioned that they are so busy trying to make a living that it leaves

Figure 5.7. Boy playing the harmonium at Vermont Gurdwara, Los Angeles, California. Photo by Jerry Berndt, courtesy of USC Center for Religion and Civic Culture.

little time for religion. Muslims in particular said that it sometimes feels awkward in their workplace to observe the daily routine of prayer, even if there is no objection from their employer. Immigrants from Asia said that, without temples being omnipresent in society, religious practice demands a different rhythm than the occasional formal observance that they followed in their home country, and this cultural difference, uncomfortable for many, is not easily addressed. A Vietnamese priest noted a different problem: namely, that it is difficult to recruit clergy in this country, since so many other alternatives are open to young men.

On the other hand, for every objection to life in Los Angeles a counter-benefit was cited. Women from Latin American countries indicated, for example, that they appreciated the view toward domestic violence that they experienced in this country. Pastors and priests teach against it, they said, whereas in their home country "machismo" practices were tolerated, if not actively accepted. Women from the Philippines said that they like the fact that religion is not as likely to be labeled "women's work" in this country, and their husbands are also expected to be active in the church. There were also expressions of appreciation with the fact that interfaith dialogue is respected in this country, at the same time there is acceptance of firmly held beliefs. In the home country, strict beliefs were often viewed as antithetical to tolerance and appreciation of others' rights to hold deep convictions. The advanced technology available in Los Angeles is also having an impact. At risk of overstatement, there seems to be a positive correlation between the marginality of a religion and the size of its Web site. Religious groups that do not command a large number of adherents have put up some of the most sophisticated Web pages. The Internet, in other words, represents an entirely new equalizing medium for achieving visibility and expanding the boundaries of communication.

THE PRACTICAL ROLE OF RELIGION IN THE LIVES OF NEW IMMIGRANTS

While much of the discussion of immigrant religion appropriately concentrates on matters of belief and worship, it is also important to catalog the very mundane, though nevertheless crucial, ways in which religion affects the daily lives of immigrants. Perhaps foremost in this connection is the role it plays as a "conduit" for people who are considering emigrating. Because of the thousands who have preceded them, those considering the move to Los Angeles know that there will be a ready-made community waiting for them when they arrive here. Leaving home is always a process fraught with considerable anxiety, an emotion that photographer Sebastiao Salgado has brilliantly captured in his documentary collection of photographs called *Migrations*.[19] But to know that there is a community at the far end of the road that shares one's values and understands the challenges one is confronting eases some of the tension associated with being uprooted and facing the challenge of starting a new life. Other institutions often develop alongside and in close association with churches, temples, synagogues, or mosques, and before long an area becomes known as "Little Saigon" or "Koreatown"—often with religious congregations as the anchor institutions. Religion addresses the problem of loneliness, in other words, by providing entry to a familiar community with familiar beliefs and practices that give structure and meaning to life—all elements of stability that are especially important in a new environment where expectations about what to believe or think are unclear. Indeed, worship and ritual have the potential to bind people together in ways that other institutions are not equipped to do.

To put it succinctly, religious institutions are a safety net for immigrants, spiritually, psychologically, and culturally. Some of the large "megachurches" approach this task by dividing their congregations into cell groups that meet in people's homes. Young Nak (Korean) Presbyterian Church, for example, has thousands of worshippers but relies on 127 such groups of twelve to twenty people, each to provide a more intimate religious experience. In addition to studying the Bible, there are times of sharing in these informal settings, followed by prayer for each other's needs. If someone is out of work, this is made known within the cell group which functions, in many ways, like an extended family. Even if someone in the group cannot supply a connection for a job, at least the person in need feels the warmth and compassion of a caring group of friends. Small storefront churches also often operate like extended family networks. Congregations are voluntary associations and even if they have paid staff they always provide multiple outlets for sharing talents and abilities—whether it be singing in a choir, directing a children's program, or cooking and serving food. Congregations of all sizes provide opportunities for expressing leadership, something that may not be possible for immigrants within their workplace or the larger society.

Religion also serves as a mediating institution, functioning as a bridge between immigrants and a culture that they fear and have not learned to navigate. Sometimes this is as simple as offering translation services for the newly arrived. At other times the mediation is more practical: connecting newcomers to various social services, advising them on a good doctor, or telling them where they can buy food cheaply. Congregations with professionals among them often set up legal clinics for immigrant members or offer health screening and referral. Young Nak employs a parish nurse; other groups have prison ministries directed to fellow immigrants who have had trouble with the law and need support as well as an advocate on their behalf. Churches and interfaith coalitions of clergy and laity have taken an active role in the defense of the rights of immigrants when police, schools, the INS, or other public agencies engage in practices that cause concern.

Advocacy, in fact, is a major role played by religious institutions. At a political level, it is to counter the nativist impulse that always arises when population shifts dramatically and individuals feel threatened that newcomers will take their jobs, work at a lower wage rate, or displace them from housing. Immigrant congregations across Los Angeles were strongly opposed to California's Proposition 187, which was intended to strip undocumented immigrants of many social services. The congregation-based Industrial Areas Foundation (IAF) went on the offensive with public demonstrations and, through its Active Citizenship Campaign, registered thousands of immigrants to vote. The IAF actively petitioned the INS to speed up the processing of applications for citizenship, so that these individuals could be turned into voters and thereby defend their rights on their own.

Cardinal Roger Mahony of the Archdiocese of Los Angeles has been a strong advocate for immigrants. In an important pastoral letter in 1993, he captured the thinking of many religious leaders when he said:

Today we are witnessing a distressing and growing trend among political leaders, segments of the media, and the public at-large, which capitalizes on prevailing fears and insecurity about the growing number of immigrants in our communities. In today's social climate, we have special reasons to study and ponder the Bible's positive view of strangers, sojourners and aliens [quoting from the New Testament book of Hebrews]. Our biblical tradition encourages us to encounter the "strangers in our midst"—not with fear and negativity—but with compassion and hopeful expectation. Our social teaching challenges us to embody this sentiment in our personal actions, in our response as a community, and in public policy.[20]

Specifically attacking the sentiment that was to later be focused in Proposition 187, he said:

We know that nothing is gained by denying citizenship and access to education to the children of undocumented workers. On the contrary, the human potential of these dynamic new Americans will be lost. Our society will not be improved by creating an even larger under-class deprived of education.

Citing papal encyclicals and appealing to scripture as well as personal empathy, Cardinal Mahony has used his bully pulpit effectively. The *Los Angeles Times* frequently publishes his opinion articles, and the press turns to him when they want a proimmigrant statement.

At a local congregational level, religious rhetoric is matched by actions, even in small Pentecostal churches such as Templo Calvario, with its "Adopt a Family" program in which church members target specific families in their community that need a helping hand. While (or because) many individuals who adopt a family were themselves immigrants only a few years previously, they believe they have an obligation to help others. One individual from this church put it this way, "We are not volunteers. We are servants doing God's work." As another member of this church explained, this dedication is fueled by the fact that the members are repaying the kindness that was offered to them by strangers when they were new to the city.

It is important to note that churches and other religious organizations do not, typically, provide services only to those within their congregation or even to those who affirm their same faith. Rather, food, clothing, citizenship, and other programs are offered, without stipulation, to everyone in the community. Informal assistance, on the other hand, often occurs because a new immigrant is a member of a cell group or participates in other church-related programs and consequently their needs are known because of the close friendships that have developed. But because of the sheer volume of requests for help, some churches have made a policy of referring individuals to Catholic Charities, the Salvation Army, or other professional charities that are capable of dealing with the complex needs of individuals and their families.

Other faith-based groups resist the idea of "charity" and instead work hard at helping individuals to be self-sufficient. For example, an Episcopal priest with an immigrant congregation decided to start a janitorial service. Father Philip Lance said that this small "capitalistic enterprise," along with a thrift store he started, is employing forty-one people. And an enterprising Jesuit priest, Fr. George Schultz, organized day laborers, creating an employment center associated with St. Joseph Center so that men and women will not be exploited simply because they are poor and not legal residents of the City of Los Angeles. With the welfare reform legislation of 1996, the Charitable Choice provision is encouraging congregations to partner with government in creating job readiness programs, which should further buttress the role that religion is playing in the areas of employment and self-sufficiency.

Because they are so consumed with problems of their own members, one might assume that immigrant congregations would be unable to think far beyond their own community, but that is not the case. During the period of our study, the Hsi Lai Temple, whose members are predominantly Buddhists from Taiwan, not surprisingly gave generously to victims of an earthquake that wreaked havoc in their homeland, but also came forward to help those affected by a devastating hurricane in Honduras and an earthquake in Colombia.

Armenian congregations have a long history of sponsoring orphans, sending money to build schools in the Republic of Armenia, and helping the elderly to cope after the collapse of the Soviet Union (and with it, the pension system), not to speak of the millions of dollars that they sent to Armenia after an earthquake in 1988 that killed 25,000 people and left a half million homeless. An Armenian priest in Pasadena told us that he recently had intervened with youth from his church who were upset that a photo in the school yearbook linked Armenian youth with gang activity, which they resented.

Islamic groups in Los Angeles have expressed their humanitarian views by encouraging discussion of State Department policy, such as the ongoing embargo of Iraq, which has claimed the lives of thousands of children because of the lack of medicine and basic nutrition. At the same time, Muslims were very pointed in their support of U.S actions and NATO troops in Kosovo. The Muslim Public Affairs Council has been very proactive in countering stereotypes about Muslims—especially those that portray them as terrorists.

Korean Buddhist temples and Korean churches have sent tens of thousands of dollars worth of aid to help counter the food shortages in North Korea, and when a destructive earthquake struck El Salvador in January 2001, a Korean church called Oriental Mission quickly raised an astonishing $3 million for medical and other supplies for the victims.[21]

THE ROLE OF RELIGION IN THE LIVES OF IMMIGRANT WOMEN

Women around the world take on a disproportionate share of religious participation and religious work in almost every dimension except formal leadership. Their participation in immigrant religion and the impact of that participation on their lives as immigrants is a topic that demands special attention. In our research, it is clear that immigrant women face the same anxieties, cultural challenges, and linguistic barriers as immigrant men, but many of those in our study described a unique set of problems and challenges of their own. We are only beginning to discover their specific needs and the ways that the faith community has responded to them. Many of the women—refugee and undocumented women in particular—have been victims of rape, have witnessed atrocities against their family members, and have lost husbands to war or abandonment. Others have come to the United States with hopes of finding the husband who left them in their home country, promising to return but not keeping that promise. These women arrive in Los Angeles feeling isolated and often helpless, unable to speak the language, and unsure of how to live. Over and over we have heard how afraid they were, how reluctant they were even to leave the house for fear of getting lost. Yet, as they have struggled to survive and adapt in a new land, they have begun to find a sense of freedom and autonomy that they did not have back home. Indeed, this is confirmed by a study conducted by one of the Center for Religion and Civic Culture's research associates, Pierrette Hondagneau-Sotelo. In her study of Mexican immigrant families she found that while women still have less power than men do in families, they generally enjoy more autonomy, resources, and leverage than they previously did in Mexico.[22] This sense of freedom is often developed in the context of religious congregations. Consider the following other examples that we have documented in our research:

- The Industrial Areas Foundation sponsored the Active Citizenship Campaign as a way to empower immigrants—and immigrant congregations—to engage the legislative process. A young Latina woman who is a member of St. John's Catholic Church told us that the community organizing process and the support from her congregation provided her with the space and place to develop her own potential. Suddenly, she said, she was given a voice as an advocate for her people. Indeed, all over Southern California, this story is repeated in churches where women have learned how to organize and how to be advocates.

- The Muslim Women's League has been teaching women to read the Koran. In this way, they are being empowered to understand for themselves their rights and privileges.

- Religious congregations, including the Swaminarayan Temple mentioned earlier, are venues where feelings of loneliness are assuaged through social interaction and community. Some women have stated that they do not mind doing the "kitchen work" at festivals because it brings appreciation and provides an opportunity for them to interact with other women and speak their native language.

- The Temple Khemara Buddikaram, as described in the introduction to this chapter, provides a place where people gather to gain healing from traumatic experiences in Cambodia. Here, women can talk to the priest, one of the few people they will trust with their pain. Rev. Kong Chhean understands the trauma that many of them have experienced, and understands both Western psychology and Buddhist healing practices. As a result, this temple has become a sanctuary for these women (see Figure 5.8).

- The women of Boyle Heights have found that Dolores Mission Catholic Church is a place where they can talk about their problems, face their fears, and take up the challenge to work for peace and safety in their communities. Every Friday, these Latina women walk through the streets, praying on the corners for peace in the barrio and an end to gang violence. Moreover, they have also learned to challenge the authorities when their sons are unjustly treated by police or become victims of racial profiling.

- Pentecostal churches maintain an aggressive stance against alcoholism and spousal abuse and are often effective in changing patterns of domestic violence and "machismo" practices in the family. As men become more involved in the church, they are motivated to change their behavior. The result, their wives often say, is that the home environment is transformed by the teaching of the church.

All over Los Angeles immigrant women are creatively finding ways to overcome financial and economic hurdles. Often, congregations serve as places where women can connect, learn about jobs, and create informal networks that enable them to augment their income. For many of the women this process is natural since informal networks were the means of

Figure 5.8. Services at the Khemara Buddhikaram, Long Beach, California. Photo by Jerry Berndt, courtesy of USC Center for Religion and Civic Culture.

survival in their home countries. But here in the new country, they often find that it is in the churches that they can connect with other women and get the mutual help that they need. The women at Dolores Mission have formed a cooperative that provides learning opportunities for them while at the same time caring for their children in a licensed child-care preschool facility. The Episcopal Diocese is working with a coalition of private and public organizations to provide legalized sidewalk vending for illegal street vendors, the majority of which are women. The focus of these efforts has been on setting up hot food carts where they can sell the *tamales* and *pupusas* that they make. Another coalition of churches and organizations is working hard to advocate for the rights of immigrant sweatshop workers in downtown Los Angeles with the hope of improving their economic standing.

Another major issue that immigrant women face is the daunting problem of health care. Often, they arrive in Los Angeles with little or no understanding of health problems and how to deal with the American healthcare system. Many refuse to be seen by male doctors and will resist getting treatment for that reason. The faith community has responded in a variety of ways to bring medical care to these women. For example, the University Muslim Medical Association (UMMA) Free Clinic was established to provide health care for women in the context of their own faith and in accordance with Muslim guidelines. Several miles to the north, Sister Diane

Figure 5.9. Outside Masjid Umar Ibn-Al Khattab, a mosque near USC, Los Angeles, California. Photo by Jerry Berndt, courtesy of USC Center for Religion and Civic Culture.

Donoghue and Nancy Ibrahim of Esperanza Community Housing Corporation established a program called "Promotoras de Salud Comunitaria" which is designed to expand access to health care and to promote wellness in the community. These trained *promotoras* are community members who are able to go door to door providing health education and offering referrals for health problems they encounter. While open to anyone in the community, it is precisely this type of outreach that meets the needs of the immigrant women. Recognizing this need, several congregations and faith-based hospitals have parish nurses who visit the community members to identify problems and offer solutions and referrals. For a woman who is afraid to go to the doctor or hospital because she does not speak English, these parish nurses become her health consultants.

CONCLUSION

The reciprocal effects of immigrants on religion and religion on the lives of immigrants are plain to see. There is no question that immigrants are changing the face of existing religious groups in Los Angeles (see Figure 5.9). Religious institutions are increasingly refocusing their mission to accommodate the growing numbers of immigrants in their neighborhoods. Religious mandates to care for strangers and the least privileged in the community are obviously behind this receptivity, but it is also borne from a recognition that the demographics of the region are changing and, hence, institutional survival is connected to inclusivity and decline is likely to be the price of turning away from the newcomers. Conversely, many of the religious "imports" to Southern California, which in their own homeland may preach exclusivity, are learning to function in a pluralistic social environment that values diversity. As minority religions here in Los Angeles, they see the value of tolerance as well as interfaith dialogue. Given the diversity of Southern California, immigrant religious groups are seldom asked to water down their beliefs and practices, but they are expected to respect the rights of others. In exchange, they are appreciated for the color and the contribution that they make to this extraordinarily metropolitan city.

Part of the postmodern mood of Los Angeles is that people need not homogenize their beliefs and practices. Quite the contrary, uniqueness and distinctiveness are valued in a city that values experimentation. Anglos are a visible presence in many immigrant congregations, sometimes because of intermarriage, and at other times because this new religious expression mediates the sacred in ways that more established religions fail to do. And there are immigrants who are switching their allegiance from the faith of their homeland. There is a small movement in Los Angeles of Latinos converting to Islam; there are Buddhist Koreans joining immigrant Presbyterian churches, and the ranks of immigrant Mormons are growing. And so the marketplace of religion evolves, with people switching allegiances in response to whoever is serving their needs the best.

What is uniformly apparent about immigrant religion, however, is that its power lies in its anchorage in communities of people. It is within these religious communities that immigrants meet their spiritual needs, find respite from their loneliness, discover marriage partners, and find support to get them past the many difficulties they face. Some of this support is formalized in programs designed to serve immigrants, and at other times it is informal, nurtured in small groups associated with congregations or in personal interactions with clergy. Indeed, clergy fill a great many roles in these immigrant congregations: pastor, social worker, immigration counselor, friend, advocate, and even psychiatrist. Religion certainly includes the search for truth, but it is also a human community that nurtures, expresses compassion, and challenges individuals to live up to their potential.

While religious institutions historically have facilitated assimilation and incorporation into American values, this part of their mission is increasingly sharing energy with the task of cultural preservation. It is in the church, temple, synagogue, or mosque that immigrants are celebrating the rites of passage, feast days, and other rituals that preserve their ties to their homeland and constantly renew the values associated with the birthplace of their ancestors. These composite identities that bridge cultures are possible because the world has changed since the Immigration Acts of 1965. In the last few decades we have increasingly become a global village in which national boundaries often feel arbitrary. This is not to ignore the political reality of country borders, which oftentimes have been created at the cost of many lives. But it is to say that the need to make mutually exclusive choices among national identities is not so important any longer, especially when the Internet can supply news about one's birthplace that may be more current than what the relatives back home are getting, and when inexpensive air travel makes it possible for many, most notably of course the more affluent, to shuttle between here and there or send their children home for vacations or extended visits.

The "melting pot" idea in the sense of convergence toward a very small list of "American" religions is certainly a dated one, but we are increasingly seeing immigrant congregations that display some similarities with that process. Many of them are organized around language or broad regional identifications. Hence, there are Latino or Asian congregations that attract people from many different national backgrounds, and yet they share an identity that is rooted in a particular language and faith tradition, finding commonalties that are different from those shared by members of congregations that are predominately comprised of Anglo Americans.

At the same time, there are congregations that are extraordinary in their inclusiveness, expanding far beyond regional or linguistic connections. In this regard, Muslims in Los Angeles undoubtedly take the prize for being the most multiethnic religious group in the city. Friday prayer in Masjid Omar ibn Al-Khattab is attended by African Americans, Persians, Egyptians, Saudi Arabians, Thais, Lebanese, and Iranians, to mention just some of the nationalities present. One person in attendance called it "the United Nations on its knees," referring to the image of people from many backgrounds kneeling shoulder-to-shoulder as they participated in the prayer service called "Salat." Indeed, even distinctions between Shi'te and Sunni Muslims, the source of tense relations elsewhere, often seem to evaporate in the Los Angeles context (see Figure 5.10).

Immigrants are a potential source of moral renewal in the United States. Concern is often expressed about the decline of civility, shared effort, and civic cooperation in Western democracies, and some of this concern is no doubt legitimate. But when we think about sources of rejuvenation, it is questionable whether middle-class Anglos are going to turn away from their individualistic ways. It is at least as likely that the source of moral renewal will come at the hands of the immigrants who know something about extended family ties, the value of community, and the importance of preserving a cultural heritage while contributing to the new society which they have chosen to help build. Religious institutions will play an important role in this process as they simultaneously incorporate new immigrants into American society and play a mediating role in helping to maintain the values connected with their places of origin.

Figure 5.10. Friday prayer at Masjid Umar Ibn-Al Khattab, Los Angeles, California. Photo by Jerry Berndt, courtesy of USC Center for Religion and Civic Culture.

NOTES

Donald E. Miller is executive director, Grace Dyrness is associate director, and Jon Miller is director of research in the Center for Religion and Civic Culture, University of Southern California (www.usc.edu/crcc). Except where we have indicated otherwise, the observations and interpretations offered here are based on our continuing study of immigrant religion in Los Angeles, with support from the Irvine Foundation, the John Randolph Haynes and Dora Haynes Foundation, and The Pew Charitable Trusts. Parts of this chapter have appeared in "Religion in the City of Angels," a report submitted to the John Randolph Haynes and Dora Haynes Foundation, January 2001.

1. Alejandro Portes and Min Zhou, "Should Immigrants Assimilate?" *The Public Interest* 116 (Summer 1994): 1–17. See also Roger Waldinger, "Not the Promised City: Los Angeles and Its Immigrants," *Pacific Historical Review* 68, no. 2 (May 1999): 253–272.

2. Dowell Myers and John Pitkin, "Demographic Futures for California" (Los Angeles: Population Dynamics Group, School of Policy, Planning, and Development, University of Southern California, 2001).

3. Patrick J. McDonnell, "Immigration to State Slows, Study Shows," *Los Angeles Times*, 22 January 2001.

4. Roger Waldinger and Mehdi Bozorgmehr, eds., *Ethnic Los Angeles* (New York: Russell Sage Foundation, 1996), 16.

5. Ibid., 14.

6. This number has been highly publicized since it was first cited. The Bureau of the Census summary where this estimate can be found appears at http://Quickfacts.census.gov/qfd/states/06/06037.html.

7. Will Herberg, *Protestant, Catholic, Jew: An Essay in American Religious Sociology* (Garden City, NY: Doubleday, 1956); Milton M. Gordon, *Assimilation in American Life* (New York: Oxford University Press, 1964); Herbert J. Gans, "Second Generation Decline: Scenarios for the Economic and Ethnic Futures of the Post-1965 American Immigrants," *Ethnic and Racial Studies*, 15(2) (1992): 173–92; Alejandro Portes and Ruben G. Rumbaut, *Immigrant America: A Portrait*, 2d ed. (Berkeley: University of California Press, 1996).

8. Immigration and Naturalization Service, "Illegal Alien Resident Population," 20 December 2000 (http://www.ins.usdoj.gov/graphics/aboutins/statistics/illegal alien/index.htm); "The New Americans: A Survey of the United States," *The Economist*, 11 March 2000, 3.

9. Alejandro Portes and Min Zhou, "The New Second Generation: Segmented Assimilation and its Variants among Post-1965 Youth," *Annals of the American Academy of Political and Social Science* 530 (November 1993): 74–98; Portes and Zhou, "Should Immigrants Assimilate?"; and Min Zhou, "Growing up American: The Challenge Confronting Immigrant Children and Children of Immigrants," *Annual Review of Sociology* 23 (1997): 63–95.

10. Gregory Rodriguez, "From Newcomers to New Americans: The Successful Integration of Immigrants into American Society," a publication of the National Immigration Forum, Washington, DC, 1999.

11. Herberg, *Protestant, Catholic, Jew*.

12. Stephen Warner and Judith G. Wittner, eds, *Gatherings in Diaspora: Religious Communities and the New Immigration* (Philadelphia: Temple University Press, 1998); Helen Rose Ebaugh and Janet Saltzman Chafetz, eds., *Religion and the New Immigrants: Continuities and Adaptations in Immigrant Congregations* (Walnut Creek, CA: AltaMira Press, 2000).

13. Edward L. Cleary, "Protestant Political Engagement and Disengagement in Latin America," paper presented to a Conference on "The Political Implications of the Rise in Protestantism in Latin America" at The Brookings Institution, Washington, DC, 3 December 1999.

14. McCarthy and Vernez, "Immigration in a Changing Economy"; James P. Smith and Barry Edmonston, ed., *The Immigration Debate: Studies on the Economic, Demographic, and Fiscal Effects of Immigration* (Washington, DC: National Academy Press, 1998).

15. Robert N. Bellah et al., *Habits of the Heart: Individualism and Commitment in American life* (Berkeley: University of California Press, 1985).

16. Robert D. Putnam, *Bowling Alone: The Collapse and Revival of American Community* (New York: Simon & Schuster, 2000).

17. Philip Martin and Elizabeth Midgley, "Immigration to the United States," *Population Bulletin: A Publication of the Population Reference Bureau* 54, no. 2 (June 1999).

18. Ibid., 8–9.

19. Sebastaio Salgado, *Migrations: Humanity in Transition*, concept and design by Lelia Wanick Salgado, 1st English Language ed. (New York: Aperture, 2000).

20. Cardinal Roger Mahony, "You Have Entertained Angels—Without Know-

ing It," *The Tidings*, weekly newspaper of the Archdiocese of Los Angeles, 10 October 1993, pp. 10–12.

21. Antonio Olivo, "Digging Deep for Quake Aid." *Los Angeles Times*, 23 January 2001, sec. B.

22. Pierette Hondagneu-Sotelo, *Gendered Transitions: Mexican Experiences of Immigration* (Berkeley: University of California Press, 1994).

6

The Third World in Los Angeles: A Metaphor Within a Metaphor

Tridib Banerjee and Niraj Verma

Our understanding of the modern metropolis has undergone a dramatic change since the early 1980s. An early 1970s smugness of taming the city through careful scientific analysis has given way to a new perspective that emphasizes the sometimes contradictory, plural, and intractable nature of the city. Theorists[1] have contributed to this new image and ideas like "edge city" and "soft city"[2] have emerged to capture this new understanding.

Following Raban,[3] we see Los Angeles as a "Soft Metropolis" that is hard to perceive, difficult to describe, and virtually impossible to capture in a deterministic way. Raban tells us that attempts to represent it in conventional ways "irritates us into metaphors." While Raban's generic metaphor of the soft city may capture the complexity of cities in general, the specific experience of Los Angeles adds a unique dimension to this understanding. We are intrigued, in particular, by the allusions to Los Angeles as a Third World city—triggered, no doubt, by its unique multicultural diversity, the swelling ranks of its immigrant population, and its polyglot cultural landscape—epitomized by the title of David Reiff's book *Los Angeles: Capital of the Third World*.[4] Might the Third World metaphor suggest a whole new class of social and economic relationships not captured by the conventional models of spatial structure and organization of cities? In this chapter we will explore such possibilities.

We should note at the outset that Los Angeles itself can be seen as a metaphor, not only because Los Angeles is an important city in its own right, but also because it is a leading prototype of future cities and of its increasingly recognized role in shaping urban scholarship. As a leading metaphor of the contemporary city, Los Angeles helps us to challenge the dominant analytical model that also was associated with another city. The Chicago School of urban analysis was not merely a preference for a particular technique or model, but also the framework within which the city was understood. It was and still remains the shibboleth for a scholarly tradition in the social sciences and of a particular way of thinking about urban policy problems.

It is not unusual for cities to represent the intellectual and philosophical discourse on social issues. Historically Athens signified order, structure, and scientific reasoning, while Jerusalem was the symbol of ethical and moral dialogues on human affairs.[5] Chicago and Los Angeles are similarly polarized. The two represent very different approaches to examining urban life. "Models versus metaphors" captures this story. If models became the vehicle to imprint Chicago on the national urban consciousness, metaphors can become the antithesis to complement our understanding of urban life and to underscore the vitality of a Los Angeles school.[6] Our goal is to contribute to the dialectical underpinnings of such a move.

Perhaps we should clarify that we recognize that models are tools that help us cope in a world of infinite possibilities. In a perplexing and bewildering world, models can provide cognitive economy and security by—to borrow a phrase attributed to William James—filing new experiences under an old head. In other words they give us a handle on things by allowing us to tame the perversities of reality.

But handles can easily become fetishes.[7] As they gather followers and gain inertia, models take on a life of their own. They acquire independent meaning and are no longer mere instruments. And since our sense of the whole is not always palpable and not always amenable to modeling, it fades in our collective consciousness and loses out to partial descriptions of reality. Reality is reduced to a model, and the model becomes the norm. Instruments become goals and the parts become larger than the whole.

The models of the Chicago School were derived from the field of human ecology, a biological-science-based generic approach to the study of human communities. Later versions of this approach took to heart the principles of competitive free market as the basis for the spatial organization of communities. Steeped in economistic values and a market rationality, the models of the Chicago School had very little to do with culture, sentiment, or symbolism in explaining the spatial order of cities and the life of communities. So mesmerizing were they, that even compelling antitheses, like Walter Firey's,[8] failed to change their tide of influence.

Today, as we challenge the hegemony of the Chicago School by a discourse focused on Los Angeles and Southern California, we are very much aware of the enduring legacy of the Chicago School in earlier as well as in recent models of Southern California. Robert Fogelson's well-known study of the fragmentation of the political space of Southern California is a classic example.[9] The legacy of the works of public-choice theorist Charles Tiebout that celebrated the fragmented metropolis as a *cause célèbre* of a political marketplace is another.[10] References to Los Angeles as a classic "Tieboutian World" or polycentric models of Los Angeles that give normative standing to its diffused spatial structure are examples.[11] Indeed, what the popular literature describes as "urban sprawl" is seen within this view of the world as efficient allocation of resources and an example of consumer sovereignty. Such is the legacy of the Chicago School, a tradition whose intellectual hegemony has shaped our understanding of American urban experience since the 1930s.

Thus little has changed when it comes to planning methods and their applications. In transportation, land use, housing, and other specializations the valiant search to measure, model, tame, and manipulate the city continues. While models and measurements may make for greater rigor, they also systematically undervalue and ignore some of the most vexing difficulties, pluralities, and ambiguities identified by recent scholarship. Like the proverbial blind men trying to describe an elephant, models are able to capture only a part of that plurality. Yet, in part because of their simple design, they dominate urban policy and pedagogy, which in turn reinforce and sustain their partial but imperious view of contemporary reality.

Our goal is to counter this trend by an alternate way of analyzing the city from the perspective of social narratives. We use metaphors rather than models to represent the city and we are particularly interested in the marginalized but transcendental qualities that comprise the "soft" metropolis. Our preference for metaphor is no accident. Metaphors are by nature vague and suggestive and unlike conventional measurements their import needs to be teased out by insightful interpretation. Given what recent scholarship has revealed as the difficult, intractable, and complex nature of the city, metaphors provide a uniquely relevant way of understanding the city. By choosing and then explicating a relevant metaphor of the city, our effort is to build on a perspective that allows us considerable latitude in interpreting the city and particularly in bringing back aspects that have been marginalized.

THE POWER OF METAPHOR

The metaphors that are used to describe Los Angeles reflect its complexity. From Joel Garreau's "edge city"[12] to Mike Davis' "fortress LA"[13] or Jonathan Raban's "soft city"[14] a rich array of such metaphors can be used to describe contemporary Los Angeles. Although choosing a metaphor to fit a particular situation is the prerogative of an individual, we maintain that this choice is neither totally arbitrary nor entirely deliberate. A systematic analysis of metaphors of Los Angeles can reveal facets of cities that are valued by scholars, humanists, and designers, sometimes visibly and consciously, and at other times tacitly or unconsciously.

In analyzing these and other metaphors, we draw on some contemporary theoretical work on metaphors and similarity.[15] Briefly, the theory suggests that metaphors derive their power and full meaning from the unsaid rather than the said. This unsaid comprises attributes that capture the similarities between the elements of a metaphor and are called its "reference class." In the popular metaphor "a city is a tree," for example, the reference class might consist of similarities between a city and a tree such as "structural or anatomical characteristics," "arterial network," or "organic nature." These similarities form the reference class, which makes the metaphor possible and gives it its power.

While all such similarities may have some utility, the ones that emphasize purpose or goals or sentiments are likely to be more valuable in planning and design than those that merely emphasize structure. For instance, structural similarities between a tree and a city may be of very limited use and might even be misleading from the point of urban planning or design. On the other hand, if we look at the role of trees in making livable environments, this reveals a similarity that resonates well with contemporary ecological approaches to city planning and city design.

The power of metaphor comes from interpreting these purposive similarities and by explicating the reference class. By tracing metaphors of the city to perspectives we find out what a person or a group or a discipline that relies on a particular metaphor values about the city. In other words, the similarities hidden within metaphors provide clues about the "values" of designers or other professionals. Aggregated together, they help us develop what is important about an artifact such as a city.

THE METAPHORICAL DESCRIPTION OF LOS ANGELES AS A THIRD WORLD CITY

Writers and other observers of Third World cities have had a love-hate relationship with their subject matter. The "City of Joy," for instance, brings simultaneous images of poverty, misery, spontaneity, and happiness.[16] We must emphasize that we do not use the Third World metaphor in either a pejorative or laudatory sense. To us the growing similarity of Los Angeles to the Third World city is not necessarily suggestive of a decline or of counterdevelopment, nor is it always nostalgic and romantic. Sociologist Peter Langer characterizes the images of the city in the humanities and social sciences by four metaphors: the jungle, the machine, the bazaar, and the organism.[17] While jungle and machine are seen as anomic, dehumanizing, and pathological, bazaar and organism are seen as communal, engaging, and spontaneous. Interestingly in this categorization the most common themes used to describe the capitalist-industrial cities (mainly of the First World) are the jungle and the machine, while the themes commonly used to describe the Third World cities are the bazaar and the organism. How far this matching is valid is not yet known. But Langer's classification is certainly suggestive of the idea that the Third Worldization of Los Angeles might mean a transition from mechanistic and anomic status to a more communal and spontaneous one.

Other writers, poets, and artists evoke dramatically different similarities between the city in the Third World and the contemporary Western city. If Langer emphasized spontaneity and community life in his metaphor, others see the Third World as denoting decline, poverty, loss, and fear. Yet others see it as pointing to an emerging global order. Since our goal is to use the Third World city to get a handle on the "soft metropolis," none of these interpretations provide ready entrée into the Third World city metaphor as we are using it. Yet an inventory of competing uses of the metaphor provides a useful contrast to our approach.

FIVE MEANINGS OF THE THIRD WORLD CITY METAPHOR

There are at least five identifiable meanings that are imputed to the Third World city metaphor. First is the idea of "New Calcutta" that signifies the struggles of living in the contemporary metropolis. Introduced in a CBS *60 Minutes* story on the homeless of New York City called "Calcutta on the Hudson," (no doubt influenced by the popular Robin Williams film *Moscow on the Hudson*) the theme was played up by *The New York Times* that ran four editorials and op-ed pieces between 1987 and 1991 under the banner "New Calcutta, an occasional series." The Calcutta metaphor signified the declining quality of city infrastructure and services, rising crime and homelessness, and even included a much-publicized subway shooting in New York. Calcutta became the symbol of ultimate urban dystopia, a benchmark of the worst urban condition. Forgotten in this analogy was that despite widespread poverty and ubiquitous pavement dwellers, Calcutta streets are much safer than New York and are without the violent crime and random shootings that they were chosen to depict. But the inaccuracy hardly came in the way of furthering hysteria and doomsday anxiety. Calcutta became an effective trope to signify decline just as the Third World had itself become an effective poster child of "counterdevelopment"[18] as chronicled in a *Los Angeles Times* article entitled "U.S. Sliding to Third World Status."[19]

The second approach is a narrative of fear and loss. It differs from the Calcutta metaphor in attributing a specific cause to the slide into Third World status but uses the growing Third World population and its impact on the changing urbanism of Western cities to fuel its interpretation. It starts with the fear of being overrun by the massive influx of dark and bloated-belly Third World immigrants and rapidly moves to the concern that too many Third World immigrants have already diluted the purity of Western culture. We see this, for instance, in the rhetoric of former U.S. House of Representatives Speaker Newt Gingrich, who claims that "the American civilization" is under attack. In the case of French xenophobes the rhetoric becomes a lament that the very purity of the French race is at stake: Jean Raspail's futuristic novel *The Camp of the Saints*, written in the early 1970s, provides a poignant description.[20]

More recent discussions in the United States about controlling immigration, proposing welfare reform ideas that deny benefits to legal immigrants, or the scandal about Third World money financing American political campaigns fan the sentiment. David Reiff's characterization of Los Angeles as the "Capital of the Third World" characterizes and epitomizes the salient issue in this rhetoric. "How can middle- and upper-class Los Angelenos be so smug and complacent?" Reiff seems to be asking. "Don't they know that Los Angeles has been already taken over by Third World Immigrants?" Tellingly, one chapter of Reiff's book is titled "Here Comes Everybody."[21]

The third idea is very much a product of the current scholarship on postcolonialism. It looks at the transitional cultural landscape and urbanism of the Western cities resulting from the settlements of previously colonial subjects in such countries as Britain, France, Holland, and Germany. This is the scenario of "The Colony Strikes Back" and it permeates the writings of comparative sociologists and cultural geographers.[22] Contemporary European cities like London, Paris, or Frankfurt are typical candidates for such analysis. The scenario is less applicable to U.S. cities.[23]

Beyond these three popular versions of the Third World city metaphor, we offer two more. These are adaptations of Reiff's reference to Los Angeles as a "capital" of the Third World" but in ways that are probably very far from his intent. Consider the word "capital." It symbolizes authority, command, control, political influence, power, and concentration, all in one place. Does Los Angeles really play such a commanding role in the affairs of the Third World? We are not sure, even though increasingly Los Angeles is emerging as a major player in the global economy, especially through its trade with Pacific Rim countries. Yet, in another sense Los Angeles may indeed have a much greater influence on the emerging consumption culture of the Third World as aptly documented by authors like Pico Iyer and Benjamin Barber.[24] As the media capital of the world, Los Angeles today has more influence and control over the changing tastes, preferences, and values of the citizens of the Third World than any other city. But this is a very different interpretation from Reiff's xenophobic narrative of the growing presence of immigrant culture in Los Angeles.

Finally, a fifth interpretation focuses on the structural transformation of the cities of the West in the context of the emerging global economic order.

This interpretation is a derivative of the "world system" view popularized by Immanuel Wallerstein.[25] It argues that the economy of cities is as much linked to the economies of other lands as it is to its own. As the national economies become increasingly integrated within a global economy, cities too become articulated in a global system of cities. With the flow of labor and capital, differences between the First World and Third World cities begin to shrink. As the Third World "ends" a "one world" view becomes compelling.[26]

The one-world approach may be the most inclusive yet, but even its catholicity cannot deny the growing polarization of income, rural-urban disparity, and the chronic poverty of the underclass. In the one-world view the "Third World" becomes the "other world." As the writings of California writers like Ruben Martinez and Richard Rodriguez[27] show, this "other side"—*el otro lado*—exists both here and in other lands across the border, often as a seamless state of being.

It is in this sense that the Third World city metaphor becomes the focus of our inquiry, although, to our knowledge, even the other interpretations have not been mined to inform urban theory. Our proposal is to explicate the reference class behind the Third World city metaphor from applications of urban theories home grown in the Third World context. The following are some elements of the reference class that give us a "handle" on the soft metropolis of Los Angeles.

DUALISM

In his classic *Peddlers and Princes* the distinguished anthropologist Clifford Geertz first introduced the idea of technological dualism.[28] Geertz showed that the productive capacities of developing countries are characterized by dual systems of modern and traditional technologies. This notion of dualism was seen as a discontinuity in the economy, and a major impediment to successful development and modernization and to the "trickledown" process. The concept became so popular that others expanded it to include economic dualism, cultural dualism, and the like. Soon, dualism became a feature of developing countries and scholars argued it was an effect of colonial underdevelopment and only partial integration of developing-country production systems with the global economy.

The pertinent question here is whether there are aspects of dualism in Los Angeles. Is dualism intrinsic to the development of the Los Angeles metropolis and therefore has it always been present? Or, should we be talking not so much of a dualism of economy or technology but of culture—the native, Hispanic, and the Anglo cultures, for example? Perhaps a new cultural dualism has come to be defined by the distinctions and divide between immigrant cultures and the existing Anglo-American culture.

DEPENDENCY

Although in disrepute in classical and Marxist theories, the idea of dependency has a strong following among Third World scholars. Several versions have arisen as dependency theory tries to keep pace with the transformations in global economic relationships. A powerful variant, "development of underdevelopment," was advanced by Andre Gunder Frank.[29] It makes the argument that the underdeveloped state of the many Third World countries was not a natural state but was the result of colonial powers subjugating native lands and profiting—developing—at the cost of the Third World. Both colonialism and neocolonialism are relevant for dependency theory. Evidence comes from "banana republics" and "coffee republics" that are permanently dependent on cash crops that in turn prevent them from autonomous and self-sustaining development.

So, how does this relate to Los Angeles? We think it raises some very potent questions. We might ask, for instance, if "dependency" is a useful category to understand the history of Los Angeles. Might dependency help us to understand metropolitan Los Angeles in its current condition or in its external relationship to the changing global economy? Could inner-city neighborhoods be seen as dependent development or underdevelopment that was influenced by its relationship to the larger society? Are Watts and East Los Angeles any different from a banana republic?

CULTURE OF POVERTY

Some more insights into the Third World metaphor of Los Angeles come from Oscar Lewis' concept of the "Culture of Poverty," made popular through his now infamous 1966 article in *Scientific American*.[30] Lewis' work was immediately grabbed by domestic politicians in the United States as a convenient explanation for what they saw as the problem of the inner-city poor. Chronic unemployment, dependency on food stamps, public housing, Aid to Families with Dependent Children, and other types of welfare programs came to be seen as a problem of the poor themselves and, in particular, of the "culture" in which they were born and bred. By the time Richard Nixon was elected president the culture of poverty hypothesis had taken root and Lyndon Johnson's programs for the "Great Society" and "War on Poverty" were being questioned, if not discredited.[31]

The scholarship on the city added to this environment. Ed Banfield's *Unheavenly Cities* had already critiqued black ghetto residents and blamed their failure to assimilate into the mainstream society on their culturally rooted—if not racial—shortcomings.[32] About the same time two well-known urban sociologists, Nathan Glazer and Daniel Moynihan, published their work on ethnicity and urban problems.[33] The flurry of these writings, critical of contemporary urban policy, and bent on explaining the complex causes of poverty—both structural and situational—created an intellectual climate predisposed to the idea that there might be such a thing as the "culture of poverty." When Moynihan became Richard Nixon's domestic policy adviser he coined the term "benign neglect" as the hallmark of the new administration's agenda toward race, poverty, and inner-city urban problems. Benign neglect signified that to the extent that inner-city poverty was a function of the culture of the poor, no amount of federal dollars and programs could solve the problem. The poor had to break the cycle of poverty on their own and a policy of benign neglect was seen as the best kind of help.

Subsequently, benign neglect would be criticized as "blaming the victim" and "regulating the poor."[34] Critics pointed out that by placing the blame for chronic poverty on the poor themselves the new policy begged the questions of structural reform.

Clearly, the theory of culture of poverty was ill-timed. Yet it is possible that the prevalent intellectual debate preordained the spawning of this article, as Lewis felt that he could shed some light on this debate from his own experience.[35] Critics blamed Oscar Lewis not only for the theory being faulty and for reinforcing popular stereotypes of certain ethnic groups and of the poor, but, more debilitating, for providing a convenient subterfuge for a conservative do-nothing, hands-off policy toward the poor. Similar arguments echoed all over Latin America against marginality theory, which, incidentally, subsumed the notion of culture of poverty,[36] as we will soon discuss.

It is interesting to note that while Lewis' background research as a cultural anthropologist was mostly conducted in the Third World context, he did not necessarily see the culture of poverty as a Third World epiphenomenon. Instead he argued (p. 21) that the culture of poverty is typically found in cash-economy settings, characterized by "wage labor and production for profit with a persistently high rate of unemployment and underemployment, at low wages, for unskilled labor." Further, he claimed that although two-thirds of the world population was poor, not all of them lived in the culture of poverty. Notably, the poor in India, the poor Jews of Eastern Europe, and the poor populations in socialist countries such as China and Cuba were singled out as not belonging to culture of poverty.

If we are to explicate the reference class for Los Angeles as capital of the Third World metaphor we must seriously examine how the concept of culture of poverty is relevant in probing the "soft" metropolis. Who are, for instance, the candidate populations to be described by the culture of poverty? Are they the homeless of Los Angeles? The impoverished blacks and Hispanics? Or, are they perhaps members in youth gangs: the "taggers"? Or illegal immigrants, much as the recent welfare reform tacitly admitted.

Lewis made four main claims about the culture of poverty that may help clarify these questions. The first, and probably the most relevant for our purpose, has to do with the relationship between the subculture and the larger society. Lewis argued that a perennial relationship of mutual distrust and alienation exists between those who are in the culture of poverty and those in mainstream society. The subculture distrusts institutions and is hostile to those who represent the mainstream establishment and convey its authority. If we take the often-confrontational relation between inner-city black and Latino youth—usually unemployed or underemployed—and the police in Los Angeles (and other cities) the criterion of mutual distrust, hostility, and alienation seems particularly relevant. Such films about Los Angeles as *Boyz N the Hood*, *Mi Familia*, and *Stand and Deliver* epitomize this relationship as do stories of Los Angeles, such as Ruben Martinez' *The Other Side* and Mike Davis' *The City of Quartz*.[37]

Even the lyrics of rap music support this conclusion. In a recent article Marshall Berman has discussed the alienation, despair, and hostility of the inner city youth through the heart-breaking lyric of the rapper Melle Mel, who remembers his recently killed subway graffiti artist friend, who unsuccessfully searched for justice. Berman also quoted lines from NWA (Niggers With Attitude), in *Straight Outta Compton*, a "LA Gansta" rap album about "lasting" in contemporary society.[38]

Although the similarity of rap lyrics with Lewis' first criterion is obvious, we still need to be careful in its application, especially given the stigma involved. Furthermore, as Berman has cautioned, for some rappers, who are indeed quite wealthy, this alienation—particularly the images of violent and "in your face" confrontation—has significant commercial value, and is carefully nurtured for its market appeal. Berman writes:

But many rappers, the more impure their music gets, the more righteously they profess a cult of racial separateness and purity. The more they fast-break and slam-dunk the English language, the louder they protest they're only talking "African." The more their lives entwine with those of whites—producers, critics, managers, editors, film-makers, not to mention lovers and wives, and an audience that marketing surveys say is as much as four-fifths white—the more they insist they have no connection with whites at all, and speak to blacks alone. The better they thrive in the multinational markets that have turned their old neighbourhoods into ghost towns—and the Reaganite years of rap's history are years of radical social polarization, among blacks even more than whites—the more they insist they are nothing but homeboys, identical with all those that they have left behind. (p. 176)

Whatever the authenticity of the messenger, is the message itself inauthentic? Clearly, neither the rappers nor the majority of their audience are a part of Lewis' culture of poverty. Yet the lyrics poignantly capture the alienation and hostility in poor neighborhoods of Los Angeles and other cities.

The second, third, and fourth points made by Lewis, which have to do with the "nature of the slum community," "the nature of the family," and the "nature of the individual," are particularly controversial. All of them hint at some form of social pathology at these levels. Thus the slum community is seen not only as physically deprived and forsaken, but also as lacking social organization, a sense of community, and effective leadership. Yet we also know that many localities in South Central or East Los Angeles proudly claim and zealously guard their sense of place and community and are indeed quite skilled in organizing their communities for grassroots initiatives. More recent scholarship underscores this understanding by showing that ghettos and slums can be seen as a positive resource.[39] In addition many counterarguments have been made to discredit the link that uses the dysfunctional family as a criterion for culture of poverty. Telling among these is Victor Urquidi's spoof, *Los Hijos de los Jones*, which uses an affluent Beverly Hills family to show that the criterion for the culture of poverty can be found in affluent middle-class individuals, families, and neighborhoods.[40]

Finally, Lewis' fifth criterion concerns individual pathology that includes such personality disorders as fatalism, inferiority complex, need for immediate gratification, and machismo. This is particularly objectionable to critics (such as Stea) because it simply reinforces popular stereotypes of "lazy Mexicans" or "drunk Indians."[41]

The lesson seems to be that if we want to resurrect the concept of culture of poverty, we have to be careful how we do it. We may have to build on the first criterion, reject the entire concept as inappropriate, or redefine the notion of culture of poverty in today's context.

MARGINALITY

If the idea of culture of poverty offers a controversial link to the Third World metaphor, the concept of marginality doesn't fare any better. After all, the idea of marginality was attacked by scholars of Latin America as a myth and a convenient subterfuge for the ruling class to wash their hands off while "blaming the victim."

In her effort to debunk the myth of marginality, Janice Perlman systematically documented both the situational metaphors and the social science theories of class, organization, personality and social pathology that have contributed to the popularity of this concept.[42] In the end, however, Perlman had to concede that marginality was both "a myth and a reality." It was a myth because the poor who lived in *barrios* or *favelas* did not necessarily fit the culture of poverty or other criteria outlined in social and psychological theories of deviance and personality disorders. Yet marginality was very real in many ways: the poor did live in the outskirts of the city or in locations that were unsuitable for mainstream housing; their housing was substandard; they were often migrants from rural areas; their informal-sector activities were in the margin of the mainstream economy; and they were likely to be of the native minority racial stock.

Marginality is essentially a concept of exclusion and inferiority. It is about hierarchy and order and has to do with the mainstream society's view of those who are considered unholy, unwashed, and untouchable. And they are the ones who dispose our waste and keep us clean. In India, the land of "homo hiearichicus,"[43] untouchables are the ones who remove the night soil, collect the garbage, cremate the dead, clean the sewers and lavatories, and dispose of society's waste. In other Third World countries the "marginals" do the hard menial service, usually at subpar wages, and collectively maintain a large pool of cheap labor. These are the people who work in the fields, plant seeds, harvest crops, and subject themselves to unrelenting exposure to chemical toxins and carcinogens. They help to maintain the comparative advantage of the economy upon which profit and livelihood of the mainstream society depend.

In another sense, the social construction of marginality is based on prescribed decorum, norms, and ideologies. Boundaries, markers, and thresholds become important devices to separate the outside from the inside. Those who do not conform or those who defy the rules or refuse to join are considered outsiders, or marginals. The Kurds in Iran, Iraq, and Turkey, the Bahai's in Iran, the Palestinians in Israel, and the Bedouins of Arabia are examples of such permanently marginalized populations. David Stea and others call them "the Fourth World."[44] From the perspective of gender studies, women are marginalized in many societies even today.

Increasingly, however, marginality is no longer just a stigma handed down from above. It is also a deliberate expression of defiance and rejection of the mainstream norms and values. The rise of counterculture in the 1960s was a form of marginality by choice. Recent writings of Henry Louis Gates and Cornell West on the identity of African Americans, Adrienne Rich's rejection of presidential award, and, most certainly, the writings of Richard Rodriguez and Ruben Martínez on the ethnic identity of Mexican Americans are eminent examples of such claims on marginality.[45]

THE INFORMAL SECTOR

A vast informal sector in Third World countries and a growing literature on the sector are ubiquitous features of the contemporary Third World landscape. Although certain features of the informal sector have been around for many years, recognition of the informal economy as a productive sector came only in 1972 when a report by the International Labor Organization urged Third World governments to recognize the contribution of the informal sector to the gross domestic product, even though its full accounting was not possible. Now, one can count such institutional champions of the informal sector as the UN Development Program and the World Bank, other international aid organizations, and local nongovernment organizations (NGOs).

Still, there is considerable ambiguity in both conceptual and operational definitions of what or who constitutes the informal sector. The idea of formal versus informal sector implies a dichotomy. Yet, empirical studies suggest a continuum between the formal and informal poles, with many workers in the gray area between these poles. Even though there may be a nexus between the two, as some empirical studies show, the overall relationship between the formal and informal sectors is one of conflict and contradiction, often manifested in contest over space and territory. Hernando de Soto interpreted this conflict as one between excessive government regulation, on the one hand, and what Mario Vargas Llosa called "the people's spontaneous and creative response to the state's incapacity to satisfy the basic needs of the impoverished masses," on the other.[46] In this libertarian view—the study being sponsored by the conservative Instituto Libertad y Democracia of Peru—informal economy is touted as the "invisible revolution in the Third World."

Another view of this conflict and tension is explained more from a theoretical perspective by Brazilian geographer Milton Santos.[47] Santos sees the coexistence and opposition of the two sectors as a dialectic relationship mediated in space.

The conflicts between the informal and formal sectors, especially in the Los Angeles context, are in part explained by concepts of dualism and marginality. But they are also in part a function of the origin of the informal economy. Recall that the precolonial, precapitalist economies of the Third World had no division between formal and informal economies. What Marx once dismissed as the "Asian mode of production" was an integrated, albeit feudal, system of production. Technological dualism would be brought by European colonial powers with the dawn of the industrial age and the rise of industrial capitalism. To the extent that the preindustrial mode of production endured, they were quickly labeled as the "traditional" sector, as opposed to the "modern sector."

This dualism was conflated with the sociological imagination of modernity and modern man, and was different from the dualism of traditional man and backward society, that found favor in Banfield and others.[48] Parallel polarities of institutions and modalities of production were invoked, as were "firm" versus "bazaar." But in recent years the informal economy has had less to do with the technology of production than it has been about resources, organizations, and mechanisms for producing and selling goods and services.

The Los Angeles metropolis is a product of the industrial era and thus offers little chance of discovering preindustrial modes of production. But recent immigrants, especially those from the rural areas of Asia, and Central and South America, bring their traditional crafts and skills. Another prospect is to look for the informal mechanisms for producing goods and services. In Los Angeles, itinerant populations sell oranges and flowers at traffic stops or offer to wash car windshields while one waits for the lights to change. Garage or yard sales—although home grown in America—are another illustration of the informal economy as are street markets, sidewalk fairs, and pushcart vendors. The Santee Alley in downtown Los Angeles, Pacific Avenue in Huntington Park, and Venice boardwalk provide visible examples.

Another category of informal economy is widespread and even prosperous. These constitute the illegal drug economy, prostitution, selling fake green cards, manufacturing knock-off apparel, illegal gambling, and garage housing. This informal sector is thriving (if not expanding!) in Los Angeles. The large informal economy of the "sweat shops" in the bowels of the garment district in downtown Los Angeles and in other industrial areas east and south of downtown is well known for its pool of undocumented workers who work as maids, take care of children, do the gardening, and work as day laborers. Like any other Third World city, this cadre of "proto-proletariats"[49] makes a significant contribution to the productive powers of the Los Angeles economy and subsidize consumer services by working at below minimum wage rate. Much of this informal economy remains invisible—other than occasional sightings of day laborers waiting patiently by the parking lots of stores—and silent and unaccounted. Like all Third World economies, where informal economy may account for about 40 percent of gross domestic product, the contribution of Los Angeles' informal economy does not appear in official records.

CONCLUSION

Inspired by Raban's work, we have suggested in this exploratory chapter that metaphors rather than models might be a more effective artifice to represent and understand the intractable and ephemeral experience of a metropolis. Raban has claimed: "The city as we imagine it, the soft city of illusion, myth, aspiration, nightmare, is as real, maybe more real, than the hard city one can locate on maps, in statistics, in monographs on urban sociology and demography and architecture."[50] There are several reasons why we favor metaphors. First, we believe that the narrative of metaphors has more expository power than conventional models. Second, the particular urban condition—the modern, industrial city—that was the basis for the Chicago model is itself an anachronism today. And finally, as Cenzatti has alluded, our understanding of a contemporary American metropolis like Los Angeles should be placed in the larger context of such ideas as the globalization of the economy, multiculturalism, and emerging notions of citizenship.[51] We have proposed that the Third World city metaphor is particularly appropriate and may open up possibilities for alternative understanding of a soft metropolis.

The bulk of the chapter was devoted to discussions of various aspects of the Third World city metaphor. We have explored the many perspectives of this metaphor and used it to see what we can learn from the literature on Third World cities, and how we might reconceptualize Los Angeles with the presence of an everyday Third World reality in contemporary Southern California. We have suggested that the possibilities are enormous, but not without caveats.

NOTES

Authors' Note: We are grateful to the Southern California Studies Center (SC2) and the Southern California in the World (SC/W) exposition at the University of Southern California for supporting work that led to this chapter. An earlier version of this chapter was published in *Planning Theory and Practice* 2, no. 2 (2001): 133–148 under the title "Probing the Soft Metropolis: Third World Metaphors in the Los Angeles Context."

1. Michael Dear, "Prolegomena to a Post-modern Urbanism," in *Managing Cities*, eds. Patsy Healey et al. (London: John Wiley, 1995); and Michael Dear, *The Postmodern Urban Condition* (Oxford: Blackwell, 2000).

2. Joel Garreau, *Edge City: Life on the New Frontier* (New York: Doubleday, 1988); Jonathan Raban, *Soft City* (London: Harvill, 1988).

3. Raban, *Soft City*.

4. David Reiff, *Los Angeles: Capital of the Third World* (New York: Simon & Schuster, 1991).

5. Martin Krieger, "What Does Jerusalem Have to Do with Athens? Roles for the Humanities in Planning." *Journal of Planning Education and Research*, 14 (1995): 217–21.

6. The idea of a Los Angeles School was formally introduced by Marco Cenzatti in a monograph published by the Los Angeles Forum for Architecture and Urban Design. Comparing the Los Angeles School with the Chicago and Frankfurt Schools, Cenzatti argued that while the Los Angeles School is similar to the Chicago School in its urban focus, it is actually closer to the Frankfurt School because its research "belongs to a broader context which begins neither with Los Angeles nor with the specificity of the urban." See Marco Cenzatti, *Los Angeles and the L.A. School: Postmodernism and Urban Studies* (Los Angeles: Los Angeles Forum for Architecture and Urban Design, 1993), p. 6.

7. Martin H. Krieger, *Marginalism and Discontinuity: Tools for the Crafts of Knowledge and Decision* (New York: Russell Sage Foundation, 1989).

8. Walter Firey, *Land Use in Central Boston* (New York: Greenwood Press, 1968).

9. Robert M. Fogelson, *The Fragmented Metropolis: Los Angeles, 1850–1930* (Cambridge, MA: Harvard University Press, 1967).

10. Charles Tiebout, "A Pure Theory of Local Expenditures," *Journal of Political Economy*, 64 (1976): 416–424.

11. Peter Gordon, Harry W. Richardson, and Hung Leung Wong, "The Distribution of Population and Employment in a Polycentric City: The Case of Los Angeles," *Environment and Planning A*, 18 (1986): 161–173.

12. Garreau, *Edge City*.

13. Mike Davis, *City of Quartz: Excavating the Future in Los Angeles* (London: Verso, 1990).

14. Raban, *Soft City*.

15. Niraj Verma, "Metaphor and Analogy as Elements of a Theory of Similarity for Planning," *Journal of Planning Education and Research*, 13 (1993): 13–25; and Niraj Verma, *Similarities, Connections, and Systems: The Search for a New Rationality for Planning and Management* (Lanham, MD: Lexington Books, 1998).

16. Larry Collins and Dominique Lapierre, *The City of Joy* (Garden City, NY: Doubleday, 1985).

17. Peter Langer, "Sociology—Four Images of Organized Diversity," in *Cities of the Mind: Images and Themes of the City in the Social Sciences*, eds. L. Rodwin and R. Hollister (New York: Plenum, 1984).

18. In a recent conference paper (Association of Collegiate Schools of Planning [ACSP/AESOP] Toronto 1996), Farookh Afshar has argued that a creeping "underdevelopment" can be seen in Canadian cities. We favor "counterdevelopment" as a more appropriate term.

19. David Gordon, "U.S. Sliding to Third World Status," *Los Angeles Times*, 8 September 1991.

20. Matthew Connelly and Paul Kennedy, "Must It Be the Rest Against the West?" *The Atlantic Monthly* 274, no. 6 (1994): 61–83.

21. Reiff, *Los Angeles*.

22. Anthony D. King, *Urbanism, Colonialism and the World-Economy* (New York: Routledge, 1990); Anthony D. King, *Global Cities* (New York: Routledge, 1990); and Anthony D. King, ed., *Re-presenting the City: Ethnicity, Capital, and Culture in the 21st-Century Metropolis* (New York: New York University Press, 1996).

23. For the obvious reason that the United States is not considered a former colonial power, unless one counts its control of the Philippines for a limited period. However, some Third World scholars have argued that the hegemonic control over almost all of Latin America and some other Asian countries is not so very different.

24. Pico Iyer, *Video Night in Kathmandu* (New York: Vintage, 1988); and Benjamin R. Barber, *Jihad vs. McWorld* (New York: Times Books, 1995).

25. Immanuel Wallerstein, *The Politics of World Economy* (New York: Cambridge University Press, 1984).

26. Bishwapriya Sanyal, ed., *Breaking the Boundaries: One World Approach to Planning Education* (New York: Plenum, 1989).

27. Rubén Martínez, *The Other Side* (New York: Vintage Books, 1992); and Richard Rodriguez, *Days of Obligation: An Argument with My Mexican Father* (New York: Penguin Books, 1992).

28. Clifford Geertz, *Peddlers and Princes: Social Change and Economic Modernization in Two Indonesian Towns* (Chicago: University of Chicago Press, 1963).

29. Andre Gunder Frank, *Capitalism and Underdevelopment in Latin America* (New York, NY: Monthly Review Press, 1967).

30. Oscar Lewis, "The Culture of Poverty." *Scientific American*, 215, no. 4 (1996): 19–25.

31. The idea of waging a war on poverty may have contributed to this as well. See, for instance, Verma, "Metaphor and Analogy" for a deconstruction of the war on poverty metaphor.

32. Although he may not have explicitly used the term "backwardness," there was more than a whiff here of his earlier arguments about the moral basis of "backward societies." (Edward Banfield, *Moral Basis of Backward Societies* [New York: Free Press, 1967]).

33. Nathan Glazer and Daniel Patrick Moynihan, *Beyond the Melting Pot: The Negroes, Puerto Ricans, Jews, Italians, and Irish of New York City* (Cambridge, MA: M.I.T. Press, 1970).

34. William Ryan, *Blaming the Victim* (New York: Vintage Books, 1976); and Frances Fox Piven and Richard A. Cloward, *Regulating the Poor: The Functions of Public Welfare* (New York: Vintage Books, 1972).

35. After all, Oscar Lewis has been studying communities and families in condition of poverty for some time. He had already published *Tepotzlan Revisited* (New York: Random House, 1961) *Children of Sanchez* (New York: Random House, 1966) and *La Vida* (New York: Random House, 1966). But these were narratives without any theorizing or without specific conclusions. In writing this article Lewis clearly addressed the contemporary debate on domestic poverty in the United States.

36. Janice Perlman, *The Myth of Marginality* (Berkeley: University of California Press, 1976).

37. Martínez, *The Other Side*; Davis, *City of Quartz*.

38. Marshall Berman, "Justice/Just Us: Rap and Social Justice in America," in *The Urbanization of Injustice*, eds. Andy Merrifield and Erik Swyngedouw (New York: New York University Press, 1997), 161–179.

39. William W. Goldsmith, "The Ghetto as a Resource for Black America," *Journal of the American Institute of Planners* 40, no. 1 (1979); and Lisa Peattie, "An Argument for Slums," *Journal of Planning Education and Research* 13, no. 2 (1994): 136–142.

40. Victor Urquidi, *Los Nijos de los Jones* cited in David Stea, "Rejecting the Culture of Poverty." *Aprovecho Newsletter*, 1980.

41. David Stea, "Rejecting the Culture of Poverty."

42. J. Perlman, *The Myth of Marginality*.

43. Louis Dumont, *Homo Hierarchicus* (Chicago: University of Chicago Press, 1980).

44. Stea, "Rejecting the Culture of Poverty." As James Scott describes it, *Seeing Like a State* (New Haven, CT: Yale University Press, 1998) was motivated by the goal of understanding how instruments, such as census data, marginalized populations on the move.

45. Henry Louis Gates and Cornell West, *The Future of the Race* (New York: Knopf, 1996); Adrienne Rich, "Why I Refused the National Medal for the Arts." *Los Angeles Times/Book Review*, 3 August 1997, p. 3; Rodriguez, *Days of Obligation*; Martínez, *The Other Side*.

46. Hernando De Soto, *The Other Path: The Invisible Revolution in the Third World* (New York: Harper & Row, 1989), xii.

47. Milton Santos, *Shared Space* (London: Methuen, 1979).

48. Edward Banfield, *Moral Basis of Backward Societies* (New York: Free Press, 1967).

49. T. G. McGee, *The Urbanization Process in the Third World* (London: Bell, 1971).

50. Raban, *Soft City*, 10.

51. Cenzatti, *Los Angeles and the L.A. School.*

PART III

SOUTHERN CALIFORNIA'S PROJECTION INTO THE WORLD

7

Global Networks, Civil Society, and the Transformation of the Urban Core in Quanzhou, China

Michael Leaf and Daniel Abramson

Global investment practices are often shown to be a source of cultural homogenization and a threat to civil society in the shaping of cities in both the developed and developing world. The model of development represented by Southern California in particular has drawn fire. In this chapter, we examine the city-building and urban-governance implications of global networks, including linkages to Southern California, through an analysis of ongoing urbanization and change in Quanzhou, in China's southern province of Fujian.

The restoration of neighborhood temples, the robust private home-building economy, and the local challenges facing conventional Chinese government-led "restructuring" of city center land use are examined in particular. As the place of origin for long-standing out-migration, Quanzhou has been able to draw upon its overseas connections—an incipient although important form of globalism—in order to offset the pressures of centralized state control. The chapter argues that in some cases global linkages may actually help to preserve important elements of local identity and lay foundations for civil society in a context of traditional strong state control over social institutions and associations.

INTRODUCTION: CITIES AND THE NETWORK PARADIGM OF GLOBALIZATION

In considering the interactions between globalization and local governance, the argument has been put forward before that although decentral-

ization may be implicit in current processes of globalization, it does not
necessarily imply an opening up of democratic governance at local levels.[1]
Instead, the strengthening of local states—that is, municipal governments—
which has resulted from globalization-led decentralization, may be coupled
with greater local social control, a tendency identified in the Chinese context as "state sprawl,"[2] "local state corporatism,"[3] or the "decentralized
command economy."[4] Other observations of the impact of global capital,
skills, and managerial approaches on China's larger cities have also emphasized the new opportunities afforded to local governments in the creation of new urban centers, or in the "remaking" of urban cores,[5] often with
no regard for existing social or physical structures.[6]

In this chapter, we would like to further explore the interactions between
globalization, governance, and city-building, by looking in particular at the
way global or transborder influences can support local identity and provide
conditions for the growth of civil society. In this instance we look to the
case of one specific Chinese city, Quanzhou, an historic city in southern
China's Fujian province, to examine how local civil society is shaped by
changing local-global linkages, and how it in turn influences the on-going
spatial development of the city. In order to undertake this examination, it
is necessary to first clarify such ambiguous terms as globalization and urban
governance.

The concept of globalization is certainly contentious, and we will not
deal here with the diversity of meanings which this term has now come to
hold. Instead, our emphasis is on the form of analysis which is implied by
Castells' notion of the "network society," which allows us a point of continuity between the diverse strands that are seen to constitute global connectedness in sociocultural terms as well as economically (i.e., as the global
expansion of capitalist relations).[7] This network perspective is critical to
understanding the geography of globalization, in particular the growing
emphasis on cities as the specific locales of connectivity, the spatial nodes
in the global network.

The role of cities in the global ecumene has in particular been recognized
and expanded upon by a significant body of analysis since the publication
of Friedmann's "world city hypothesis."[8] As Douglass points out, the significance of this discussion lies in the reconfiguration of development theory
which it implies, with the movement away from earlier formulations which
emphasize the nation-state as the fundamental unit of analysis.[9] How specific cities and urban societies articulate (or consciously seek to articulate)
with globalization, particularly the global economy, is a critical although
so far understudied question, in that such connectivities certainly underlie
the historical processes of what Douglass refers to as "world city formation."

It should be remembered, however, that conscious attempts at long-
distance interconnectedness by cities and through cities are by no means

only a recent phenomenon, as seen in interpretations of the rise of the city in Western Europe[10] and in the expanding frontier of nineteenth-century North America.[11] The acknowledgment of the historical rootedness of such processes is important, as this underlies to a great degree the specificity of place, and thus determines how a locality engages with the global.[12] This is certainly the case with the city of Quanzhou.

Another concept we wish to highlight is the particular traditional mode of urban governance which characterizes local state-society interactions in many Asian localities. Here we use the term "traditional" not so much to imply the historical roots of such governance practices, but rather in the Weberian sense to stress the contrast with modern, rationalized, bureaucratic structures. For this we rely upon the metaphoric use of the pyramid to illustrate not only the formal hierarchical administrative structures, but also to emphasize the essential verticality of power relations within these governmental systems. Thus, the pyramid of governance refers to both the formal administrative system composed of a nested hierarchy of geographic spaces, from the central state down to the local neighborhood, as well as to the web of clientelistic interpersonal relations which are overlaid upon this formal framework.[13]

Reflection on these concepts raises the question as to whether the widening and deepening of network-based globalization have the potential for opening up cracks in the lower strata of the pyramids of governance, thereby challenging the dominance of the central state at the pinnacle. Lower echelons in the hierarchy of governance may now be able to take advantage of new opportunities which arise through the aegis of globalization, opportunities which increasingly may be accessed directly while circumventing the center entirely. The generalizations implicit in this argument require examination at lower levels of the hierarchy, and yet we know that among localities there is great diversity. The specific means by which any particular place engages with the global will be shaped by its own particular circumstances.

Like "globalization," the concept of "civil society" is also both compelling and problematic, and we will not give a full recounting of the diversity of definitions of the concept here. Broadly stated, the term refers to the composite of social organizations and institutions which function outside of the direct control of the state. Civil society is a long-standing concept in the political economy literature of the West, yet it is striking how discussions of civil society have been revived, or even invented anew, in light of recent theorizing regarding globalization. One prominent stream of argument which has arisen from the alternative development, or "empowerment," literature presses for a view of the rise of civil society as being in direct response to or in opposition to forces of globalization.[14] A network view, as we are putting forward here, can help us get beyond this narrow dualistic framework of local versus global. Following Castells, the emphasis is on the characteristics of network connectivity which underlie both the expansion of globalization and the perceived rise of the institutions of civil society. The question of autonomy remains central to the discussion, and, in fact, may be seen to be even more problematic, as the potential for intricate networks of personalistic connectivity at local levels may obviate the possibility for true independence of civil society groupings from the myriad agencies of the state.[15]

This would seem to apply especially to China, where networks of inter-connectedness between the agencies of the state and the ostensible institutions of civil society work through a diverse set of channels. Despite the identification of such new creatures in the civil society bestiary as "semi-civil society"[16] and the seemingly paradoxical "state-led civil society,"[17] autonomy remains elusive in the understanding of Chinese social structures. In his analysis of this "search for civil society" in China, Gordon White differentiates between political interpretations of civil society and a socio-logical view which emphasizes more broadly the associational structures within (nonstate) society, rather than focusing on explicitly political organizations and actions.[18] This emphasis on the associational structures of Chinese civil society prompts a line of thinking first formulated by de Tocqueville in his interpretation of nineteenth-century American civic culture and championed in recent years by Robert Putnam in his influential work on Italian politics.[19] By Putnam's analysis, it is the horizontal linkages inherent in social organizations which allow for the development of trust or "social capital," creating a counterweight to the verticality of traditional political structures.

The value of such an interpretation of social relations based upon the networks of individual actors is that it helps us to break apart monolithic views of "the state" in relation to society. Any individual actor may experience multiple webs of relationships. Leaders of community organizations, in particular, may have both strong vertical, personalistic connections to local officials and important horizontal linkages to others within their organization. From liberal theory, it is the dominance of horizontal linkages in aggregate which is at the root of a strong local civic community and which underpins civil society,[20] an idea which is helpful for thinking about local governance in Quanzhou, a city whose development trajectory indicates a divergence from state-dominated forms elsewhere in the country.

In the case of Quanzhou, the current situation derives as much or more from the city's history of international linkages as it does from the present economic reforms of the Chinese state. In the following sections of this chapter, we will therefore look at the connectivities of Quanzhou and its people to cities around the Pacific Rim, and examine how certain sets of linkages, such as those associated with the restoration of the city's many neighborhood temples, are presenting new challenges for local governance.

QUANZHOU IN ITS NETWORKS

No visitor to any part of Quanzhou today would mistake it for Orange County, or even Monterey Park. That this should be so is by no means self-evident, however. The city depends heavily on foreign investment, and Southern California has an important place in Quanzhou's ties to the world beyond China. According to the Quanzhou Municipality Overseas Chinese Gazetteer, more Quanzhou-originated emigrants to the United States live in Los Angeles than in any other American city, and, of a number of specific "well-known" entrepreneurs with roots in Quanzhou who are listed in the Gazetteer, 40 percent are in Los Angeles (pp. 118–126).[21] Quanzhou has discussed becoming sister cities with Monterey Park, a major new Chinese-American "ethnoburb" of Los Angeles,[22] and many of its listed business-men in the United States are also active in kinship associations and cultural organizations like Chinese language schools. The same Indonesian-Chinese tycoons who are central to the "crony capitalism" that has imported Southern California models of development to Jakarta are part of the Overseas Chinese community originating in Fujian, and their conglomerates have invested heavily in their Chinese "hometowns" (*qiaoxiang*): Riady (Li Wen-zhang)'s Lippo Group in Fuqing; Sudono Salim (Liem Sioe-liong)'s Salim Group in Putian, and Widjaja (Oei Ek-tjong)'s Sinar Mas Group in Quan-zhou itself.[23] These and other ethnic Chinese (mainly Fujianese) investors from Southeast Asia and Taiwan also figure prominently among Asians investing in Southern California.[24]

Nevertheless, links between Quanzhou and Southern California and even the entire United States are slender, sparse, and indirect, compared with those connecting it to Southeast Asia. Looking at the receiving end, the bulk of American direct investment in Quanzhou is small and limited to toy, clothing, and cosmetics manufacturing. In real estate, there is comparatively little direct investment from outside mainland China, and no investment from the United States at all.[25] The story of Quanzhou's links with the West is much older and more complex than any simple listing of current investment amounts and sources could tell, and yet an appreciation for this story is necessary to understand the way these links have influenced the city's urban development patterns.

Quanzhou's position as a cosmopolitan trading center began at least over a thousand years ago, before the Tang dynasty (sixth–ninth centuries). By the end of the fourteenth century, Quanzhou was the most prominent port on the Chinese littoral.[26] Like Venice, at the other end of the "Maritime Silk Road," Quanzhou was an entrepreneurial city with strong global link-ages, long before globalization was identified as an historic force. In more recent times, this outward orientation has been expressed in the city's role as a place of tremendous out-migration, with the descendants of Quanzhou's migrants now accounting for large portions of the Hokkien-speaking population of the Chinese in Southeast Asia.[27]

It is useful to contrast these sets of Quanzhou's overseas connectivities with the linkages implicit in being part of the modern nation-state of the People's Republic of China. In comparison to what might be put forward as being typical of Chinese urbanism today,[28] Quanzhou exhibits a number of exceptional qualities, derived from its specific historic and geographic circumstances. In this, three basic factors may be identified: (1) the relative lack of state investment in the region during the period of the centralized command economy, due to what was seen as Quanzhou's vulnerable position directly across the straits from Taiwan; (2) the high degree of private control of property in the city, even during the most radical periods of China's recent past; and (3) the importance of the city's *huaqiao* (Overseas Chinese) connection—that is, that Quanzhou has been a place of great out-migration with actively maintained connections to overseas relatives.

Each of these three factors is tightly intertwined with the other two, giving rise to a particular political economy of development that differs from what might be considered to be the Chinese urban norm. This underscores the need to carefully examine local factors within the Chinese polity in order to understand processes of development and change. To give an example, the low level of central state investment in the area translates in practical terms into a lower proportion of state-sector ownership in the local economy and a significantly less-developed presence of *danwei* (work units) in the city. The "front line" position of Quanzhou across the strait from Taiwan has thus been a contributory factor to the persistence of private or collective ownership throughout the period of state socialism. One instance of this is that, unlike most of urban China, the Quanzhou government never carried out a program of housing collectivization. By the end of the 1970s, more than 90 percent of the city's housing stock was still in private hands.

Private ownership at the household level is linked even more importantly to the influence of the *huaqiao* connection, in that city officials have always worked to maintain good relations with overseas expatriates, and have therefore been careful not to implement policies which could be seen as disenfranchising those components of the local community who have connections to the outside. The former mayor who, more than any other single official, was responsible for the city's decision not to implement housing collectivization during the Great Leap Forward and the Cultural Revolution, roughly estimates as much as 40 percent of inner-city residential property was wholly or partially owned by Overseas Chinese.[29] The local government generally estimates that more than 5 million Overseas Chinese (mostly in Southeast Asia and Taiwan) can trace their roots to Quanzhou and its immediate environs.[30] The investment and development implications of the *huaqiao* connection are historically rooted, with major initiatives for development and change originating from returned expatriates in the 1920s and 1930s, and a special district of elegant mansions (the Huaqiao Xincun) set aside in the 1950s to reward the wealthiest overseas supporters of the Revolution. In short, the *huaqiao* connection has long been crucial to the local economy. In the context of low levels of central state spending, it has provided the local government with a significant degree of leverage vis-à-vis the central government in Beijing.

The transborder connectivity of Quanzhou is thus critical for both local politics and the local economy. For analytical purposes, flows of overseas money into the city may be looked upon as falling into three categories. The first is foreign direct investment; this is what shows up on the record books and attracts the attention of businesspeople, scholars, and others who are interested in the vicissitudes of international trade and other matters of consequence. The second is what is often seen as charitable donations, and this results in new schools, new roads, rebuilt temples, and so forth. This shows up in different record books and hence is much more difficult to get a handle on, although it may be no less consequential than foreign direct investment. In certain respects, it may be somewhat spurious to pretend that there really is a clear separation between the first category (business investments) and the second (charitable donations).

The third category, referred to as household remittances, is even harder to track, as this does not necessarily show up on anyone's record books. The city of Quanzhou is at the moment undergoing tremendous reconstruction and reworking of its historic urban fabric. Much of this is resulting from household-by-household redevelopment. The three-, four-, and five-storey white tile buildings—the physical expression of household remittances from Overseas relatives—are transforming the old city of Quanzhou (see Figure 7.1).

For Quanzhou's planners and administrators, this form of capital movement is also of great consequence, even if it is not an issue that has heretofore attracted much research attention. The urban impacts of the remittance economy, like charitable donations and foreign direct investment, are all indications of the continuing connectivity of the city and its region with the rest of the world.[31] The globalization of Quanzhou which is implicit in these observations has implications for local social structures. The historically rooted and contemporaneously continuing flows of capital, people, and ideas shape the local character of social relations, and, in particular, underlie the establishment and maintenance of autonomous social organizations in the city. Such organizations have long characterized Chinese society—for example, the craft guilds, literary societies, and native place associations of the late Qing period.[32] It was only during the recent historical period of centralized state socialism that state and society were for ideological reasons understood to be exactly equated, and such autonomous organizations were suppressed.[33] Since the advent of the reforms at

Figure 7.1. Private houses built in 1994, and a traditional courtyard house in Quanzhou's Old City. Photo by Daniel Abramson.

the end of the 1970s, China has experienced a flourishing of new organizations, including hundreds of thousands of business and professional associations, academic societies, and recreational and cultural clubs.[34]

In the following section, we lay out some preliminary ideas about one particular type of organization, which, despite its lack of official recognition, has become prominent once again in the social fabric of Quanzhou—the many local associations for the restoration and maintenance of the city's neighborhood temples.

FENXIANG NETWORKS AND THE TEMPLES OF QUANZHOU

A notable finding in Putnam's work on Italian political culture is how the vitality of civic community in Italy is negatively correlated with the local presence of the Catholic Church and the degree of religiosity among local residents.[35] Thus, the church was found to play a much more central role in the clientelistic south than in the more democratic north. This interpretation should not be taken as an indictment of the civic role of religion *per se*, but rather as an indication of the long-standing historical linkages between church and state in the southern Italian context.

The question of the civic community implications of religion in southern China is much less straightforward than the Italian situation, owing in part, no doubt, to the historical lack of an institutional monopoly by a state-sanctioned religion. In order to appreciate the complexities of current conditions, it is useful to first point out a few aspects of the role of religion in China's prerevolutionary past. In his interpretation of late imperial China's religious life, Stephan Feuchtwang stresses the distinction between the temples of official religion and popular religion.[36] Official religion, incorporating elements of Taoism and Buddhism, utilized a system of temples and rites closely paralleling the formal administrative hierarchy of the state—the traditional pyramid of governance—and designed to reinforce the leading agency of the imperial throne. In contrast, the various sects and temples of popular religion were locally initiated and were able to develop into noncentralized networks of similar temples through the ritual referred to as the "division of incense" (*fenxiang*), which allows for the nonhierarchical propagation of new temples. In this distinction between official and popular temples we can see very different respective roles, with the temples of the official religion focused on maintaining the legitimacy of the imperial state and the temples of popular religion playing a critical function in the construction of local community mores.

It should be pointed out, however, that when viewed historically, these two aspects of Chinese religion cannot be seen as being mutually exclusive. Feuchtwang, in his analysis, emphasizes the overlaps between the official and popular religions. As the gods of popular religion were almost invariably once living beings who were canonized through the popular religion, good administrative practices from time to time required their official recognition, resulting in the co-optation of certain of the *fenxiang* temple networks into the administrative hierarchy of the official religion. The Tian Hou Gong Temple in Quanzhou is a good example of this, with Mazu, the "goddess" of the temple, now looked upon as a bodhisattva, indicative of the assimilation of Taoist and Buddhist strands in the official religion of imperial China.

Historically, assimilation works in both directions, as the practices surrounding the City God (Cheng Huang) Temple illustrate a downward appropriation: this temple is characteristically part of the official religion, yet its ceremonies allowed for broader popular participation than what would be necessitated by formal ritual. As it was at the lowest end of the official religious hierarchy, the City God Temple was thus closest to the citizenry, a factor resulting in adaptive ritual practices over time. Ritualistic celebrations at a revived Temple of the City God in Quanzhou are now characteristically similar to the public ceremonies of other temples of the popular religion.

In contrast to the hierarchy and exclusivity of the temples of the official religion, a "popular temple's area is defined purely territorially—all those within a given territory, whatever their rank or class, are expected to participate in its major festivals, at least by paying the ritual maintenance tax."[37] This inherent egalitarianism allowed for the creation of locally based social capital (i.e., horizontal social ties, in contrast to the verticality engendered by the official religion), and has no doubt been an important factor in the proliferation of *fenxiang* temples wherever *huaqiao* Chinese have settled.[38] *Fenxiang* temples served local communities in multiple ways, by functioning as points of focus for a number of different social services and collective undertakings, such as the organization of small-scale rotating credit associations.[39]

In its prerevolutionary past, the city of Quanzhou contained well over 100 temples. Many were closed down or converted to other uses in the 1950s or before, with many more destroyed as relics of feudalism during the Cultural Revolution in the 1960s and early 1970s. In response to both the interests of local residents and the increasing influence of Overseas Chinese after the opening up of China in the early 1980s, a priority list of major temples to be restored was established in the mid-1980s. A major criterion for this prioritization was that the buildings to be restored must be recognized as belonging to one of the five recognized religions in China today (Buddhism, Taoism, Catholicism, Protestantism, and Islam), which is, in a sense, a new, postrevolutionary definition of Chinese "official religion." Other criteria included historical importance and the expression of interest in restoration by the appropriate body of the religion in China. Thus twenty-seven structures were put on this list, including, for example, the only Arab-built mosque extant in China today. As they are not part of any officially recognized religion, the dozens of other *fenxiang* temples, *ancestral halls*, and other neighborhood altars were not included.[40] Nonetheless, it is estimated that nearly one-half of these smaller temples have at this point been restored and reopened by informal groups operating within the neighborhoods of the city (see Figure 7.2).

One may now observe in this region of Fujian a major resurgence of the practices and landscapes of traditional popular religion.[41] The Quanzhou city government is at a loss as to how to formally respond to the phenomenon of neighborhood temple restoration, as there are no official instructions coming down from Beijing in regard to this. There is, however, a recognition that since this is something which can influence both the social and physical development of the city, there is a need for a management response, and local officials have been surveying the situation for a number of years.

The potential social implications of temple network revivals may be understood from the case of the Ciji Gong Temples, one of the most prominent *fenxiang* networks in the region. The Ciji Gong Temples are dedicated to the god Baosheng Dadi, the canonization of a ninth-century doctor historically identified by the name Wu Tao. The original Baosheng Dadi Temples are located at a distance from Quanzhou, near the modern-day port city of Xiamen, yet the popularity of this "divine doctor" and his impor-

Figure 7.2. Typical neighborhood temple restored between 1993 and 1997 with private donations from local residents and overseas relatives. Photo by Daniel Abramson.

tance as a protector of life have led to the spread of Baosheng Dadi Temples throughout the region, throughout Taiwan, and in the many parts of Southeast Asia where Hokkien migrants have settled. In southern Fujian alone, it is estimated that there are currently more than 300 temples in this *fenxiang* network.[42] In the past, the ceremonies and rituals associated with Baosheng Dadi were a major source of traditional medical knowledge for the people of the region, a role which the temple has modified and modernized over time. The most prominent Baosheng Dadi Temple in Quanzhou today, known as the Huaqiao Ciji Gong, has maintained a free clinic since 1878, serving the people of Quanzhou with both Chinese and Western medical treatments.[43] A noteworthy point is that despite the closure of temples elsewhere in the city, the Huaqiao Ciji Gong was able to remain open throughout the struggles of the Cultural Revolution due to its important social service orientation.

The Huaqiao Ciji Gong (Flower Bridge Temple of Charity), as its name implies, also functions as a critical point of connectivity to overseas compatriots from the city and its region. The temple has been able to maintain its free clinic with significant funding from other Taiwanese and Southeast Asian Baosheng Dadi Temples in its *fenxiang* network, a point which no doubt was also a factor in being able to maintain its operations throughout China's socialist period. Such networks are important to examine in that they begin to blur the distinction between local and global; in this, the functioning of Quanzhou's *fenxiang* networks are emblematic of much broader forms of local-global connectivity.

GLOBAL NETWORKS IN QUANZHOU'S URBAN LANDSCAPE

The importance in Quanzhou of maintaining *qiaoxiang* (hometown or place-of-origin of overseas Chinese) networks, and the persistence of many of the traditional cultural institutions through which these and other social networks operate, has had a notable influence on the recent development of the city's land and buildings, especially in the historic city center. At first, the municipal and central district governments attempted to follow the pattern of urban redevelopment that began to sweep China in the early 1990s—a pattern that took little account of existing community networks and physical structures. Through typical large-scale demolition, street widening, and construction of mass housing and commercial space, government-sponsored developers succeeded in rebuilding nearly 17 percent of the Old City. However, while this is a significant proportion of an area that is only about 6.5 square kilometers in its entirety, the redevelopment is remarkable in that it has accommodated to an unusual degree the existing scale of commerce (predominantly small shopfronts on the ground floor of mixed-use buildings), and the existing residents who wished to remain in their old neighborhoods. Although their old houses were demolished, nearly all residents could afford to buy new units on site—a remarkable contrast to redevelopment projects in Beijing, for example.[44]

Both the design of the public spaces and the architectural style of the redevelopment went to extraordinary lengths to respond to local construction traditions and other local features of the urban landscape: characteristic arcaded shophouses, small plazas for traditional civic activities like opera and amateur *Nan Yin* (Southern music; the musical form popular in Quanzhou and elsewhere in Southern Fujian Province that traces its lineage back to the Tang Dynasty) performances, and fanciful Minnan (South of the Min River); Southern Fujian-style stone and brickwork on the building facades. Even the small neighborhood temples were given places to rebuild among the new structures. In one telling twist of the typical tale of Southern California-style globalization, a shopping mall that was built by a Philippine *huaqiao* investor with promises of attracting world-famous American brand-name department stores like Saks Fifth Avenue and J.C. Penney ended up housing only a McDonald's, while the rest of the complex was occupied by local small wholesale textile dealers, who treated the interior atrium much as they would a city street, complete with motorcycle access (see Figure 7.3).

Furthermore, while the developer's prospectus showed the McDonald's

Figure 7.3. Developer's rendering of the interior of a shopping mall proposed for a site in the Old City of Quanzhou, c. 1996. Photo by Daniel Abramson.

in a typical automobile-dominated suburban setting with a towering sign, drive-in, and parking lot, the actual McDonald's as built occupied a three-story arcaded streetfront building designed to respect the neighboring early-twentieth-century shophouses (see Figure 7.4).

Moreover, the actual city-center redevelopment that has been accomplished is far less than the 65 percent that the local government expected to rebuild by the year 2000.[45] A combination of concern for the historic fabric of the city,[46] a reaction by local residents angry over the prospect of demolition, and the sheer expense of relocating a population overwhelmingly of private homeowners has driven the local government to seek alternative approaches to improving the Old City's infrastructure and environment. Not only private ownership, but also private informal construction, has dominated the Old City of Quanzhou even since 1949. Standard collective apartment-style housing did not appear in Quanzhou in any significant number until 1980. In 1977, work-unit housing throughout the entire municipality of 11,015 square kilometers (including extensive mountain areas, six counties, and two county-level cities) represented only about one-fifth of all urban housing at the county-level or higher. Within the

Figure 7.4. Actual McDonald's in Quanzhou's Old City, with early twentieth-century arcaded shophouses in background. Photo by Daniel Abramson.

historic center of Quanzhou proper, *xin cun* (planned housing estates) only occupy about 115,000 square meters, or 2 percent of all the land.

Private construction, by contrast, was much more dynamic than the public or collective sector before 1990, and has kept apace up to the present. In 1990, private, "scattered" housing represented 71 percent of all urban housing in the Quanzhou municipal administrative area. Within the Licheng District, which is comprised of the Old City and some of its near suburbs, individual houses accounted for twice the built floor area of work-unit housing by 1990. In the 1980s alone, private home-builders invested 11.7 billion RMB to build 590,000 square meters—about as much floor area as had been built privately over the previous three decades. Even in the year 1998, after eight years of wide-ranging professional real estate activity,[47] private investment in all types of building in the Licheng District amounted to 136 million RMB, not much less than the 170 million invested by the real estate industry.[48]

The combination of a dynamic private construction sector and a land tenure system that has continued with little disruption since the first half of the twentieth century has produced a traditional urban core that in some ways resembles an informal village, but with an urban density and greater mix of uses. The ground floors or front rooms of many houses have become shops or restaurants. Households have wholly or partially replaced their old one-storey wood structure houses with new granite, brick, or, most recently, reinforced concrete structures of two to five storeys. Many of these houses are extremely large (up to 500 square meters) for the small plots of land on which the owners, frequently, have lived for many generations. Moreover, it is not uncommon for large private houses to be partially empty for much of the year. The factors which contribute to this phenomenon include a custom of sinking savings into house construction, and a high frequency of shared ownership or investment. Although Quanzhou undertook quite early to reestablish an open and clear system of property registration,[49] shares in ownership by Overseas relatives, like the extent of remittances, are rarely revealed.

Again, therefore, official figures tend to underestimate the importance of *huaqiao* relations, not only to individual resident families, but also to the overall development of the city center. One further indication of this importance is the fact that the above-mentioned Huaqiao Xincun, a subdivision of lots given to wealthy returned Overseas Chinese to build their own villas between 1954 and 1965, was actually the first planned government housing project to be built within the Old City. Even after confiscating some property for public purposes during the three decades following 1949, a major feature of the Reform era in Quanzhou has been the restoration of such property to original owners, especially if these owners wish to return from overseas. A legal precedent was set in 1979 when Lin Pingguo, a Philippine *huaqiao* from Quanzhou, sued the municipality to have his family *citang* (ancestral temple), in which his immediate family had been living before 1949, returned to him. Built during the reign of Qing emperor Daoguang, the *citang* had been confiscated in the 1950s for public offices, and ultimately occupied and then demolished by the Bureau of Agriculture. The government pinned its legal defense on the argument that because the property had been a "superstitious"[50] facility rather than a proper home, it was not required to compensate the owner for its expropriation. The court decided in favor of the plaintiff, however, and the government was required to find another plot of land in the city center suitable for the construction of a new home.

This case gives some clue to the complexity of the web of social and political relations in which property rights and the shaping of urban space are patterned in Quanzhou. Since then, an alliance between local residents and overseas relations all belonging to one kinship association has succeeded even against the powerful Public Security Bureau in a dispute over the right to rebuild their ancestral temple on land that had been appropriated by the Public Security Bureau (See Figure 7.5).

At first appearance, the urban landscape of Quanzhou's Old City appears quite chaotic—the jumbled product of a multitude of unrelated individual decisions carried out in the security of established private tenure and relatively high household incomes. This landscape has nothing in common with the accretion of standardized, collective living and workspaces that

Figure 7.5. Ancestral temple funded by an international kinship association being built on land previously expropriated by the Quanzhou Public Security Bureau, 2000. Photo by Daniel Abramson.

characterize most other, larger Chinese cities. In fact, Quanzhou's Old City is also the subject of constant negotiation between the interests of local residents and authorities, and overseas individuals and communities. It is difficult to overestimate the importance of embellishing the private home in the world of coastal South China's migratory families. Denise Chong's account of her own Chinese-Canadian grandfather's obsession with building a house in his home village in Guangdong vividly illustrates the human dimensions of this tradition. Moreover, besides wielding influence as familial relatives, these overseas actors also have an impact as entrepreneurs, as public benefactors, or as custodians of cultural traditions that have persisted in spite of radical revolution. And sometimes they have been the purveyors of revolution themselves.[51]

CONTINUITY AND DISCONTINUITY IN QUANZHOU'S REDEVELOPMENT

It is a common misconception that the desecration of temples and the destructive transformation of traditional urban space in China are exclusively the project of the Communist regime.[52] In fact, throughout China during the early years of the Republic, the new Nationalist government undertook to "modernize" China in part precisely by overturning a broad array of urban spatial principles that had come to be seen as sacred by the supporters of the Qing and other *yi lao yi shao* (young and old cultural conservatives).[53] In Quanzhou, the role of Overseas Chinese in this undertaking was especially pronounced. A clique of progressive young *huaqiao* Nationalists, mainly from the Philippines, established a new bureaucracy to oversee public works in the 1920s, which succeeded in demolishing part of the city wall, replacing the main Song dynasty stone bridge across the Jin River with a new reinforced concrete one, widening the city's existing two main streets, and clearing a swath through the center of the city to build a new tree-lined avenue of arcaded shophouses.[54]

The new avenue, now named Zhongshan Road, was designed by Lei Wenjin, an engineering graduate of Cambridge University. He drew heavily on British colonial experience in construction, and the *huaqiao* entrepreneurs who attempted to capitalize on the new public works also brought physical forms from colonial Southeast Asia to the city. A Vietnamese Chinese entrepreneur, who had already built a "French-style" avenue in Saigon and named it after himself, attempted to do the same in Quanzhou by buying up land along one of the major widened streets.

Most of the reformers' schemes were compromised or stopped by local speculators or conservatives, or the inert resistance of existing social institutions.[55] Zhongshan Road, for example, was forced to take many twists and turns to avoid the homes of influential people and important temples. One of the most notable of these was the previously mentioned Huaqiao Ciji Gong. The street was also built narrower than intended, due to the Urban Construction Bureau director's preference for selling off the land that abutted it instead of providing the commodious sidewalks that Lei Wenjin designed. In 1922, when the Urban Construction Bureau attempted to demolish the ancient Song dynasty Arab-built Qingjing Mosque (now one of three nationally protected monuments in the Old City) in order to widen the street that ran past it, the local Muslim *Hui* community protested to a prominent *Hui* official in the Nationalist government, who successfully interceded.

In this instance of conservation, ethnic networks were far more important than any professional concept of what constitutes valuable architectural heritage. There was no official Nationalist preservation policy extended to the important monuments and temples of Quanzhou. Indeed, the relative importance of various social networks is indicated in the fate of all of Quanzhou's temples during the Republican era. The major ones suffered during the *pochu mixin* (eradicate superstition) movement. With the exception of its famous twin pagodas, which were restored in 1926–1928 by two *huaqiao* philanthropists, Kai Yuan Temple fell into disrepair; the Confucian temple's front plaza became a market in 1931 and the buildings were occupied by a school; and the Tian Hou Gong Temple to Mazu, Goddess of the Sea, also became a school. Smaller or more popular Taoist and folk temples like the Guanyue Miao, the Xuanmiao Guan, and the myriad neighborhood *pujing* temples, on the other hand, were left untouched for fear of angering too many people.

If DeGlopper's account of community definition in nineteenth-century Lu-kang, a city in Taiwan populated predominantly by people from Quanzhou, is reflective of Quanzhou before 1949, then we can extrapolate to suggest that the differential treatment of Quanzhou's temples during the Republican era reflected a general weakening of traditional elite or more widely dispersed networks, such as those of the Buddhist orders, scholar-official society, and even maritime society, leaving the more local, territorially defined social groups in a relatively strong position.[56]

After 1949, the Maoist regime extended the attack on traditional social structures to include the more local institutions. The Taoist Xuanmiao Guan was completely destroyed and, as mentioned above, the number of territorial neighborhood temples declined during the 1950s and 60s to a point during the Cultural Revolution when none openly functioned as such, though a few original structures remained to house health clinics, neighborhood committees, police stations, and other secular services. The rapid, unregulated revival of this level of religious space and life after 1980, however, has shown that the social networks associated with neighborhood temples were never eradicated. Rather, the same respected community elders who served on the neighborhood committees and in the secular elderly associations were also members of the temple committees and were in charge of raising funds from local residents for the temple restorations. Larger restorations, like that of the Xuanmiao Guan or the Chan-Buddhist Chengtian Si, have cost millions of RMB, and have required significant contributions and political lobbying from Overseas Chinese religious and commercial leaders.

It is ironic that at the end of the twentieth century, this generation of Quanzhou's overseas progeny has reversed the attack on traditional religious space which their Overseas Chinese forebears brought back to the city at the beginning of the century. The reaction is perhaps explained by the greater success that a more home-grown, sometimes-xenophobic brand of nationalism (i.e., Maoism) obtained in continuing this attack. And yet it is striking that in both eras, local social networks in Quanzhou have survived, aided by their own global ties. It is also remarkable, as David Strand phrased it, how Republican urban reformers "pre-visioned" the end-of-century urban transformation in China.[57] In the 1920s, Philippine *huaqiao* investors introduced the two- and three-storey arcaded shophouse to Quanzhou; in the 1990s, Philippine *huaqiao* introduced the glass-atriumed shopping mall. The street widenings and straightenings; the raising of multistorey buildings; the commercialization of the urban core—all are resumed.

Of course, one important difference is that the preservationist reaction to this is no longer only the expression of an inward-looking, nativistic cultural conservativism; rather, late-twentieth-century preservationism also has its global networks and vocabulary, and these are being applied in Quanzhou as energetically as are the global flows of capital. Moreover, these flows of capital are being filtered through the fine sieve of small entrepreneurs and individual households. Zhongshan Road in the 1920s represented a unified urban vision, but was built out bay by bay, house by house; the city-center mall of the 1990s, though presented as a vision of international corporate standardization, ended up also occupied on a shop-by-shop basis with a minimum of corporate regulation applied to it.

CONCLUSIONS: CONNECTIVITY, URBAN SPACE, AND CIVIL SOCIETY

The city of Quanzhou, like other cities in China, is now in the midst of profound changes, changes driven in large part by the emergence of new actors on the urban development stage, in contrast to the near-monopoly of the state in prereform times.[58] Intensive and extensive investment in the built environment of the city, from the most top-down construction projects, including widening of roads and upgrading of major infrastructure, to the bottom-up construction of the myriad new individual houses by city residents, has resulted in an unprecedented transformation of the city over the past decade. While Quanzhou's suburban development does include one example of a Western-style villa subdivision and is otherwise rather typical of Chinese metropolitan development with high-rises and high-density housing estates, the rebuilding of the historic center itself is taking a different path.

Contrasting the case of Quanzhou to Jakarta, despite the fact that some of the same marketing influences are at work in China as in Indonesia, and even some of the same people are part of the global network that brings Western-defined aspirations to these two cities, the effect of global influence is evidently quite different. Southern California and other late-twentieth-century Western influences in Quanzhou are undoubtedly present but indirect, filtered through the aspirations and activities of Philippine and Indonesian investors who were exposed to American influence in those countries, and who then sought to import it to Quanzhou. How are these influences "preservationist" in nature? After all, the usual stated social goal of most investments by *huaqiao* in China's rural and urban environment is to "modernize" the "backward" place from which they originated. There are three ways.

First, in tandem with efforts to modernize their homeland, many Overseas Chinese have explicitly promoted the restoration of temples, ancestral halls, and other historic structures that are, for them, landmarks and monuments to their roots. Life-cycle rituals like weddings and funerals, also,

continue to reflect the influence of remittances sent back by Overseas relatives, often to the point of wasteful extravagance in the eyes of local authorities. Second, even Overseas Chinese investment in the modernization
of China's southeast coast is, from a cultural perspective, unintentionally
preservationist, relative to the development trajectory of China's hinterland
and northern areas. *Huaqiao*-driven modernization is already a relatively
continuous, century-old tradition in China's southern littoral; has taken
place on a very small but broad-based scale, at the level of clans, villages,
and individual families; and has enfolded deference to tradition within its
progressive tendencies: "Overseas Chinese who originated from Quanzhou
have an historic tradition of building [modern] multi-storey buildings (*lou-
fang*) in one's hometown for the glorification of their ancestors (*yaozu
rongzong*)."[59]

The definition of modernization in the rest of China, on the other hand,
has been subject to wildly shifting political winds at the level of the central
government throughout this century. In Quanzhou especially, where private
housing was rarely expropriated for fear of alienating *huaqiao* relations,
the influence of these relations has had a calming effect on the transformation of urban fabric, even taking into account the disappearance of
many individual old houses. Although the current preservationist municipal
administration considers the unrestrained self-building activity of individual
households to be a serious threat to the city's historic character, the plot
pattern, streets, and social structure of most urban neighborhoods have
remained essentially intact. And even when larger-scale, speculative development is undertaken, it is rooted in the earlier tradition of self-building,
and in many ways responds to the dwelling-cultural aspirations of the local
market which that tradition bred.[60]

Finally, and most intangibly, the familiarity of local Quanzhou community leaders with the world outside China seems to have engendered a
kind of homely cosmopolitanism that allows global influence to coexist
more comfortably with local tradition than in other cities where the mayor,
bedazzled by a developer's flashy images of a Bonaventure-style (referring
to the American style of glass tower and fortress-like street front type of
development that has been so popular in Chinese planning schemes during
the past 15 years or so, a classic early example of which is the Sheraton
Great Wall Hotel in Beijing) hotel scheme, unilaterally arranges to build it
in the heart of the city's historic center. This is not to say that such schemes
have not been placed before the eyes of Quanzhou's leaders, or even that
certain factions within the local government have not gone ahead and built
them; rather, at the same time, a constituency has grown around the idea
that such schemes can and should be wed to the local building style and
to the urban fabric without sacrificing the city's modernity.

The role of global networks in the preservation of Quanzhou's local
identity has implications that go well beyond urban form. This instance of

the ability of traditional, community-based institutions and relationships to "tame" state power and global capital flows seems to possess some of the characteristics of civil society. In this regard, the resurgence of interest in temples is particularly useful to examine in further detail for a number of reasons.

First, there is a lesson here about the complex nature of Quanzhou's overseas connectivity. In practice, the analytical clarity implied by categorizing capital flows as foreign direct investment, charitable donations, and family remittances becomes blurred. Clearly such flows are imbedded in the web of personal, familial, and institutional connections which link Quanzhou to the rest of the world. The high level of household remittances shapes the local economy and makes possible the pervasiveness of temple restoration activities, which notably occur without official sanction. Official charitable donations, as seen, for example, in the much more costly restorations of the major (i.e., official religion) temples of the city, are ostensibly of a different nature, as these occur through the intermediary of local government agencies, follow an official priority list, and are duly recorded by the government. Yet the two phenomena cannot really be seen as being any more distinct than the official religion of China's imperial past was from the activities of the cults of popular religion. From the practical standpoint of doing business in this part of China, foreign direct investment, which for the most part is based on connections to "overseas compatriots,"[61] is also intimately linked to local charitable contributions, a practice with deep historical roots.[62]

Second, the restoration of neighborhood temples tells us something about the persistence and vitality of local associational forms. Conversations with members of these informal, unregistered organizations reveal that certain of the social capital-building activities which have long been associated with the *fenxiang* temples were not fully suppressed during the period of the Cultural Revolution; the large collective feasts and celebrations which are integral to the rituals of *pudu* (universal salvation, more commonly known in English as the Hungry Ghost Festival, a kind of Halloween and All Souls Day for Chinese Buddhists), for example, were merely carried out indoors in a much more atomized and dispersed fashion,[63] a practice which by necessity required the passive collusion of local authorities. The question which this presents us with today is whether the persistence of such traditions has the potential to underpin the development of new civil society institutions, and, if so, how the activities of such self-organizing groups will articulate with the needs and interests of officialdom. One might hypothesize that in the case of Quanzhou we are seeing a trend which could facilitate the further localization of state practices within the broader Chinese polity.

And third, this raises the idea that these two forms of connectivity—the transborder connectivity of globalization and the local connectivity of self-organizing civil associations—are not only linked, they are inseparable. At the most rudimentary level of monetary flows to finance the restoration of temples, whether through official charitable donations for the larger temples or through family remittances for neighborhood temples and altars, foreign capital is implicit throughout. Traditional carved stone tablets which publicly record donations now group contributions according to the currency in which they were remitted, whether in Renminbi, Hong Kong dollars, New Taiwan dollars, or U.S. dollars. But connectivity is by no means limited to the movement of money. It can be argued that such capital flows are denotative of the much more consequential connections between individual actors, and, by extension, between interconnected groups of individuals. Possible consequences of connectivity may be most visible in the changing physical fabric of the city of Quanzhou. The social, cultural, and even political implications may be less apparent—although no less critical for the future of the city and its people.

NOTES

1. Michael L. Leaf, "Globalization, Governance and the Cities of Pacific Asia," in *Proceedings of the Fourth Ritsumeikan-UBC Seminar*, ed. Matsubara Toyohiko, The Steering Committee of the Fourth Ritsumeikan-UBC Seminar, Kyoto, 1999.

2. James S. K. Chen, "Land Management Practice in Fuzhou, People's Republic of China," master's thesis, School of Community and Regional Planning, University of British Columbia, Vancouver, 2000.

3. Michael L. Leaf, "Urban Planning and Urban Reality Under Chinese Economic Reforms," *Journal of Planning Education and Research*, 18 (1998): 145–153.

4. Vivienne Shue, "State Sprawl: The Regulatory State and Social Life in a Small Chinese City," *Urban Spaces in Contemporary China*, eds. Deborah Davis et al. (New York: Cambridge University Press, 1995), 90–112.

5. Kris Olds, "Globalization and the Production of New Urban Spaces: Pacific Rim Megaprojects in the Late 20th Century," Asian Urban Research Network, Working Paper no. 9, UBC Center for Human Settlements, Vancouver; Piper Gaubatz, "Changing Beijing," *The Geographical Review*, 85, no. 1 (1995): 79–96.

6. Daniel Abramson, "Marketization and Institutions in Chinese Inner-city Neighborhood Redevelopment: A Commentary on 'Beijing's Old and Dilapidated Housing Renewal' by Lü Junhua," *Cities* 14, no. 2 (1997): 71–77.

7. Manuel Castells, *The Rise of the Network Society* (Cambridge, MA: Blackwell Publishers, 1991).

8. John Friedmann, "The World City Hypothesis," *Development and Change*, 17, no. 1 (1986): 69–84.

9. Mike Douglass, "World City Formation on the Asia Pacific Rim: 'Everyday' Forms of Civil Society and Environmental Management," in *Cities for Citizens: Planning and the Rise of Civil Society in a Global Age*, eds. Mike Douglass and John Friedmann (New York: John Wiley, 1998), 107–137.

10. L. H. Lees and P. M. Hohenberg, "How Cities Grew in the Western World:

A Systems Approach," in *Cities and Their Vital Systems*, eds. J. H. Ausubel and R. Herman (Washington, DC: National Academy Press, 1988), 71–84; Fernand Braudel, *Civilization and Capitalism, Volume III: The Perspective of the World* (New York: Harper and Row, 1984).

11. Christopher G. Boone, "Real Estate Promotion and the Shaping of Los Angeles," *Cities* 15, no. 3 (1998): 155–163.

12. Michael L. Leaf and Ayse Pamuk, "Habitat II and the Globalization of Ideas," *Journal of Planning Education and Research* 17 (1997): 71–78.

13. Michael L. Leaf, "Vietnam's Urban Edge: The Administration of Urban Development in Hanoi," *Third World Planning Review*, 21, no. 3 (1999), pp. 297–315.

14. John Friedmann, *Empowerment: The Politics of Alternative Development* (Oxford: Blackwell, 1992); John Friedmann, "The New Political Economy of Planning: The Rise of Civil Society," in *Cities for Citizens: Planning and the Rise of Civil Society in a Global Age*, eds. Mike Douglass and John Friedmann (New York: John Wiley, 1998), 19–37; Leonie Sandercock, *Towards Cosmopolis: Planning for Multicultural Cities* (New York: John Wiley, 1998).

15. This is a theme which is central to Bakti Setiawan's, "Local Dynamics in Informal Settlement Development: A Case Study of Yogyakarta, Indonesia" (University of British Columbia, School of Community and Regional Planning Ph.D thesis, Vancouver, BC: University of British Columbia, 1998), an analysis of squatter communities in Yogyakarta, Indonesia. In this study, Setiawan found that the communities which have been the most successful in upgrading are also those which have the thickest web of ties to local agencies. The strength of informal personalistic linkages between community leadership and local officials often overrides specific legal strictures on settlement formation and upgrading, thus allowing for a much higher degree of perceived tenure security than might be supposed on legal grounds alone.

16. He Baogang, *The Democratic Implications of Civil Society in China* (New York: St. Martin's Press, 1997).

17. Michael B. Frolic, "State-Led Civil Society," in *Civil Society in China*, eds. Timothy Brook and B. Michael Frolic (Stanford, CA: Stanford University Press, 1977), 46–67.

18. Gordon White, "The Dynamics of Civil Society in Post-Mao China," in *The Individual and the State in China*, ed. Brian Hook (Oxford: Clarendon Press), 196–221.

19. Robert D. Putnam, *Making Democracy Work: Civic Traditions in Modern Italy* (Princeton, NJ: Princeton University Press, 1993).

20. Ibid.

21. The Gazetteer estimates that a total of about 150,000 Chinese-Americans originated from Quanzhou. The Gazetteer, it should be noted, is a compilation of the Quanzhou branch of the national Overseas Chinese Liaison Association (*Qiao-Lian*), itself a kind of "government (Party)-organized" nongovernmental organization (GONGO) whose mission is to foster relations with Overseas Chinese and attract their investment.

22. Zhuang Yancheng et al., eds. 1991. *A Comprehensive Review of Investment Environments in China's Coastal Cities: Quanzhou Volume* (Shanghai: East China Teacher's University Press, 1991); Li Wei, "Anatomy of a New Ethnic Settlement:

The Chinese Ethnoburb in Los Angeles," *Urban Studies* 35, no. 3 (March 1998): 479–501.

23. Scott Waldron, "Indonesian Chinese Investment in China: Magnitude, Motivations and Meaning," Australia-Asia Paper No. 73, Centre for the Study of Australia-Asia Relations, Griffith University, Queensland, 1995; Constance Lever-Tracy, David Ip, and Noel Tracy, *The Chinese Diaspora and Mainland China: An Emerging Economic Synergy* (New York: St. Martin's Press, 1996).

24. "How the Missiles Help California," *Time*, 1 April 1996, 45; Damon Darlin, "How Do You Say Cockatoo Inn in Chinese?" *Forbes*, 18 November 1996, 54; "The Global Finance 600: The World's Most Powerful Financial Players," *Global Finance*, September 1997, 35–44.

25. Quanzhou Municipality Overseas Chinese Gazetteer Editing Committee, *Quanzhou Shi Huaqiao Zhi (Quanzhou Municipality Overseas Chinese Gazetteer)* (Beijing: Zhongguo Shehui Chubanshe [China Social Publishing House], 1996), p. 220.

26. Alfred Schinz, *Cities in China* (Berlin: Gebrüder Borntraeger, 1989); Hugh R. Clark, *Community, Trade, and Networks: Southern Fujian Province from the Third to the Thirteenth Century* (Cambridge: Cambridge University Press, 1991); David Selbourne, *The City of Light* (London: Little, Brown and Company, 1997).

27. Zhuang Guotu, "The Social Impact on Their Home Town of Jinjiang Emigrants' Activities during the 1930s," in *South China: State, Culture and Social Change during the 20th Century*, eds. Leo Douw and Peter Post (Amsterdam: North-Holland, 1996), 169–181.

28. Leaf, "Urban Planning and Urban Reality."

29. Interview with former Mayor Wang Jingsheng, 15 June 2000.

30. Zhuang Yingzhang, "God Cults and Their Credit Associations in Taiwan," in *South China: State, Culture and Social Change during the 20th Century*, eds. Leo Douw and Peter Post (Amsterdam: North-Holland, 1996), 69–76; Dai Yifeng, "Overseas Migration and the Economic Modernization of Xiamen City during the Twentieth Century," in ibid., 159–168.

31. In his attempt to build a global model of migration and development, Ronald Skeldon, *Migration and Development: A Global Perspective* (Essex, England: Longman, 1997) places particular emphasis on the global implications of family remittances, estimating that this flow of real capital is second only to that associated with the oil industry when looked at in aggregate. Skeldon also emphasizes the unevenness of the global remittance economy; Quanzhou is undoubtedly one of the locales in the world whose local economy is highly dependent upon overseas remittances.

32. G. William Skinner, "Introduction: Urban Social Structure in Ch'ing China," in *The City in Late Imperial China*, ed. G. William Skinner (Stanford, CA: Stanford University Press, 1977), 521–553.

33. Timothy Brook, "Auto-Organization in Chinese Society," in *Civil Society in China*, eds. Timothy Brook and B. Michael Frolic (Armonk, NY: M. E. Sharpe, 1997), 19–45.

34. He Baogang, *The Democratic Implications of Civil Society in China*.

35. Putnam, *Making Democracy Work*.

36. Stephan Feuchtwang, "School-Temple and City God," in *The City in Late*

Imperial China, ed. G. William Skinner (Stanford, CA: Stanford University Press, 1977), 581–608.

37. Ibid., 591; Kenneth Dean, *Taoist Rituals and Popular Cults of Southeast China* (Princeton, NJ: Princeton University Press, 1993), 178–180.

38. Kristofer M. Schipper, "Neighborhood Cult Associations in Traditional Taiwan," in *The City in Late Imperial China*, ed. G. William Skinner (Stanford, CA: Stanford University Press, California, 1977), 651–676.

39. Zhuang, "God Cults and Their Credit Associations in Taiwan."

40. Although it is notable that three of the major *fenxiang* temples, including the Tian Hou Gong Temple, mentioned above, were included in the list for restoration despite their roots in popular religion.

41. Dean, *Taoist Rituals and Popular Cults of Southeast China.*

42. Ibid., 85.

43. Ibid., 91

44. Lü, "Beijing's Old and Dilapidated Housing Renewal."

45. Tao Tao, "Problems in the Implementation of Quanzhou's Old City Redevelopment Plan," in *Renewal and Development in Housing Areas of Traditional Chinese and European Cities*, International Conference Proceedings, Xi'an, Quanzhou, Beijing. 1995.

46. Since 1981, Quanzhou has been officially designated a *Lishi Wenhua Mingcheng* (Famous Historic and Cultural City), a national designation similar to the international World Heritage Cities list.

47. Beginning in 1990, for example, commodification of real estate extended to industrial and commercial buildings, mixed-use retail and housing, villas, apartments, and so on, and often in the form of comprehensive, large-parcel development complete with infrastructure and social services.

48. Quanzhou Municipal Statistics Bureau, *Quanzhou Tongji Shouce* (*Quanzhou Statistical Handbook*), 1998.

49. Land and housing property registration was resumed in 1981, a comprehensive cadastral survey undertaken in 1984–1985, and the registry open to the public in 1989.

50. Ancestor worship, like any of the popular folk religious activities that do not fit within the government's five categories of established religions, is officially proscribed in China, despite its widespread revival in fact (Dean, *Taoist Rituals*).

51. Denise Chong, *The Concubine's Children* (Toronto: Viking, 1994).

52. For example, see Geremie Barmé's Introduction to L. C. Arlington and William Lewisohn, *In Search of Old Peking* (New York: Oxford University Press, 1987).

53. Shi Mingzheng. "Beijing Transforms: Urban Infrastructure, Public Works, and Social Change in the Chinese Capital, 1900–1928," Ph.D. dissertation, Columbia University, New York, 1993.

54. We owe much of the following account of the Republican-era urban history of Quanzhou to interviews with Mr. Wang Lianmao, Curator of the Quanzhou Maritime Museum, who interviewed many of the historic actors between 1961 and 1963.

55. Perhaps the most telling evidence of the passions aroused by the reformers' idealistic efforts was the fate of Ye Qingyan, a Philippine *huaqiao* leader of the public works bureaucracy: loudly condemned by conservative local scholars and

officials for destroying the city's ancestral tradition, he eventually resigned and became a monk.

56. Donald R. DeGlopper, "Social Structure in a Nineteenth-Century Taiwanese Port City," in *The City in Late Imperial China*, ed. G. William Skinner (Stanford, CA: Stanford University Press, 1977), 651–676.

57. David Strand, "Beyond Coast and Capital: Pressures and Previsions in the Making of the Modern Chinese City," in *Wall and Market: Chinese Urban History News* 1, no. 1 (1996), electronic journal.

58. Michael L. Leaf, Daniel B. Abramson, and Tan Ying, "Social Research and the Localization of Chinese Urban Planning Practice: Some Ideas from Quanzhou, Fujian," in *The New Chinese City: Globalization and Market Reform*, ed. John R. Logan (London: Blackwell, 2000).

59. Quanzhou Municipality Overseas Chinese Gazetteer Editing Committee, *Quanzhou Shi Huaqiao Zhi*.

60. The Gazetteer states: "As early as the late 19th century in the main cities and towns the landscape is dotted with villas built by *huaqiao*. But not until the late Qing dynasty did the sale and rental of property become the main purpose of this construction" (p. 220).

61. Yue-man Yeung and David K. Y. Chu, "Development Corridor in Fujian: Fuzhou to Zhangzhou," Occasional Paper No. 42, Hong Kong Institute of Asia-Pacific Studies, The Chinese University of Hong Kong, Shatin, Hong Kong, 1995.

62. Zhuang, "The Social Impact on Their Home Town of Jinjiang Emigrants' Activities during the 1930s."

63. Dean, *Taoist Rituals*, gives other examples of the persistence of ritual during this period, albeit carried out surreptitiously in the dark of night, in spite of the closure and dismantlement of temples.

8

Exporting the Dream: Hollywood Cinema and Latin American Suburbia

Rafael Pizarro

Interpretation of our own reality through foreign schemes only contributes to make us every time more unrecognizable to ourselves, every
time less free, every time more lonely.

Gabriel García Márquez

Sprawled, low-density middle- and upper-class residential suburbs usually
thought of as characteristic of North American cities[1] became ubiquitous
and commonplace in many Latin American cities during the 1950s, 1960s,
and 1970s. One of those cities was Bogotá, Colombia. It is feasible to
believe that the rise of the suburban pattern may have been related to
similar institutional and technological factors that triggered the massive
suburbanization of the United States in the post-World War II period. Of
these factors, lower land values in the periphery, increase of car ownership
among a rising middle and upper class, and the expansion of freeways are
the most commonly acknowledged. Nonetheless, some Latin American
scholars suggest that the suburban pattern and its associated landscapes are
direct borrowings from the United States.[2] Indeed, the similarities seem to
indicate a transfer of these urban ideas from North America. Yet it is not
clear how and why the idea of suburbia was transferred to Latin America
and why was it embraced so readily among home-buyers.

This chapter explores the notion that a less-conventional factor such as
the influence of cinematic images may play an important role in shaping
the form of the built environment and in bringing the suburban ideal to

Latin America. In this chapter, I claim that the idealized depiction of suburbs and the negative image given to the "city" in Hollywood films, added
to the fact that the Latin America city is in many ways similar to the "mean
city" of Hollywood cinema, may have led Latin American audiences to
ideologically embrace the suburb, try to re-create it in their own environments, and even develop a negative attitude toward their own cities. The-
oretically, this chapter questions the production of space and urban design
as autonomous and particular to a specific cultural context. Instead, I see
it as a result of, at least partially, readings and interpretations of foreign
spaces in the cinematic text.

The method I use to make the following assertions is interpretive. Empirical data to support causal connections between what audiences see in
movies or television and their behavior is questioned in critical studies of
the two media. Nonetheless, theoretical speculations such as the one I present in this chapter may serve as a platform to launch empirical research to
study these connections.

I will show, first, evidence of suburbia in Latin America and the claim
by some scholars that it might be the result of American influence. Second,
I will illustrate how the notion of suburbia can be transferred between
foreign cultures. Here, I put emphasis on the role of visual media in these
transfers. My claim is that the power of Hollywood cinema to affect people's impressions about the city resides in the tension it creates between
"city" and "suburb," pitching one against the other. The effect of this
dialectical antagonism between those two landscapes may result in the audience's affection for the suburb and disdain for the city.

At the end of the chapter, I argue that in the United States the tension
between city and suburb is not as problematic as it is in Latin America.
Considering that both landscapes have been present in North America for
almost a century, the public has had a reference to both, thus creating a
sense of balance between the two in the mind of the American viewer. In
Latin America, however, where the American-style suburb was practically
unknown until recently, the tension between city and suburb is resolved by
re-creating the missing part of the dichotomy, the suburb.

INTRODUCTION

For the past three decades, Hollywood cinema has interpreted the American urban landscape as a dichotomy between the city and the small town
or the suburb.[4] On the one hand, film narratives have fabricated an idealized suburban landscape characterized by a peaceful, healthy, and pleas-
urable environment, an urban utopia embedded in a small-town
atmosphere. On the other hand, the same narratives have constructed an
unhealthy, dangerous, dark urban landscape, an urban dystopia represented in the "city."

This city-suburb dichotomy is undoubtedly rooted in the American agrarian tradition that vilified the city and idealized the country, the small town, and later the suburb. And, while it may have a mild impact on the North American audience, I argue that it may have a great one on the Latin American. After all, the development of suburbia in the United States in the eighteenth century made Americans well acquainted with the suburban landscape and allowed them to compare through first-hand experience the advantages of the country and the disadvantages of the city. I claim that the effect of this antagonistic dialectic in a Third World country's culture may be of particular significance. I argue that because, on the one hand, the "vile" city portrayed in Hollywood filmography is, unfortunately, very close to the reality of some Latin American cities and, on the other, the "benign" small town or suburb does not have a match in those cities, Latin Americans have tried to recreate the suburban ideal by constructing their own suburbs mirroring the American model.

DIFFUSION OF THE CITY AS IDEA AND THE POWER OF CINEMATIC MEDIA

The diffusion of technological innovations has been a fundamental factor in shaping the physical dimension of civilizations. The final form and meaning of an object in material culture are largely the result of several transfers and transformations of the same idea from culture to culture.[5] In the diffusion of innovations, "an invention or a new institution adopted in one place is [usually] adopted in neighboring areas and in some cases continues to be adopted in adjacent ones until it may spread over the whole Earth."[6] Although studies in the diffusion of material culture usually refer to artifacts as objects ranging in size from small tools to buildings, the fact that the city is a manufactured reality resulting from the collective effort and genius of individuals does indeed qualifies it as another "artifact."[7] In fact, scholars argue that "the city can be analyzed . . . as an instrument subject to the evolution of any [other] technological product."[8] Thus, the evolution of urban form as an intrinsic characteristic of the city-object can be traceable from one geographical location to another and from one culture to another.

Discussions about how artifacts are invented in different cultures and how their representations diffuse from one culture to another sit at the center of the literature on material culture.[9] Archeological findings and ethnographic studies suggest that ideas did not sprout spontaneously in different parts of the world but rather in specific geographic nodes and from there to the rest of the world. These findings suggest that either humankind has been "uninventive" or the same solution for similar problems has been devised independently in different geographical areas.[10] The processes whereby ideas spread "often involve change and adaptation, so that there is a constant interplay between borrowing and innovation"[11] and this is the case with the transfer and adaptation of architectural and urbanistic ideas from one culture to another. Similarity in architectonic styles and urban patterns among ancient civilizations gives evidence to this "borrowing" among separate cultures.[12] Today, however, the process and media for borrowing and adaptating urban ideas among cultures are far more complex than in the past, and I argue that they involve new informational and entertainment technologies as those devised in Southern California.

The multiplicity of media possibilities, ranging from "real" to "virtual" traveling, makes difficult to pin down which medium is most influential. Nevertheless, the cinematic representation is undeniably one of the most powerful media to influence our ideas about the world. "Cinematic images react with other elements of culture, including television, music, legend and folklore, and literature" to generate powerful "metaphors about the . . . city"[13] and to structure understandings of ourselves and of our place in the world. Cinematic landscapes and places are very telling about the city because they "establish the nature of a geography grounded in representation."[14] As such, cinema "helps [to] structure the cultural context within which urban affairs take place."[15] Further, "the way spaces are used and places are portrayed in film reflects prevailing cultural norms, ethical mores, societal structures, and ideologies. Concomitantly, the impact of a film on an audience can mold social, cultural, and environmental experiences"[16] deeply affecting our conception of real places.

When the meaning attributed to images on the screen are transferred by an audience to the material and social world . . . the hyper-real become[s] a model for reality. If film images can influence clothing style, musical taste, toys, and our vocabulary [they may also] . . . participate in the structuring of our values, our social behavior, and . . . our relation in, and the construction of, the "real world."[17]

The appearance of a foreign urban landscape, such as the American suburb in Latin America, may be closely related to representations of "real life" suburbia in Hollywood cinema.

SUBURBIA IN LATIN AMERICA: THE CASE OF BOGOTÁ

Today's Latin American cities show evidence of middle- and upper-class suburban residential developments in the inner city and peripheral areas[18] (see Figure 8.1). Literature on the subject not only shows evidence of a "centrifugal movement of . . . high income groups away from the center of the city"[19] with characteristics similar to the American suburb,[20] but it also suggests that the new urban pattern is imported from the United States.

Figure 8.1. Suburban residential development in Phoenix, Arizona. Photo by Rafael Pizarro.

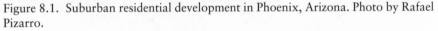

Alien cultural practices have swept through [Latin America]. [I]ts cities have naturally taken on a similar look, not only to one another, but also to the principal source of new technology, investment, and culture: North America. . . . Differences are apparent but, apart from the writing of the signs, it is sometimes difficult to distinguish the streets of Caracas from those of Los Angeles. . . . Latin America's affluent suburbs featured . . . California style housing during the 1950s and 1960s. Today, most elite residential areas feel much like North American suburbs. Indeed, the whole suburban life-style is imitative of the United States, based on the car and its associated retail structures such as the supermarket and shopping and entertainment malls.[21]

Bogotá, Colombia, for example, "manifests a strong 'dependency' relationship with . . . the United States. . . . [R]esidential segregation, traffic congestion, and employment patterns are to some extent imported phenomena."[22] The history of suburbia in Bogotá dates back to the first part of the century and it actually resembles that of the United States.[23] In the 1920s, the Bogotá elite started to abandon their homes in the heart of the city to move their families out to the peripheral agricultural areas,[24] immediately followed by Bogotá's upper middle class.[25] Undoubtedly, and as in the United States, other forces such as government housing policies,[26] increasing population densities in the city center, improved transportation and service facilities, and superior environmental conditions in the northern edges of Bogotá were also instrumental for the outward pull toward pe-

Figure 8.2. Supermarket in Bogotá, Colombia. Photo by Patrick Rouillard.

Figure 8.3. Retail commercial strip in Phoenix, Arizona. Photo by Rafael Pizzaro.

ripheral suburban expansion. But the reason for the particular form the suburbs took cannot be accounted for only by these forces. Latin American scholars insist that the similarity between the suburban patterns in both countries is related to the cultural influence of the United States.[27] In Bogotá, the "ever expanding sprawl, . . . shopping malls, cinemas and entertainment complexes . . . look[s] more and more like a North American city[28] (see Figures 8.2 and 8.3, and Figure 8.4).

Figure 8.4. Commercial Center in Bogotá, Colombia. Photo by Patrick Rouillard.

By the 1970s, American-type suburbanization with its associated problems[29] was well established in Bogotá. Today, the penetration and adaptation of suburban landscapes into the older fabric of the city are such that it is difficult to believe those suburbs were not developed there,[30] in a situation similar to what occurred with the suburban pattern in the United States. The "American middle-class adopted the English model of bourgeois suburbanization [in the 1800s] so decisively that ever since Americans have been convinced that it was they who invented suburbia."[31]

DIFFUSION OF URBAN IMAGES THROUGH FILM

Cinema, more than any other medium, greatly enhances and intensifies meanings through real and figurative signs. "The pleasure [and power] of film lies . . . in its ability to create its own cinematic geography, . . . an ideologically charged cultural creation whereby meanings of place and society are made, legitimized, contested, and obscured."[32] Movies "expand our experience vicariously by showing us what is it like to live in another fashion . . . offer[ing] a 'virtual experience"[33] Semiologists tell us that in these representations we are "confronted with complex symbolic structures [as] mediations of social reality."[34] This "impression of reality through a rapid succession of iconic signs"[35] makes place in the cinematic landscape a "spectacle, a signifier of the film's subject, a metaphor for the state of mind of the protagonist"[36] thus creating a deep impression in the mind of the viewer.

Although the cause-effect relationship between the cinematic images and the audience's behavior is still contested,[37] it has strong support among some scholars. "A recent analysis of the relationship between television habit and general attitudes toward crime, found that frequent television viewers seem to suffer from the 'mean world syndrome,' being more likely to overestimate their chances of encountering violence."[38] There is also evidence that a recent increase in the production of " 'hood" films has triggered renewed interest in problems of the "inner cities."[39]

Because cinema "helps structure the cultural context within which urban affairs take place,"[40] representations of urban life in movies seem to affect not only our opinion about the social group protagonist of the action but also our perception of the physical location where the action takes place. Because space and place "are inextricably integrated with social, cultural and political dynamics [they] have become indispensable to cinematic communication."[41] Stereotyped images of places are seemingly extremely powerful to trigger action in the mind of the receiver for they are idealized images of a real place.[42] Place stereotype is a "highly simplified generalization[s] about people and places which carry within them explicit assumptions about their characteristics and behavior."[43]

My contention is that the tension between the image of the "real place" and the "stereotyped place" created in film makes the cinematic suburb a magnet for the viewer. Research in Brazil suggests that Brazilian TV soap operas, which idealize life in the city, may have affected rural-urban migrations. "[P]eople are attracted to cities that appear on television. The projected image of the [city] as a modern place full of opportunities in which a modern person can get ahead only if she or he is sufficiently shrewd" seems powerful enough to trigger population migration.[44] Also, Burgess and Gold argue that human migrations in earlier times might have been triggered by the power of descriptive images of foreign places. They claim that the "the establishment of agriculturist settlements in the highly marginal environment south of Salt Lake City valley by the Mormons was largely a consequence of Brigham Young reading, and believing a propagandist emigrant guide-book."[45]

The tension or polarity between two different and opposed places—one invested with positive and the other one with negative connotations—is especially pervasive in Hollywood cinema and television.[46] This tension can be interpreted as the creation of a dystopia and a utopia. The dystopia is the "city" and the utopia the small town or suburb. This point and counterpoint projected in the mind of the viewer can shape his or her attitudes toward both landscapes. For the North American viewer, there is no real tension between both places because the U.S. public is thoroughly familiar with the two. The city and the suburb coexist in the daily reality of North Americans. In Latin America, however, the inexistence of one of the two, the utopian suburb, may trigger unfulfilled desires to live "suburban lives."

THE CITY/SUBURB DICHOTOMY IN HOLLYWOOD
CINEMA AND TV

Representations of the city in Hollywood cinema and TV seem to share with contemporary literature the same intellectual bias against the city.[47] To put it in the simplest terms, film and TV narratives depict the city as "bad" and the small town (and later the suburb) as "good." This dichotomy is perhaps the legacy of a resilient agrarian tradition in the United States characterized by an anti-urban bias.[48] "The city of the last twenty-five years has been kinetically projected as a dehumanizing place of corruption and immorality, as a jungle, as mean streets, as a reservation/killing fields, as racial tinderboxes, . . . and as . . . Hell and . . . Apocalypse."[49] American cinema[50] tends to portray the cities as "alienating and hostile places in which . . . there is a seamy underlife all too ready to rise to the surface."[51] Almost invariably[52] the city is portrayed in film as

too big, too noisy, too dusky, too commercial, too crowded, too full of immigrants, too full of Jews, too full of Irishmen, Italians, Poles, too artificial, destructive of conversation, destructive of communication, too greedy, too capitalistic, too full of automobiles, too full of smog, too full of dust, too heartless, too intellectual, too scientific, insufficiently poetic, too lacking in manners, too mechanical, and destructive of family. . . .[53]

Small towns in cinema and suburbs on television, on the other hand, have been portrayed as benign places of good morals and traditional family values. An urban paradise of tranquillity basking in balmy weather under sunny skies, and sitting on clean, neat, manicured greenery. In particular, "television has glorified the single family house as the standard American home, enshrined the low density neighborhood, and . . . provided an unrelentingly negative picture of the city as the haven of crime and violence."[54] In the United States of the 1950s, when television became more popular than movies, the ideal of a suburban home became fixated and perpetuated in the minds of an audience that watched suburban movies sitting in their very own suburban homes.

[O]ne of the longest-running and most popular of all the programs dealt with the trials and pleasures of suburban life. Ozzie and Harriet Nelson became staples across the land as households followed the progress of David and Ricky from infancy through young manhood. . . . *My Three Sons, Father Knows Best, The Brady Bunch, Leave it to Beaver*, and *Life with Riley* suggested that the appropriate setting for family life was the detached home and that the ideal symbol of making it in America was to trade a small suburban house for a large one. Even the hugely successful *I Love Lucy* shifted locales from an urban apartment to a suburban house.[55]

This antagonistic relationship between suburb and city has been accentuated by movies such as *The City* (narrated by Lewis Mumford, 1939), *Avalon* (1990), and *True Stories* (1991) which explicitly pitched the suburb against the city.[56]

This polarized image of the urban landscape in film can be all the more impacting when the viewer has limited opportunities to compare one of the two landscapes in real life. Such may be the case with some lower-income groups residing in cities such as New York or Chicago but specially in Third World megacities such as Bogotá, Rio de Janeiro, São Paulo, and others. "The impressions, the images, the rhetoric, the noise of the city found in movies (and in television) comprise the only frequent contact that many [people in these groups] have with their [own] cities."[57] When such is the case the remote possibility of living the "reality" of the suburb becomes all the more tantalizing for Latin Americans used to living in megacities, whose experience of the city is akin to the urban dystopia shown in Hollywood films.

Studies on the impact of television on viewers suggest that the fascination and appeal of suburban environments and their neighborhoods do not come so much from the physical attributes of the landscape represented but rather from the illusion of living in a place where the possibility of living the same idyllic private life of the characters becomes real.[58] This aspect of the effect of cinema on the audience is particularly critical in Latin America, where the hyperreal suburban landscape created by film does not have a reflection on reality. Most Latin American megacities did not have, at least until recently, widespread upper- and middle-class low-density residential suburbs. On the contrary, the Latin American city has been characterized by high densities, high-rise apartment buildings, high crime rates, insecurity, congested streets, grimy places, and afflicted by all sorts of urban maladies (see Figure 8.5).

Bogotá is undoubtedly a crime-ridden and violent city. Petty crime, which has always been rife, is currently rampant and rates of car jacking, armed robbing and kidnapping have recently escalated. Few homes, even in the low income settlements, fail to take elaborate precautions against burglary. Higher income families long ago started moving into estates with armed security guards or into high-rise apartment blocks. In the first eight months of 1993, 5,600 people in the city died violent deaths, and 2,000 of these were shot. The . . . city has now overtaken Medellín [the second largest in Colombia with population of 5 million] as the most violent city in Colombia. Nationally, Colombia's murder rate in 1992 stood at 86 per 100,000 population, compared to 9 per 100,000 in the US.[59]

THE CITY-SUBURB TENSION AND THE LATIN AMERICAN AUDIENCE

Cinematic images are said to show representations of place in "context" but devoid of true "content." This distortion of reality is due to the nature

Figure 8.5. Middle-class mixed-use residential area in Bogotá, Colombia. Photo by Rafael Pizarro.

of film-making which attempts to translate "complex stories of daily life to a sequence of images upon a depthless screen."[60] In the case of commercial Hollywood cinema, this disparate image of reality is reinforced by locations chosen for filming movies. "Hollywood, Beverly Hills, and Bel Air, with a little Malibu and Venice Beach thrown in for a coastal touch . . . nurture and reify a particular set of urban signs: palm trees, sun, abundance, paradise."[61] Thus, Hollywood cinema "has provided a common dream life, a common fund of reference and fantasy to a society divided by ethnic distinctions and economic disparities."[62] These disparities become particularly magnified when the culture receiving these images is the Latin American.

It is possible that for a Latin American audience residing in a megacity, where the *real* dystopic city is part of their everyday existence, images of a *reel* dystopic city reify what the movies are telling them, that life in the "city" is perilous. This connection between a *reel* and a *real* dystopic city notion was reinforced with the black action films of the 1970s. Coincidentally, this film genre became popular at a time when Latin American capitals started to experience tremendous expansion as a result of rural-urban migrations, densification, and an unprecedented rise in urban crime.

The black action film genre of the early seventies . . . incorporated subject matter and thematic concern in which inner city impoverishment and crime acted as primary conditions for the narratives. . . . Films like . . . *Shaft* (by Gordon Parks, 1972) placed urban living conditions . . . at the core of their thematic concerns. In doing so, they presented narratives structured around crime, drugs, prostitution, and the effects of poverty on urban life to an audience who read these images as [being close] to their own situations.[63]

Although the audience Massood is referring to in the above quote is North American, the situation may well apply to the Latin American context. Negative depictions of cities in Hollywood film may even have deeper resonance in a Latin American audience. At least Americans have the alternative to the "mean city" in a charming small town or the quiet residential suburb, but in Latin America this alternative is the poverty-stricken rural village. In Latin America high urban primacy reflects extreme cultural polarization between city and country. The urban dwellers of the Latin American megacity usually regard the rural village with disdain and contempt. For them, it is a shoddy place where the unsophisticated, uneducated, vulgar, and poor peasants live.[64] Latin Americans, then, are left with no alternative: the city is "bad" and the country is "bad." As a reaction to this blind alley or lose-lose situation, I argue that Latin Americans have absorbed and interpreted the cinematic images of the American suburb as the equivalent of the "country" (in the North American context) and the Latin American city as the "city" in the *cinematic* context. This suggests the strong possibility that Latin Americans would want to re-create the charming lifestyle of small-town America represented in the suburb of cinema in an attempt to grab a piece of the American Dream and plant it in their own lands. Or, at the very least, that their attitude toward the introduction of new suburban development in their cities is rather positive, embracing, and welcoming.

NOTES

1. Kenneth Jackson, *Crabgrass Frontier: The Suburbanization of the United States* (New York: Oxford University Press, 1985).

2. Richard M. Morse and Jorge E. Hardoy, *Rethinking the Latin American City* (Baltimore: Johns Hopkins University Press, 1992).

3. Jackson, *Crabgrass Frontier*; and Robert Fishman, *Bourgeois Utopias: The Rise and Fall of Suburbia* (New York: Basic Books, 1987).

4. John R. Gold. "From 'Metropolis' to 'The City': Film Visions of the Future City, 1919–1939," in *Geography, the Media and Popular Culture*, eds. Jacquelin Burgess and John R. Gold (New York: St. Martin's Press, 1985); and Douglas Muzzio, "Decent People Shouldn't Live Here: The American City in Cinema," *Journal of Urban Affairs* 18, no. 2 (1996): 189–215.

5. P. G. Duke et al., *Diffusion and Migration: Their Role in Cultural Development* (Calgary, Canada: Archeological Association, Department of Archeology, University of Calgary, 1978); and Peter J. Hugill and D. Bruce Dickinson, eds., *The Transfer and Transformation of Ideas and Material Culture* (College Station: Texas A&M University Press, 1988).

6. Yehoshua S. Cohen, *Diffusion of an Innovation in an Urban System: The Spread of Planned Regional Shopping Centers in the United States 1949–1968* (Chicago: University of Chicago, Department of Geography, 1972). See the chapter written by Kroeber.

7. Michel de Certeau, *The Practice of Everyday Life* (Berkeley: University of California Press, 1984); and Arthur Asa Berger, *Reading Matter: Multidisciplinary Perspectives on Material Culture* (New Brunswick, NJ: Transaction Publishers, 1992).

8. Oscar Saldarriaga, "City, Territory and Memory," in *Pobladores Urbanos: Cities and Space*, vol. 1, ed. Julian Arturo (Bogotá, Colombia: TM Editores, 1994), 104.

9. Daniel Miller, *Material Culture and Mass Consumption* (New York: Basil Blackwell, 1987); and Hugill and Dickinson, *The Transfer and Transformation of Ideas and Material Culture.*

10. Some scholars suggest that this is also because humankind has the same mental origins (Hugill and Dickinson, ibid., p. xiv).

11. See chapter by Kelley in Duke et al., *Diffusion and Migration.*

12. Cohen, *Diffusion of an Innovation in an Urban System*; A.E.J. Morris, *History of Urban Form: Before the Industrial Revolutions* (New York: John Wiley, 1979); and Lewis Mumford, *The Culture of Cities* (London: Secker and Warburg, 1938).

13. Muzzio, "Decent People Shouldn't Live Here."

14. Jeff Hopkins, "A Mapping of Cinematic Places: Icons, Ideology, and the Power of (Mis)representation," in *Place, Power, Situation, and Spectacle: A Geography of Film*, eds. Stuart C. Aitken and Leo E. Zonn (Lanham, MD: Rowman and Littlefield, 1994).

15. Muzzio, "Decent People Shouldn't Live Here," p. 190.

16. Stuart C. Aitken and Leo E. Zonn, eds., *Place, Power, Situation, and Spectacle: A Geography of Film* (Lanham, MD: Rowman and Littlefield, 1994).

17. Hopkins, "A Mapping of Cinematic Places," p. 61.

18. The suburbia I am concerned with in this chapter refers to the Latin American equivalent of the middle- and upper-class segments of the United States, not the lower-class developments so conspicuous in the urban edges of most cities in Latin America. The nature, causes, and dynamics of these two types of urbanization are completely different. On the one hand, lower-class suburbia in Latin America has rarely been planned (see, for example, Luis R. Rodriguez, *El Dessarollo Urbano en Colombia* (Bogotá, Colombia: Universidad de los Andes, 1967); Morse and Hardoy, *Rethinking the Latin American City*; Peter M. Ward, *Mexico City: The Production and Reproduction and Reproduction of an Urban Environment* (Boston: G. K. Hall, 1990); Josef Gugler, ed., *The Urbanization of the Third World* (New York: Oxford University Press, 1991); and Michael Pacioni, ed., *Problems and Planning in Third World Cities* (New York: St. Martin's, 1981); on the other hand, the values embedded in the "design" of this kind of urbanization are directly borrowed from the indigenous milieu from which its inhabitants come from the rural areas.

19. Walter D. Harris, Jr., *The Growth of Latin American Cities* (Athens: Ohio University Press 1971), 61.

20. In Hermosillo, Mexico, for example, Ford Motor Company has established

a satellite town which includes not only residential but also commercial, office, recreational, and manufacturing facilities (Bryan Roberts, "Transitional Cities," in *Rethinking the Latin American City*, eds. Morse and Hardoy [Washington DC: Woodrow Wilson Center Press, 1992]).

21. Alan Gilbert, *The Latin American City* (London: Latin American Bureau, 1994), 30.

22. Ibid.

23. Peter Amato, *An Analysis of the Changing Patterns of Elite Residential Areas in Bogota, Colombia* (Ithaca, NY: Cornell University Press, 1968).

24. The role of the government in structuring the Bogotá suburbs has also been important. Zoning, in the way it was conceived in Europe and the United States, was very popular among Bogotá's elite during the early 1960s. The elite was alarmed that "their new residential areas might be undermined by the encroachment of undesirable uses" at a time when rapid growth was occurring in the city. Gilbert cites Amato who says that "the early zoning of the city permanently fixed the spatial distribution of socio-economic groups and bears testimony to the desire and an ability of the elite to structure the city in conformity to their own interests" (p. 95). In the early parts of the century European planners (e.g., Le Corbusier, Jose Luis Sert, and Karl Brunner) fully endorsed standard zoning practices in their plans for Bogotá, to the point that an industrial area designated on the western side of the city to separate the poor from the rich was termed the "Maginot Line." See Alan Gilbert, "Bogota: Politics, Planning, and the Crisis of Lost Opportunities," in *Metropolitan Latin America: The Challenge and the Response*, eds. Wayne A. Cornelius and Robert V. Kemper, Latin America Urban Research, vol. 6 (Beverly Hills, CA: Sage Publications, 1978).

25. Amato, *An Analysis of the Changing Patterns.*

26. As in England and the United States in the late 1800s (see Fishman, *Bourgeous Utopias*; Jackson, *Crabgrass Frontier*; and John J. Palen, *The Suburbs* [New York: McGraw-Hill, 1995]), government policies toward low-income housing fostered segregation between upper and lower classes. Amato in Gilbert, "Bogota."

27. Ibid.

28. Gilbert, *The Latin American City*, p. 6.

29. Gilbert reports that "rising levels of car ownership combined with existing trends in land use are beginning to generate traffic congestion. . . . The principal cause is the . . . separation of housing and jobs; the CBD [central business district] contains about 210,000 jobs but less than 10,000 workers live in the area. Thus about 2,000,000 travel into the central area for work, creating major traffic jams four times each day. The physical expansion of the city will worsen congestion and will lengthen the journey to work" (Gilbert, "Bogota," 96).

30. Not all suburban developments in Bogotá, however, resemble the North American pattern. The affluent, "well planned," suburbs with "green zones, good services, paved roads, and street lighting" refered to by some of these authors have developed in stark contrast with poor residential areas in other parts of the same periphery. See Alan Gilbert and Peter M. Ward, "Land for the Rich, Land for the Poor," in *The Urbanization of the Third World*, ed. Josef Gugler (New York: Oxford University Press, 1988), 130.

31. Fishman, *Bourgeois Utopias*, 14.

32. Hopkins, "A Mapping of Cinematic Places," 47.

33. J. Cassiola, "Political Values and Literature: The Contribution of Virtual Experience," in *Reading Political Stories: Representations of Politics in Novels and Pictures*, ed. M. Whitebrook (Boston: Rowman and Littlefield, 1992), 62, cited in Muzzio, "Decent People Shouldn't Live Here," 208.

34. Jacquelin Burgess and John R. Gold, eds. *Geography, the Media and Popular Culture* (New York: St. Martin's Press, 1985), 24.

35. Hopkins, "A Mapping of Cinematic Places," 47.

36. Aitken and Zonn, *Place, Power, Situation, and Spectacle*, 17.

37. The argument goes further than whether cause-effects can be established. There are two distinct "schools" of thought in these subjects, both arguing against each other: the European school, which "focuses on the relation of media to other cultural and political forms and is dominated by structuralism and semiotics," and the American school, which "is concerned with the effect of media on individual attitudes and behavior and is dominated by social and cognitive psychology" (J. Burgess in Aitken and Zonn, *Place, Power, Situation, and Spectacle*, 9). Some cultural geographers argue that "the experience of more than 60 years of mass communication research demonstrates the futility of pursuing cause-and-effect relationships outside of the broad matrix of social communication, of which mass communication is but part" (Gold, "From 'Metropolis' to 'The City,' " 125).

38. E. Kolbert, cited in Nancey G. Leigh and Judith Kenny, "The City of Cinema: Interpreting Urban Images on Film," *Journal of Planning Education and Research* 16 (1996), 51–55.

39. Paula J. Massood, "Mapping the Hood: The Genealogy of City Space in *Boyz N the Hood* and *Menace II Society*," *Cinema Journal* 35, no. 2 (1995): 85–97.

40. Muzzio, "Decent People Shouldn't Live Here," 190.

41. Aitken and Zonn, *Place, Power, Situation, and Spectacle* ix.

42. In film studies the concept of "image" of place is defined as a representation of a real place rich with actual information about the true characteristics of that place. See Burgess and Gold, *Geography, the Media and Popular Culture*.

43. Ibid., 8.

44. Robert Wilheim, "Urban Modernity in the Context of Underdevelopment: The Brazilian Case," in Morse and Hardoy *Rethinking the Latin American City*, 194.

45. Burgess and Gold, *Geography, the Media and Popular Culture*, 9.

46. Muzzio, "Decent People Shouldn't Live Here."

47. Gold, "From 'Metropolis' to 'The City,' " 125.

48. Muzzio, "Decent People Shouldn't Live Here."

49. Ibid., 200.

50. Martin Scorsese's *Taxi Driver* (1976) is a "nightmare vision of New York City as one of the middle levels of Dante's Inferno. The film opens with a taxi emerging from the steam bellowing. It is a vision of a hellish netherworld where . . . bilious vapors rise slowly from the bowels of the city, colored by the harsh glare of flashing neon" (Magill's *Movie Guide*, 1994, in Muzzio, "Decent People Shouldn't Live Here," 201).

51. Gold, "From 'Metropolis' to 'The City,' " 125.

52. Woody Allen is a rare exception in this tradition of American cinema. In *Manhattan* (1976) and *Annie Hall* (1979), for example, Allen uses New York City

as a place for romance, intellectuality, leisurely strolls, and spontaneous encounters with friendly people.

53. M. White and L. White, *Intellectuals Versus the City: From Thomas Jefferson to Frank Lloyd Wright* (Cambridge, MA: Harvard University Press, 1962), quoted in Muzzio, "Decent People Shouldn't Live Here," 190.

54. Fishman, *Bourgeois Utopias*, 203. Shows such as *Ozzie and Harriet* (1950s), *Leave It to Beaver* (1960s), *Happy Days* (1970s), *Wonder Years* (1980s and early 1990s) glorified suburbia in an almost infantile and naive way.

55. Muzzio, "Decent People Shouldn't Live Here," 282.

56. Leigh and Kenny, "The City of Cinema."

57. Muzzio, "Decent People shouldn't Live Here," 190.

58. Miller, *Material Culture and Mass Consumption.*

59. Gilbert, *The Latin American City*, 7.

60. Massood, "Mapping the Hood."

61. A. Schlesinger, Jr. Foreword, in J. E. O'Connor and M. Jackson, *American History/American Film: Interpreting the Hollywood Image* (New York: Frederick Unger, 1979), ix–xiii, quoted in Muzzio, "Decent People Shouldn't Live Here."

62. Massood, "Mapping the Hood," 87.

63. It is outside the scope of this chapter to elaborate on the origins and pervasiveness of this image of rurality in Latin America, but no doubt it has to do with the strong urban orientation that Spanish colonizers brought to the Americas. A Jeffersonian agrarian ideal as it developed in the United States was never promoted by any prominent figure in Latin American history.

64. Kenneth Jackson is among the advocates for this last possibility. In opposition to Robert Fishman, another scholar of suburbia, he argues that suburbia is not a trademark of America. Rather, that it is the logical decision of the middle and upper classes to move to the suburbs once certain socioeconomic conditions and advances in technology have been achieved—that is, car ownership, lower land values on the urban periphery, and a desire for segregation and exclusivity. Jackson's claim is that the desire to live in quiet single-family detached residential neighborhoods, set in a park-like environment, organized along green lawns and tree-lined streets is "a common human aspiration. . . . Given enough access to automobile ownership, highways, and disposable wealth [suburbia] will work elsewhere. . . . [I]ts achievement depends on technology and affluence . . ." (Jackson, *Crabgrass Frontier*, 303).

9

Orange County, Java: Hybridity, Social Dualism, and an Imagined West

Robert Cowherd and Eric J. Heikkila

INTRODUCTION

Until 1997, when Southeast Asia's economic boom came to an abrupt halt, suburban housing developments sprouted from the carefully cultivated rice fields surrounding the region's cities from Manila to Mandalay. In Indonesia, the world's fourth most populous country, a nascent real estate industry set out to promote an explicitly "modern" lifestyle inspired by the images and projections of the forms and values of the West in general and Southern California in particular. Encouraged by the market response to their emulation of the products of the Southern California real estate industry, the larger developers of the Jakarta Metropolitan Area, or Jabotabek,[1] came increasingly to employ planners and architects based in Southern California. Together, they offered the wealthiest Jakartans houses and communities implied to be authentic foreign imports from the most sophisticated cities of Western Europe, North America, Australia, and Japan.

This chapter examines the larger real estate developments or "new towns" of Jabotabek in two apparently contradictory ways. First, in emulation of the Southern California real estate industry's forms and methods, the new towns have served to fulfill Indonesian aspirations of both a wealthy consumer class and the national political elite to display the status symbols of Western-style suburban housing indicative of increasing living standards. And second, as an adaptation of a foreign cultural import conforming more closely with local norms, the new towns offer an example of hybrid architecture caught between an imagined world of the West and the continuity of the daily practices of a complex socioeconomic tableau. A third section moves beyond the scales of architecture and urban design to examine some of the broader social and environmental consequences of the path taken in Jabotabek's urbanization, in which the models imported from Southern California play a special role. In the context of a stronger than usual confluence between the political and capital elite—the infamous Crony Capitalism of Soeharto's New Order regime—the outcomes of applying these models take on new dimensions and significance. In Jabotabek, the Southern California development models have been at the heart of a process that has led to the undermining of well-intentioned efforts to provide affordable housing in the new towns. At the regional scale, the far-flung consumer-class enclaves of the new towns serve to promote both a greater social segregation and an acceleration of environmentally destructive practices, similar to, but far more potentially devastating than, precedents in Southern California. The experience of the Jabotabek new towns demonstrates the power and malleability of the images being broadcast from Southern California, the complexity of hybrid cultural construction, and the dangers of uncritical adoption driven by the lure of commercial imagery.

CONJURING AN IMAGINED WEST

The dominance of the Jabotabek region in Indonesia is indisputable. Not only is it the largest population center with over 10 percent of the country's 225 million people, Jakarta and its environs occupy the economic, administrative, and symbolic center of the nation—a situation likely to persist despite recently passed legislation designed to foster greater local autonomy.[2] Jabotabek boasts 22 percent of the country's gross real domestic product (GRDP), 80 percent of its circulation of money, and well over 80 percent of all bank head offices. Almost half of all international arrivals and departures are routed through Jakarta's Soekarno-Hatta International Airport, and a stunning 85 percent of the country's labor force in financial, real estate, and business services is located in Jabotabek.[3] During the 1980s and 1990s, the economic liberalization policies of President Soeharto's New Order regime (1965–1998) succeeded in attracting foreign investment, stimulating the Indonesian private sector, and planting a long line of tinted glass office towers along Jakarta's *axis mundi* (see Figure 9.1).

This trophy case of international architecture represented a substantial accomplishment in Soeharto's role as "Father of Development."[4] In contrast to the socialist-modernist public monuments set in grand public spaces built by Indonesia's first President Sukarno (1949–1965), Soeharto's tastes leaned more toward the symbols of advanced capitalism: the glass-box of-

Figure 9.1. Modern Jakarta skyline. Photo by Robert Cowherd.

fice tower, the freeway overpass, the shopping mall set in a sea of cars, and the golf course surrounded by sprawling mansions.[5]

With the development of service-sector employment, Jakarta became the center also of Indonesia's rising affluence and aspirations. A new class of consumers flocked to the gleaming shopping malls filled for the first time with foreign goods. But the "middle class" who could afford to purchase these goods came to include only the top 7 to 10 percent income earners. During the economic crisis this figure dropped to a paltry 2 percent.[6] These figures beg the question: In what way is the "middle class" in the middle? To avoid misrepresenting the situation in Indonesia, we instead adopt the convention of referring to this group as the "consumer class." For most of the rest of the population, never before had the target of personal aspirations been so clear, so attractive, so near at hand, yet still so out of reach. With a television placed in every village, the state-led "development" agenda and commercial marketing campaigns converged to reinforce a clear message to candidates for entry into the new consumer class: the physical forms and social practices of "backward" local cultures were in need of replacement by "modern" forms and practices, in large part emulating those of the developed West. It was a demonstration of what Armstrong and McGee have identified as the "convergence of consumption," in which the flooding of local markets with goods and images from an international market have fostered a greater homogenization of consumer tastes throughout the world while reducing consumer choice by driving out local competitors. Nowhere, they claimed, would this be more obvious than in "the built environment, transportation and lifestyles."[7] This claim has proven particularly valid in the case of Jabotabek.

Since the late 1970s, the Indonesian real estate industry has been aggressively marketing a decidedly cosmopolitan way of life to guide the formation, attainment, and reformation of consumer-class aspirations that is the business of consumption. This vision was constructed in part by reinforcing images of the bleak physical realities of Jakarta as its opposite: garbage-strewn streets, the stench of waterways, traffic-clogged arteries, and a negative portrayal of life in the *kampung* (urban village).[8] Home to the majority of Indonesian urbanites while occupying a relatively small percentage of the land, the *kampung* plays a crucial role in the social and cultural life of Indonesian cities. Despite the socioeconomic diversity and close-knit nature of communities in most *kampung* in Jakarta, its general lack of formally provided infrastructure and the presence of the poor have made the word *kampung* into a derogatory term and source of shame.

Against this image of environmental degradation, traffic congestion, and the aura of the *kampung*, the real estate marketers set out to construct its opposite from images of an idealized, modern, developed West. Their task was to appeal to the imaginations of the emerging consumer class by presenting a residential complement to the mode of consumption found in the new shopping malls. If the real estate developers were looking for a means of conjuring an idealized West to offer the consumer class, they need have looked no further than the ready-made imagery of America and the developed West already firmly lodged in the consciousness of Indonesians via the television, film, advertising, music, and other industries of cultural production based in Southern California.[9] With this as the goal, what better model for Indonesian developers to emulate than that of the Southern California real estate industry?

ORANGE COUNTY, JAVA

In his examination of Orange County, California, Edward Soja[10] invokes the concept of *simulacra* first defined by Jean Baudrillard as a cultural artifact that lays claims to being an "authentic" reproduction of an original that may or may not have ever existed as such.[11] Home to a plethora of amusement parks including Disneyland, Soja portrays Orange County as the birthplace and capital of theme-park-inspired residential communities which require residents to maintain the architectural style of the neighborhoods used to invoke cultural fantasies. The neighborhoods of Orange County's Mission Viejo community are given the names Spanish Colonial, Greek Island, Cervantes' Spain, Capri Villa, and Uniquely American.[12] Emulating these marketing strategies, the first real estate developments in Jakarta were satisfied to simply employ naming schemes that refer to foreign sources. Names of European and North American cities and regions were used in the naming of house models and gated neighborhoods as a means of tapping into the imaginary projections by Indonesians of the "good life" in the developed West.

Naming strategies quickly escalated in the 1980s and early 1990s to the creation of elaborate "costumes" of historic architectural elements and roof forms in which to clothe standardized house plans as a more direct evocation of an imagined West congruent with the images from Western film, television, and advertising. Increasingly, architectural firms from Southern California were called upon to design these exterior flights of fancy. One of the earliest and deepest involvements of an American architectural firm was the 2,000-hectare (4,940-acre) new town Kota Legenda (Legend City), which features a range of house sizes and plans, each available in either "Mediterranean" or "American Colonial" style. The "83/144" house,[13] for example, is available in either the model named "Malta" (the "Mediterranean" variant) or the "Dallas" (the "American Colonial" variant). The two styles are applied to houses that are identical in plan. The only difference between the "Malta" and the "Dallas" lies in the use of hip versus gable roofs, stucco versus brick, and a difference in door, window, and ornamental details. These elements offer an appearance of variety of consumer choice, which is taken as a prerequisite for successful commodification. Underlying the ornamental symbolism of the facades, there is an oppressive uniformity of house plans, site planning, parcel division, street layout, and subdivision planning exhibited across the Jabotabek real estate industry. This careful balance of the tamed exotic and the safely familiar reflect the formulations of symbols and codes developed in the real estate design and marketing practices of Southern California—"imagineering," to use the term of the Walt Disney Company. As such, Indonesia's "Mediterranean" style developments are not directly inspired by anything found in Europe. Instead, what is imagined to be the "good life" of the developed West comes to Jabotabek via Orange County (see Figure 9.2).

The significant number of architectural, engineering, and planning firms located in Southern California employed by Indonesian developers makes the Indonesian real estate industry in many ways an extension of the Southern California real estate industry. The 770-hectare (1,900-acre) Alam Sutera housing estate was planned by SWA Group of Laguna Beach, Orange County. The 3,000-hectare (7,400-acre) Citra Raya new town developed by Ciputra is based on a master plan and architectural designs of RNM Architects of Newport Beach, Orange County. The 30,000-hectare (116-square-mile) Bukit Jonggol Asri series of new towns employed the same planners as the 35,000-hectare (135 square mile) Irvine Ranch, which constitutes over one-fifth of Orange County (see Figure 9.3).

There is also a significant overlap between the two professional com-

Figure 9.2. Entrance to the Rodeo Drive neighborhood in a new town in Jabotabek, Indonesia. Photo by Robert Cowherd.

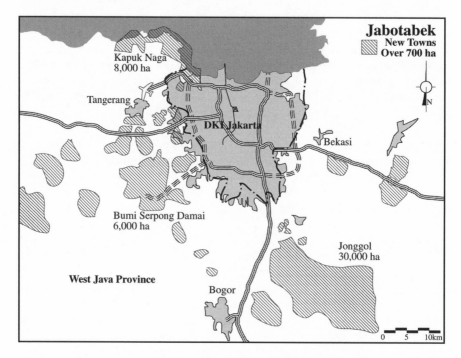

Figure 9.3. New towns outside Jakarta. Map by Robert Cowherd.

Figure 9.4. Photo collage used on the cover of the marketing brochure for the Beverly Hills neighborhood in the new town of Kota Wisata (Tour City), south of Jakarta. Photo by Robert Cowherd. No credits appear for the Brochure's artist.

munities in terms of finance and affiliations, including membership by many in both Real Estate Indonesia and the U.S.-based National Association of Home Builders. With the bulk of imported television and film programming already coming from Hollywood, the convenience of Southern California as a one-stop source of cultural production appears to be greatly appreciated in the Indonesian real estate industry (see Figure 9.4). The imagery is neatly complementary as if to say: "You've seen it at the movies. You've shopped for it in the mall. Now you can *live* it in your very own little piece of *Beverly Hills 90210*."

To the extent that objections to the dominance of foreign imagery in the real estate developments of Indonesia are raised at all, they come from a vocal segment of Indonesian architects and *budayawan* (people concerned with issues of culture). They ask: Why not refer to the cultural roots of Indonesia's rich cultural heritage? Sometimes appealing to a sense of national pride, the styles of these developments are portrayed as "arrogant" foreign intrusions by foreign architects. Responding to such accusations Gordon Benton, Town Manager of Lippo Karawaci, appeals to the necessity of deferring to market forces:

Today, clients want to be international, because of their extensive travels to Europe and the US. They are also highly influenced by television. They aren't too keen on ethnic architecture. . . . They want Mediterranean style, Los Angeles style and Bev-

erly Hills style. Our marketing people have been successful in identifying the market
and we are very sure of what they want.[14]

Benton predicts the eventual replacement of local styles with an "international style, heavily influenced by the U.S." citing poor sales of the few
houses that offer references to indigenous styles. Seconding this position,
housing industry magnate Ciputra is quoted in the same article as saying
that 99 percent of real estate is sold to locals who are not interested in
Indonesian styles, suggesting instead that the latter be preserved in interior
decoration as seen in the lobbies of several of the biggest hotels in Jakarta.

LIFE IN A THEME PARK

The California Office of Tourism advertises Orange County as "a seven
hundred and eighty-six square mile theme park" where "the theme is 'you
can have anything you want.' "[15] Soja writes that it is no longer necessary
to make a special trip to experience the pleasures of the artificial theme
park, for the land of make-believe has come to envelop the world that more
and more people live in. Even as he was warning of the replication of
Orange County on the peripheries of cities across America, the creators of
Tour City (Kota Wisata), less than an hour's commute south of Jakarta,
were busy constructing a 1,000-hectare (2,470-acre) new town completely
integrated with the features and facilities of a theme park evoking the cultural capitals of the imagined West. Tour City sets out to make it possible
to experience a tour around the world without ever leaving the security of
your own gated real estate development. The town center is planned as an
"International Village," evoking fragments of London, Paris, Amsterdam,
and Rome in a multicultural version of Disney's Main Street. Crossing over
"Jurassic Lake" via replicas of the "Sydney Harbour Bridge" and London's
Tower Bridge (here called "London Bridge") you will reach "Fantasy Island" where a water park and amusement park rides are mixed with in-
vocations of "River Walk New Orleans" and "Caribean [*sic*] Plaza," all in
the heart of the town center. The explicit theme park strategy is extended
to the residential neighborhoods as well, with each gated community assigned a different identity invoking the most visited places of an imagined
West: Florence, Paris, Marseilles, Monaco, Madrid, Amsterdam, Den
Haag, *Amerika*, California, and Kyoto.[16] The monuments of each of these
places are replicated in miniature in each of the neighborhood *simulacra*,
with a Mt. Rushmore in *Amerika*, a windmill in Amsterdam, and an Ise
Shrine in Kyoto. Outside of the world of theme parks, rarely has the translation from imagination to built environment been executed so directly. But
then the creators of Tour City intend to pose the question: Wouldn't we
all rather live *inside* a theme park?

HYBRIDITY BEHIND THE HOLLYWOOD FACADE

With the brand of an imagined West firmly established by the symbols embedded in the larger environment of real estate development and explicitly imprinted on the facades of their homes, the *orang realestat* (literally: real estate people) live lives more closely related to the way Indonesians have long lived than the form and imagery of their new housing would suggest. With the imaginations of new town dwellers captured, it is not necessary for either the day-to-day practices, or the forms most directly related to those practices, to match either the place for which their neighborhood is named or Southern California from which the custom of naming neighborhoods is duplicated. The form their interior architecture takes behind the facade of Western symbols reflects a way of life much closer to the lives of the wealthiest of their counterparts in the *kampung* than is suggested by the imagery of the new town.

This disconnection between the marketing imagery of the facade and the lived experiences of the interior corresponds with a distinction made by Henri Lefebvre in his categorization of the three realms of spatial experience that characterize the human relationship to space:

(i) Spatial Practices: the physical and material experience of space in daily practices;

(ii) Spatial Perceptions: the representation of spatial experience encoded in referential symbols, language and perception; and

(iii) Spatial Imagination: utopian visions and invented landscapes of the imagination, dreams, planning visions and marketing images.[17]

By distinguishing between these three realms of spatial experience, Lefebvre's categories are useful in examining how the form of our built environment contributes to our conception of the world, and sets the limits within which we imagine the past, present, and future. More significantly for the present examination, these categories are useful in understanding how imagined realities of other times and other places both inform our perceptual experiences of space and influence the form of the material world that is then constructed. In the realm of the imagination, we have examined the marketing imagery and design references employed in the development of the new towns of Jabotabek, as well as their projections of what life in the modern developed West is imagined to be.

Working simultaneously, but in apparent contradiction to the operation of the spatial imagination, is the persistence and social cohesion of habitual preferences and daily practices of life that coexist alongside, and possibly quite independently of, the symbolic system of the spatial imagination. This corresponds with Lefebvre's first category of spatial practices. This conflict registers in only the most subtle ways to influence the perception of the living environment (Lefebvre's second category), which in the new towns is dominated by the reference to the other worlds being conjured in the spatial imagination. The aspirations of the consumer class require that life in the new towns be perceived as cosmopolitan—elsewhere labeled "transnational space"—regardless of what little resemblance Jabotabek new town life may actually bear to life in Madrid, Kyoto, or Beverly Hills. What follows is an examination of the partial ways in which the symbolic codes invoking an imagined West extend into the interior space of the house, where they run up against the resistance offered by "spatial practices." The result is the formation of a hybrid architecture of domestic space: forms and their associated use and meaning that do not directly correspond to either Western or Indonesian precedents.

A body of literature from sociology and anthropology supports Lefebvre in finding a dialectic relationship between social and cultural norms and practices on the one hand and the physical forms of the built environment on the other.[18] This relationship of mutual encoding is associated with a high degree of resistance to rapid change as persistent spatial forms will work against attempts to change the social order and vice versa. The uniformity of house, site, and neighborhood planning noted above, along with the need to offer a range of house and lot sizes in order to satisfy buyers of different means, has yielded several house designs that exhibit an almost systematic progression from small and simple to large and more complex. Starting from the most basic house plans, the progressive elaboration and addition of elements provides evidence of the designer/marketers' priorities and thus offers a portrait of the relative values of the lifestyle envisioned for the new consumer class of Indonesia. These attributes lend the real estate housing of Jabotabek to an analytic method usually reserved for long-established vernacular traditions. A comparison of several features of the Indonesian private-sector houses with their closest American equivalents as indicated by their architectural attributes or in their labeling conventions are used here to trace the origins of form back to foreign and indigenous sources.

WHITE HOUSE STYLE

Most of the features of the private-sector housing of the New Order period were already highly evolved by the time they were injected into the new "clothing" of the new towns. They demonstrate a link to the earlier architectures of either the Dutch colonial period or the housing of the *kampung* and rural traditions. The most significant link between these earlier forms and the new towns of the New Order period is found in the form of the so-called White House style. It is important to mention briefly this phenomenon as the most immediate precedent to what soon followed, which Indonesians call simply *Realestat*, and we will refer to as the "Real

Estate style" house. Many if not most of the Real Estate style interior plan elements are already present in a highly developed form in the proliferation of the White House style.[19]

The White House style earned its name for its large white concrete facades, with a central *porte cochere*, neoclassical columns and cornices, balconies with stainless steel railings, and stained glass windows. It is characterized by its grand scale with ceilings of four meters (13 feet) or more on two floors. Favoring size over landscaping, these houses fill the entire lot except for a setback from the front lot line to accommodate the display of a car or two. While this particular formula has its origins in the communities of successful Chinese Indonesian entrepreneurs, it appears to share characteristics with examples of large white mansions that have emerged throughout Southeast Asia.

Given the history of violence against the ethnic Chinese in Indonesia, the White House style is built as an urban fortress with barbed wire on top of high concrete walls and steel fences complemented by a guard post and, increasingly, surveillance cameras.[20] The house is commonly built all the way to the rear wall of the lot. Only between a portion of the family room and the rear wall is there a break in the roof, permitting a small space for a "garden" reminiscent of the central light wells of the Southeast Asian shophouse. This is the only landscaped space in the White House style and performs a symbolic function in keeping with the rules of Feng Shui to ensure the success and prosperity of the household. Floors are covered in large white ceramic tiles or, better yet, white marble, one of the primary objectives being to display material wealth.

Interestingly, the White House style is understood in the context of Indonesian towns as an "international" style emulating its own imagined version of Western architectural culture, although only the highly altered reference to classical elements of columns, cornices, and broken pediments (and perhaps a certain Baroque overexuberance) hints at any such connection. This is an earlier version of the imagined West and demonstrates the power the spatial imagination can have over reality. The Chinese Indonesians who were the primary clients for the White House style were motivated to reject local and Chinese historical cultural referents in favor of more "international" associations for several reasons. In contradiction to the theories of political economy at work elsewhere, the wealthy minority of Chinese merchants and industrialists have been prevented from wielding significant political power. In 1967 a series of regulations banned any printed matter using Chinese characters, required the adoption of Javanese names, and demanded that all ethnic Chinese either apply for Indonesian citizenship or leave the country.[21]

Unable to express their own ethnic identities and with the long-standing enmity between the Javanese and the Chinese limiting options for assimilating into an Indonesian identity, Chinese were left to appeal to a relatively neutral third party to negotiate the cultural minefield presented to them. Both the White House style and the Real Estate style are a manifestation of what is perceived as the safe haven of an imagined West conjured as a means of transcending the local conflicts of race and class. While Chinese Indonesians have a particularly compelling set of reasons for invoking the imagery of the West, members of the indigenous ethnic groups of the archipelago share similar motivations for transcending both the categorizations of traditional cultures and any associations with the *kampung*.

LIVING ROOM/*RUANG TAMU*

The houses produced by the Indonesian real estate industry of even the smallest size typically feature a room labeled "living room." As shown in marketing plans, this room is furnished with a sofa, easy chairs, end tables, lamps, and rugs similar to the manner of a living room found in North American homes. But the location, adjacencies, and use of the Indonesian "living room" do not directly correspond to those of North American living rooms. Marketing plans that are labeled in Indonesian employ the term *ruang tamu* (literally: guest room) for this space. Unlike the Anglo-American usage of the term "guest room," the *ruang tamu* is the semipublic space found in the front of houses throughout Indonesia. They are typically screened off from the rest of the house, protecting the more intimate realm of the family living space from the probing gaze of visitors. This screening permits polite, albeit tentative, admittance to the home for the duration of a conversation and the requisite niceties exchanged over tea.[22]

The Indonesian real estate industry has produced houses that feature a space that fits the location, orientation, adjacency, and many of the functions of the *ruang tamu* while breaking with tradition by integrating it visually with the dining space and the rest of the house in the manner of an American living room. The foyer that mediates between the front door and the living room in typical Anglo-American houses is not included here. In the enlarged and elaborated version of the *ruang tamu* of the Real Estate style there is an overlap in the form, function, and meanings with the North American "living room" that justifies its label. But with its cramped size, function as a circulation space, and omission of the foyer, the relationship is not one-to-one. The differences are significant enough to identify this Indonesian living room/*ruang tamu* as a hybrid element demonstrating characteristics of both traditions while not entirely satisfying either.

PEMBANTU REALM

It is interesting to note that almost all housing produced by the formal sector includes separate quarters for domestic servants or *pembantu*. Even in the 21-square-meter (226-square-foot) "Very Small House" category, these quarters are planned for as part of the optional later extension of the house into the backyard space. The presence of the *pembantu* is imprinted on the physical form of the house plans in several ways, none of which correspond with California models even where quarters for domestic servants are provided. The most obvious difference is in the size of living quarters allotted to *pembantu*. Marketing plans show these within a range of sizes from 5.9 square meters (64 square feet) down to 2.2 square meters (24 square feet)—barely room enough to stand at the foot of a twin-sized bed.[23] In larger model houses *pembantu* quarters are located up a spiral staircase on the second floor off of the garage or the rear yard. This space is inaccessible from the rest of the second floor and the spiral staircase duplicates the main stairway of the house. Although living quarters for domestic servants have long been a feature of upper-class indigenous housing, the extension of the *pembantu* realm into a more distinct spatial segregation of the house both horizontally and vertically, as well as the duplication of elements such as stairs and, most dramatically, kitchens, is a recent development with the White House and Real Estate styles.

POTEMKIN KITCHEN

The kitchen of the Real Estate style house is a space where the divergent needs of persistent daily practices and the invocation of an imagined West apparently cannot be accommodated as it might be in a single, hybrid kitchen. Instead, to use Lefebvre's terms, the needs of the aspiring "spatial imagination" and the mundane daily "spatial practices" each require their own kitchen. To foreign eyes, the kitchens of the owner-built housing prevalent in the *kampung* are coarse affairs: small, dimly lit spaces with concrete floors. Dishes are washed in a bucket on the floor and dried on racks. A one or two-burner kerosene or propane stove is also on the floor where most cooking is done in a squatting position. In "improved" kitchens the addition of a concrete countertop raises some of these tasks up to counter height, while much of the food preparation, such as cutting and the grinding of spices, still occurs at the floor level. Despite appearances, these kitchens are highly functional, producing a vast majority of what is eaten in Indonesia. Many Indonesians, given the choice, still prefer cooking at floor level, but this practice is incompatible with the image of a cosmopolitan lifestyle exuded by the Real Estate style housing.

The real estate developers feel understandably compelled to take advantage of the opportunity presented by the new availability of imported kitchen appliances, countertops, and cabinets employed to display wealth and status. The two kitchens resulting from this Solomonaic solution are distinguished as the *pembantu*'s "wet" or "dirty" kitchen, and the family's "dry," "clean"—or, as labeled on marketing plans, "pantry."[24] Almost all of the cooking is done by the *pembantu* in the "wet" kitchen, while the sophisticated appliances of the "pantry" remain off limits unless supervised by a member of the family. This resolution accommodates both the persistence of Indonesian cooking practices and consumer-class aspirations that demand the display of a "trophy" kitchen. The "pantry" is a set piece behind which the real kitchen is concealed. The hybrid expression is thus a house type with two separate kitchens. As in the separation of the *pembantu* quarters with its contrasting set of standards in both space and amenities, the counterdistinction between the *kampung* and the modern city is brought into the space of the home.

THE NEW SPACES OF SOCIAL DUALISM

Beyond the architectural hybridization of the Real Estate style architecture, the larger impact of the new towns has taken on dimensions and meanings within the context presented by Jabotabek that are dramatically different from Southern California precedents. The Crony Capitalism of the Soeharto era and the formidable pressures on infrastructure and environment resources, to name but two factors, have contributed to the new towns serving as vehicles for the further enrichment of the business and political elite at the expense of even greater housing pressures and environmental degradation experienced by the majority of Jakartans. This section looks first at the structure of the real estate industry and its role in undermining the stated housing policy goal of providing housing for middle-income groups. Second, it looks at how Jakarta's increasing privatization of urban space operates to broaden the gap between the consumer class and the majority aspiring to join their ranks. Third, this chapter ends with a brief look at what was to have been Southeast Asia's largest new town project and the new capital of Indonesia imported directly from Orange County, California.

In the early 1970s, President Soeharto's New Order regime established a housing policy with the intention of achieving two primary goals: the provision of housing for the majority of the growing population of the Jakarta Metropolitan Area; and the transformation of the image of Jakarta from the sea of *kampung* to a modern, ordered cosmopolitan city. The state-led housing development policies that were carried over from the Sukarno period fell short of providing the necessary housing for the growing population by several orders of magnitude. Soeharto's foreign advisers led Indonesia to be an early adopter of what has since become known as a Market Enabling Strategy designed to stimulate private-sector activity guided by government incentives and restrictions to achieve the goals of society. The profit motive along with government programs to facilitate land consolidation and housing finance were the incentives used to mobilize a dynamic private sector to build housing far in excess of, and higher in quality than, what the state could possibly provide by its own efforts and limited resources. The restrictions, however, were consistently weakened by lack of enforcement to the great benefit of developers and the consumer class, while conditions for the targeted beneficiaries worsened significantly.

To require housing production that matched the needs of the majority of Jakartans, a 1974 decree established a quota of standard house types imposed on developers who wished their housing to qualify for the government program of subsidized home ownership loans. For every single luxury house built, developers are required to build three "Small Houses" at 22 to 36 square meters (237 to 388 square feet) and six "Very Small Houses" at 21 square meters (226 square feet) or less. This ratio of 1:3:6 reflected the overall perception of income stratification at the time. The intention of this program was for the subsidized loans and the smaller nine out of ten houses produced to benefit the 20 to 80 percent middle-income group.[25] The decree also states that the different house types must be "mixed" to encourage a greater social integration without giving details as to what might be meant by the word "mixed."[26]

Unfortunately, this decree has been undermined in a wide variety of ways by both developers and administering agencies. The required smaller houses are often built far away from the main developments and with inadequate infrastructure. In violation of development permit requirements, developers have been known to sell the smaller lots without building any houses on them.[27] In some cases, administrators exact a fee (often equivalent only to land costs) ostensibly for the government to use in building the required housing elsewhere, although it is not clear if and where this housing has ever actually been built.[28] In justifying these actions, government officials and developers alike are fond of propagating the conventional wisdom that the rich and poor "prefer to live apart." Leaf estimates that until 1990, the number of Very Small Houses actually built resulted in a ratio that was more in the range of one to one.[29]

Regulations also require developers to supply a certain capacity of "Public Facilities," and "Social Facilities" referring to mosques, churches, sport and recreation facilities, public open space, and so on. These are often omitted by tacit agreement between the developers, who are reluctant to pay for construction, and public administrators, who are reluctant to take on responsibility for maintenance.[30] Golf courses and country clubs are often offered as fulfillment of requirements, although exclusionary fees and fences hardly qualify these as "Public." Another weakness in implementation has stemmed from the practice of some of the largest developers to employ as "consultants" the very planning officials responsible for regulating their activities.[31] Even if a greater degree of class integration and social amenities were being achieved *within* the new developments, the housing policy missed its target group by a wide margin, excluding most of the intended beneficiaries from the new developments. Even before the

1997 monetary crisis, the smallest units of 21 square meters or less were affordable by only the top 40 percent income groups.[32]

NEW ORDER CRONY CAPITALISM AND THE REAL ESTATE INDUSTRY

In part, the failure to meet social goals despite the impressive productive output of the Indonesian real estate industry becomes clear only upon examining the makeup of the industry itself. The shift in housing policy to a Market Enabling Strategy coincided with the realization on the part of the large, ethnic-Chinese-controlled corporate groups that great opportunities for expansion and investment diversification could be found in the suburbanization of Jakarta. The rise of the ethnic Chinese in corporate Indonesia is personified by Liem Sioe Liong, whose contracts in the 1950s to supply the Diponegoro Division of the Army, under the command of a then young General Soeharto, was the basis of what has since become an historic alliance of capital and political power.[33] As Adam Schwarz documents in *A Nation in Waiting*, a book that was banned in Indonesia, an implicit accommodation was reached under Soeharto between what has become the two interrelated, yet distinct, dominant groupings of Indonesia's private sector: the ethnic-Chinese family-based corporate empires and the close friends and relatives of Soeharto.[34] In return for substantial shares in the Chinese corporate holdings, a powerful *bumiputra* (native) political elite, with backing from the military, safeguarded their now common interests of protecting and favoring the economically powerful ethnic-Chinese conglomerates. Although Chinese Indonesians make up only 4 percent of the population, they are estimated to control about 70 percent of private domestic capital.[35]

Given the history of social jealousy between the Javanese and the Chinese in Indonesia, the 1967 ban on Chinese written language and other symbols of Chinese identity was part of a larger deracination campaign seeking to subsume ethnic divisions under a national "Indonesian Culture" and a denial of the "Chinese Problem" altogether.[36] Soeharto's sustained attempts to render less-conspicuous the coincidence of class and race, represented by his partnership with the Chinese corporate elite, were complemented by the establishment of professional associations and preferential policies aimed at favoring the stimulation of an indigenous business class, albeit one largely dependent on state contracts.[37] This campaign assumed that the use of the terms "Medium- and Small-Business (loans, incentives, supports, etc.)" was silently understood as meaning "non-Chinese."

It is interesting to compare this with the open rhetoric of the approach taken by Prime Minister Mahathir Mohamad, Soeharto's autocratic counterpart in Malaysia, where no comparable alliance has been made. Mahathir's decidedly politically incorrect response to communal race riots of

1969, *The Malay Dilemma*[38] propagated the rationale for Malaysia's subsequent aggressive national affirmative action program designed to counter
ethnic Chinese economic dominance over the ethnic Malay majority. Such
a head-on approach in Indonesia is found only in the ban on Chinese cultural expressions designed to satisfy popular resentment of the ethnic Chinese. This left the Chinese-based conglomerates, a minority within the
minority, to play a free hand in dominating the corporate economy.

Despite attempts to mobilize *bumiputra* entrepreneurs, indigenous developers were to play only a minor role in the property market dominated
throughout its three-decade history by the large, ethnic Chinese development groups closely connected with the center of power. The 1972 expansion of the Liem Sioe Liong Group into the property market came with the
investment in a record 450 hectares (1,112 acres) through the Metropolitan
Development Company headed by the Chinese-Indonesian architect Ciputra. That same year the professional association Real Estate Indonesia (REI)
was founded by Ciputra who served as its first president. By 1975, membership in REI was a prerequisite for applying for a development permit,
leading some to consider it Ciputra's means of limiting participation in the
industry.[39]

STIMULATING DEVELOPMENT THROUGH ARTIFICIAL
LAND SCARCITY AND HOUSING DEMAND

A concentration of resources in the hands of a few corporate groups
combined with an unwillingness of government enforcers have distorted
the land market and shaped the housing supply of Jabotabek in ways not
predicted by either the intentions of government regulations or even the
precedents of the Southern California development model. The 1995 *Indonesia Property Report* published a list of the largest developers (by area
of land held under development permit) showing that the ten largest companies controlled about 70 percent of a total 62,000 hectares (240 square
miles) of land under development permits.[40] But this portrayal fails to account for the underlying structures of the industry in which separate development ventures are part of a handful of family-based corporate
empires. Ciputra heads the Si Pengembang Group of five development corporations, which together dominate the industry. Two of these corporations made it to the top-ten list on their own. Ciputra is also a partner in
the colossal 6,000-hectare (15,000-acre) Bumi Serpong Damai new town
that is listed as the second largest developer in Jabotabek. The son of Liem
Sioe Liong is another partner in the Bumi Serpong Damai consortium and
head of the Salim Group, which tops the list as controlling the most land
under permit. While Ciputra is the driving force behind the new town development in Jabotabek, the Salim Group has developed very few of its
properties, preferring instead to hold onto them as investments in the

future. This reflects a more general practice by real estate developers to purchase and hold under development permits more land than they intend to develop at any given time. This has resulted in the removal of a vast area of land from the Jabotabek land market. In the three regencies that comprise the ring around the Special Capital Province of Jakarta, referred to as Botabek, over 120,000 hectares (463 square miles), an area almost twice the size of Jakarta itself, have been held off the market by developers.[41] Of this area only 14 percent has actually begun development despite a government requirement that projects be completed within a period of three years from the issuance of a development permit.[42] This privately held land bank has created a scarcity responsible for artificially inflating the cost of land and housing further constricting the housing options for the majority of Jakartans.[43]

The artificial scarcity created in land supply is complemented by an artificial demand created through the mismanagement of state-subsidized home ownership loans. Targeted to help the middle 20 to 80 percent income group of Indonesia, the program has instead been heavily skewed to the upper end of the market. Between 1976 and 1990, the median monthly income of households benefiting from the subsidy to buy private-sector housing (83 percent of the program's funds) exceeded the 80 percent income group cut-off point of the program.[44] The primary beneficiaries of the subsidies have been the wealthiest purchasers of new housing and the real estate industry itself. In fact, the housing credit program has been abused by some to purchase a dozen or more houses, not to occupy or even to rent, but as an investment motivated by the strong performance of real estate in comparison with other investment opportunities. Government weakness in the implementation of both incentives and restrictions of their Market Enabling Strategy has greatly benefited a small circle of Soeharto's friends while largely ignoring social goals of affordable quality housing for the masses.

With this overstimulation of the property sector, the long-term goal of moving *kampung* residents into "proper" formal-sector-produced housing on fully regulated parcels in effect degenerated into a race to simply eliminate the *kampung* to make way for skyscrapers, shopping malls, toll roads, golf courses, and the new ring of luxury suburbs. The banking system contributed to the property boom through lax regulations which allowed real estate developers to set up what were in effect private banks. These received massive infusions of overseas financial capital from investors eager to partake of the Southeast Asian Miracle.[45] Together, these excesses combined to feed the economic "bubble" that significantly exacerbated the depth and duration of Indonesia's suffering in the wake of the monetary crisis that struck the region in mid-1997.

SPATIAL SEGREGATION OF INFRASTRUCTURES

The loss of *kampung* areas and the inflationary pressures of the property boom have contributed to a significant decline in both the security and quality of housing for a majority of Jakartans.[46] Competition for urban space has displaced people from the space of the street as well. In 1988, bicycle taxis, called *becak*, were banned in Jakarta. Despite providing an income, albeit meager, for over 100,000 Jakartans and providing low-cost, environmentally friendly transport for countless others, *becak* did not fit the image of "Jakarta, the Metropolitan City." Given the dominant paradigm of Soeharto's development agenda, it was seen as inevitable progress that the *becak* should be forced to yield their street space to a rapidly expanding traffic of private automobiles. Tens of thousands of *becak* were not only confiscated but with theatrical flourish they were dumped into the Java Sea.[47] Similarly the public bus system has been allowed to continue a steady decline of service levels in recent decades, characterized by rising crime, delays of traffic congestion, broken air conditioning, and black smoke spewing from the aging fleets. Even buses have been seen as a hindrance to the flow of private automobiles.

The new towns were originally intended to be not only self-sufficient but also to relieve the heavy burdens on Jakarta. Instead, 60 to 80 percent of the workforce commutes from homes in the new towns to the central city.[48] An estimated 310,000 daily commuter trips into Jakarta in 1986 are expected to increase to over 500,000 by 2010.[49] The lower densities of the new towns make public transit uneconomic even if it were not considered a threat to the image of the town. The resulting increase in automobile dependence of Jabotabek has exacerbated Jakarta's already infamous traffic congestion, air pollution, and dangers to nonmotorized users. The increased use of private automobiles harms those left in the city by reducing urban livability and forcing them off the streets, into buses or, if they can afford it, into cars and out to the new towns. Everyone in Jakarta is caught in this vicious cycle.[50] But it will be the lucky few able to afford the price of admission who will view the playing out of this vicious cycle from the comfort and security of the spaces of the consumer class: the *Realestat* house, the air-conditioned automobile, the luxury shopping mall, and Jakarta's new privatized realms of wired urban exclusivity, the corporate executive Superblock.[51]

It is within the space of the consumer class that the advances of architecture and urban design are concentrated. Within Lippo Karawaci, an effort has been made to counteract the privatization of the street space by providing bicycle lanes on its largest streets and adopting the methods of traffic calming on its smallest residential lanes. But in the new towns, the streets are already private property. The defensive perimeter, which fortified

each individual house in the White House style, is here moved out to en-
close entire gated neighborhoods. These are then further enclosed by a
second barricade around the entire town with a single point of entry connecting the new town with the rest of the world. Within this outer defensive
perimeter, individual neighborhoods feature single-gated and guarded
points of entry. In Lippo Karawaci, the planners built streets that connected
the otherwise isolated gated enclaves internally, assuming that two layers
of defensive walls and guarded entryways would suffice. Residents, however, have forced the private government of the town to fence off these
streets, returning Lippo Karawaci to the world of dead end *cul de sac*.[52]

The new towns, like shopping malls and the new Superblocks, foster a
deepening social dualism that provides a higher quality environment and
more sophisticated infrastructure for the consumer class without having to
provide it for all. This increasing segregation of space and infrastructure is
defended through a range of means from the subtleties of surveillance to
actual physical barriers dividing the mobile from the place-bound; the cosmopolitan from the tribal; and the connected from the unconnected.[53]
Prominent among the aspirations of modernity that held great currency in
the twentieth century was the ideal of publicly provided "universal infrastructures." The United States has led the movement to displace this ideal
by the logic of the marketplace and the strategies of privatization.[54] In their
examination of the new towns of Jabotabek, Dick and Rimmer point out
that the compact cities and scarce agricultural land of Europe would seem
to serve as a more appropriate urban model for Indonesia.[55] Instead, Indonesian developers have been attracted by the sociospatial aspects of the
American model. America's highly skewed income distribution and discom-
fort with public space resonate with Indonesian consumer-class fears of
racial violence and striving for social differentiation. But the American paradigm, exemplified by the new spaces of Orange County, takes on entirely
different and largely unpredictable consequences when applied uncritically
to the context of Indonesia.

JONGGOL: THE IRVINE RANCH OF JAVA

In 1996 President Soeharto's son, Bambang Trihatmodjo, called a press
conference to unveil the plan for Bukit Jonggol Asri (Beautiful Jonggol
Hills), a series of new towns encompassing 30,000 hectares (116 square
miles). The project was five times larger than any new town that had been
ventured up to that point. The project consortium was sold on the concept
during a trip to Orange County to tour the 35,000-hectare (135-square-
mile) Irvine Ranch development in Orange County that was to serve as the
prototype for the Jonggol project. Back in Jakarta, the consortium set out
to ensure the project's success through a number of extraordinary measures.
To sidestep the area's status (pending approval at the time) as a protected

water catchment area for Jakarta, the project was mandated by Presidential Decree.[56] To ensure sufficient demand to support such a massive enterprise, the consortium was "negotiating" with the government to make it the new capital of Indonesia. And to guarantee the authenticity of the copy, the same Orange County-based consultants who designed the towns of Irvine Ranch were engaged to prepare the plans.[57]

The project was designed to standards comparable to those of the Irvine Company's communities, boasting a wealth of wildlife preserves, parks, and, most conspicuously, a land-use pattern dominated by single-family houses. Internally, Jonggol would achieve a great deal in terms of high-quality living environments and infrastructure associated in the marketing literature with environmental sustainability. But the realization of Bukit Jonggol Asri would reproduce the social and environmental burdens of the earlier new towns of Jabotabek, only now on a much larger scale. The first phase of the project, interrupted by the economic crisis, was to have been Waskita, the most exclusive and residential in character of Bukit Jonggol's many planned new towns. Low-density residential land uses were planned for two thirds of Waskita's 665 hectares (1,640 acres) of developable land, generating daily automobile trips per household at a rate approaching, for the first time in Indonesia, that of Southern California.[58]

CONCLUSION

The powerful imagery emanating from Southern California offers a ready-made vision of "the good life" imagined to prevail in the developed West. But is the cultural-spatial model of Southern California capable of offering this same "good life" to the rest of the world? The case of the Jakarta Metropolitan Region's real estate developments would suggest not. While the Orange County-inspired commodification of architecture is taken to extremes in Jabotabek, behind the fanciful facades, interior spaces exhibit characteristics of a hybrid architecture accommodating the persistence of daily practices. Ultimately, the elements identifiable as having origins in the West are altered first in their representation by the industries of cultural production and again in their reception by other societies. Having touched their hearts and minds, the members of the Indonesian consumer class have claimed ownership of the images they receive. The actual manifestation and impacts of this imagined West have proven to be very much a product of the new context.

The international marketplace of personal aspirations affects not only consumer choices in malls and new real estate markets, but also the personal visions of the political and business elite. The lure of the biggest, brightest, tallest, and most lavish futures has proven compelling even if gained at the cost of increased exclusion and immiseration of the majority. A cultural shift seems to have transferred responsibility for the future to the private sector and to have excused a responsible leadership from asking any longer how better conditions could be extended to the city and society as a whole. The privatization of space itself is one of the primary sources of worsening conditions for the majority. This only serves to further justify in the minds of the privileged minority the necessity of defending and extending their privileged position—a position measured against standards that are updated in daily broadcasts from what is seen as the ultimate position of privilege, Southern California.

NOTES

1. The geographic label "Jabotabek" is a composite of the first syllables of the four administrative units that comprise it: the Special Capital Province *Ja*karta, and the surrounding Regencies of *Bog*or, *Tang*erang, and *Bek*asi.

2. Tellingly, despite their larger goals, the recent Decentralization Laws (no. 22 in 1999 and no. 25 in 1999) have sparked off a new wave of competition among the ministries of the central government vying for control of lucrative new decentralization initiatives funded by generous overseas assistance.

3. B. S. Kusbiantoro, "Sustainability of Jabotabek-Indonesia: Lessons Learned from the Asian Crisis," *Perencanaan Wilayah Dan Kota*, 10, no. 3 (November 1999): 130–139.

4. For a thorough examination of the language and rhetoric of development under Soeharto, see Ariel Heryanto, "The Development of 'Development,' " *Indonesia* 46 (1988): 1–24.

5. Although rendered in modernist forms, the Jakarta built by both presidents Sukarno and Soeharto fulfills the requirements of the Javanese tradition of capital city building in which the physical manifestation of the ruler's power in the capital serves as a divine instrument for controlling the conditions and events of the periphery. See Paul Wheatley, *Nagara and Commandery: Origins of the Southeast Asian Urban Traditions* (University of Chicago Department of Geography Research Paper Nos. 207–208, 1983), 430; Timothy Earl Behrend, "Kraton and Cosmos in Traditional Java" (unpublished master's thesis, University of Wisconsin, Madison, 1982); Robert Heine-Geldern, *Conceptions of State and Kingship in Southeast Asia* (Ithaca, NY: Cornell University Southeast Asia Program, Data Paper No. 18, 1956).

6. Solvay Gerke quotes Indonesian Minister of Education and Culture Juwono Sudarsono citing a middle-class population of 5 million. Later in the same piece she refers back to this figure as .2 percent of the population. We infer that this discrepancy is the result of an unintended slipped digit. Solvay Gerke, "Global Lifestyles under Local Conditions: The New Indonesian Middle Class," Chapter 6 in *Consumption in Asia: Lifestyles and Identities*, ed. Chua Beng-Huat (London: Routledge, 2000), 136, 154; Richard Robison, "The Middle Class and the Bourgeoisie in Indonesia," chapter 4 in *New Rich in Asia: Mobile Phones, McDonald's and Middle-class Revolution*, eds. Richard Robison and David S. B. Goodman (New York: Routledge, 1996).

7. Warwick Armstrong and T. G. McGee, *Theatres of Accumulation: Studies in Asian and Latin American Urbanization* (London: Methuen, 1985), 180–190.

8. *Kampung* are rural or urban villages that grow incrementally through both

expansion and densification by informal means. Though generally lacking in formally provided urban services, they are not considered slum or squatter settlements. Residents typically hold traditional land-use rights or rent from those who do. They are often chaotic-looking areas of owner-built housing with mixed land uses and socioeconomic classes. The *kampung* continues to be a basic element of cities throughout Indonesia.

9. On this point, see Rafael Pizarro, chapter 8 in this book.

10. Edward W. Soja, "Inside Exopolis: Everyday Life in the Postmodern World," Chapter 8 in *Thirdspace: Journeys to Los Angeles and Other Real-and-Imagined Places* (Cambridge: Blackwell, 1996), 237–279. An earlier version of this chapter is also found in Michael Sorkin, ed., *Variations on a Theme Park: The New American City and the End of Public Space* (New York: Hill and Wang, 1992).

11. Jean Baudrillard, *Simulations*, trans. Paul Foss et al. (New York: Semiotext[e], 1983), 146–147.

12. Soja, "Inside Exopolis," 269.

13. House layouts are identified according to a two-number sequence corresponding to the areas of the house and the parcel in square meters. A house measuring 83 square meters in area on a parcel of 144 square meters is identified by the sequence 83/144.

14. "RI Enters Post-mo in Architecture," *Jakarta Post* (19 March 1995): 1.

15. From an advertisement for *The Californias*, California Office of Tourism. Quoted in Soja, 237.

16. Tellingly, the Japanese appear to enjoy a status in the eyes of Indonesians more closely associated with the developed West than Asia, as demonstrated whenever a Japanese foreigner is referred to as a *londo* (literally a person of Dutch descent, from the word *Belanda*, meaning The Netherlands) usually reserved for Caucasians. This reinforces the point that the operative distinction to be considered worthy of simulation of an imagined West is not ethnic or geographic, but membership in the developed First World.

17. Henri Lefebvre, *The Production of Space*, trans. Donald Nicholson-Smith (Oxford: Blackwell, 1991). See also the work of David Harvey: *The Condition of Postmodernity: An Enquiry on the Origins of Cultural Change* (Cambridge: Basil Blackwell, 1990), 218–19; and *Social Justice and the City* (Cambridge, MA: Johns Hopkins University Press, 1988), 307–313.

18. Claude Lévi-Strauss, *Structural Anthropology* (Hammondsworth: Penguin, 1963); Pierre Bourdieu, *Outline of a Theory of Practice*, trans. Richard Nice (Cambridge: Cambridge University Press, 1977); and Michel de Certeau, *The Practice of Everyday Life*, trans. Steven Rendall (Berkeley: University of California Press, 1984).

19. The authors are obliged to Johannes Widodo, Dean of the Architecture Faculty of Parahyangan University, for entertaining and correcting early speculations on the topic of the "White House" style.

20. Periodic outbreaks of mob violence targeting Chinese Indonesians have a centuries-old history in the region. This pattern was repeated most recently during the monetary crisis riots which toppled Soeharto. These peaked in May 1998 when the shops and neighborhoods favored by Chinese Indonesians were targeted for burning, looting, and rape in Jakarta, Solo, Medan, and several other Indonesian cities.

21. For a fuller examination of the so-called China Problem in Indonesia, see *Symposium Proceedings: The Role of the Indonesian Chinese in Shaping Modern Indonesian Life* in a special issue of the journal *Indonesia* (1991); and Ariel Heryanto, "Ethnic Identities and Erasure: Chinese Indonesians in Public Culture," Chapter 4 in *Southeast Asian Identities: Culture and the Politics of Representation in Indonesia, Malaysia, Singapore, and Thailand*, ed. Joel S. Kahn (Singapore: Institute of South East Asian Studies, 1998), 95–114.

22. For an interesting look at the rituals surrounding the *ruang tamu* and its form, see Saya Shiraishi, "Silakan Masuk, Silakan Duduk" (Please Come in, please Sit Down), *Indonesia* 41 (1986): 89–131. The authors thank Ben Zimmer for pointing out this reference.

23. The smallest *pembantu* quarters found so far are in the relatively large 95-square-meter (1,023-square-foot) house "Nice/Berkeley" model at Kota Legenda. This bedroom measures 1.0 meter by 2.2 meters (3.3 feet by 7.2 feet).

24. This counterdistinction replicates the pairing of the traditional *pasar* (bazaar) or "wet" market and the modern *swalayan* (supermarket) or "dry goods" store. The term "pantry" is chosen perhaps as a shortened version of "butler's pantry," as in the optional, additional space associated with the main kitchen that is included in only the largest and most well-appointed houses. The connotations of the "butler's pantry" would seem to be more congruent with the other naming strategies of the Indonesian real estate industry than associating the fancy kitchen with "pantry" as a place to store food.

25. Michael Leon Leaf, "Land Regulation and Housing Development in Jakarta, Indonesia: from the 'Big Village' to the 'Modern City' " (Ph.D. dissertation., University of California at Berkeley, 1991), 246–252.

26. Ibu Ramalis S. Prihandana, Head of the West Java Province Department of Public Works, interview with Robert Cowherd, Bandung (3 April 1998).

27. Harald Leisch, "Gated Paradise?: Quality of Life in Private New Towns in JABOTABEK," *Proceedings of the Second International Conference on Quality of Life in Cities*, National University of Singapore, School of Building and Real Estate (8–10 March 2000), 257–264. The consistent undermining of the 1:3:6 regulation is further described by Dalhar Susanto, "Kota Baru di Jabotabek: Optimalisasi Bisnis" (New Towns of Jabotabek: Business Optimization), paper presented at the seminar *The Planning of New Town and Restructuring Urban Centers*, Universitas Pelita Harapan, Lippo Karawaci, Indonesia (29 March 2000), 7–8.

28. Ibu Ramalis interview.

29. Rather than the required 1:6 ratio. Leaf, "Land Regulation and Housing Development," 247–249.

30. According to Ibu Ramalis, these two categories are required to make up 40 percent of the total land area. A story in the *Jakarta Post* ("N. Jakarta Gets Public Facilities from Realtors," 28 January 1991) relates the tale of a group of developers who turned over schools, sports facilities, a mosque, a church, and a market to the city government in a public ceremony despite the fact that none of these facilities had yet been built. Cited in Leaf, "Land Regulation and Housing Development," 207–209. See also Gunawan Tjahjono, "New Town: Urban Future for Expanded Metropolis in Indonesia?" *Journal of Southeast Asian Architecture*, no. 1 (November 1997): 13–24.

31. This assertion is based on confidential communications with the authors by

reliable observers. Widespread popular resentment of "KKN"—*korupsi* (corruption), *kolusi* (collusion), and *nepotisme* (nepotism)—was a major factor in Soeharto's downfall. Thus, while corrupt practices have been commonplace in Indonesia, it would be wrong to argue that they are acceptable within Indonesian culture.

32. Leaf, "Land Regulation and Housing Development," 246–252.

33. Sori Ersa Siregar and Kencana Tirta Widya, *Liem Sioe Liong dari Futching ke Mancanegara* (Liem Sioe Liong from Fytching to Overseas) (Jakarta: Pustaka Merdeka, 1988). Cited in Leaf, "Land Regulation and Housing Development," 239–240.

34. Adam Schwarz, *A Nation in Waiting: Indonesia in the 1990s* (Boulder, CO: Westview Press, 1994).

35. *South China Morning Post* (1 September 2000); Richard Robison, *Indonesia: The Rise of Capital* (Sydney: Allen & Unwin, 1986); and Schwarz, *A Nation in Waiting*. Soeharto's invocation of tradition in the construction of an "Indonesian Culture" was aimed at satisfying local aspirations for specific local identities while ensuring the integrity of the nation-state that has been the primary task of government since independence. See John Pemberton, *On the Subject of "Java"* (Ithaca, NY: Cornell University Press, 1994).

36. See *Symposium Proceedings*; and Heryanto, "Ethnic Identities and Erasure."

37. Robison, "The Middle Class and the Bourgeoisie in Indonesia," 93–95.

38. Mahathir Mohamad, *The Malay Dilemma* (Singapore: Asia Pacific Press, 1970).

39. Leaf, "Land Regulation and Housing Development," 242–245.

40. Jess C. Lukas, Chief Operating Officer, PT Lippo Village, "Township Development: A Situational Analysis," in *Indonesia Property Report* 1, no. 2 (3rd Quarter, 1995): 20–25.

41. National Land Board Director of Land Use, Maryudi Sastrowihardjo, is quoted as putting this figure at 150,000 hectares in "Gubernur DKI Soal Jonggol: Jangan Jadi Penyakit Bagi Jakarta" (Jakarta Governor on Jonggol: Don't Become a Problem for Jakarta), *Republika* (14 November 1996). But based on two other 1996 sources, we believe he was adding the proposed 30,000 hectares of Bukit Jonggol Asri to the lower figure given by Tommy Firman, "The Restructuring of Jakarta Metropolitan Area: A 'Global City' in Asia," *Cities* 15, no. 4 (1998): 229–243; and "Proyek Kota-Baru Jonggol, Bisa Merusak Tata Air Jakarta" (Jonggol New Town Project, Could Harm Jakarta's Water Supply), *Republika* (13 November 1996).

42. Leaf, "Land Regulation and Housing Development," 206–207.

43. Michael Leaf, "The Suburbanisation of Jakarta: A Concurrence of Economics and Ideology," in *Third World Planning Review*, no. 1 (April 1995): 41–57.

44. Ibid., 76.

45. The property-sector bubble in Thailand accounted for over 50 percent of that nation's bad loans credited for bringing on the crash of the baht. Thailand's currency crash was the spark that set off the crisis that eventually engulfed its neighbors. Koichi Mera and Bertrand Renaud, eds., *Asia's Financial Crisis and the Role of Real Estate* (Armonk, NY: M. E. Sharpe, 2000); and Tjahja Gunawan, "Jangan Lagi Memberi Kredit Berlebihan ke Properti" (Never Again Give Excessive Loans to the Property Sector) *Kompas* (15 July 2000), 15.

46. Leaf, "Land Regulation and Housing Development," 290–296.

47. Jakarta Governor Sutiyoso has vowed to defy a recent court order lifting the twelve-year *becak* ban. "Pedicab Drivers Win Lawsuit Against Jakarta Governor," *Jakarta Post* 18, no. 96 (1 August 2000): 1.

48. Susanto, "Kota Baru di Jabotabek," 5.

49. Tommy Firman and Ida Ayu Indira Dharmapatni, "The Challenges to Sustainable Development in Jakarta Metropolitan Region," *Habitat International* 18, no. 3 (1994): 5.

50. The most recent and carefully argued of the extensive literature on the impact of cars on cities and the environment are Peter Newman and Jeffrey Kenworthy, *Sustainability and Cities: Overcoming Automobile Dependence* (Washington, DC: Island Press, 1999); Michael Brower and Warren Leon, *The Consumer's Guide to Effective Environmental Choices: Practical Advice from the Union of Concerned Scientists* (New York: Three Rivers Press, 1999). See also a review article of three recent books on the topic: David Banister, "Review Essay: The Car Is the Solution, Not the Problem," *Urban Studies* 36, no. 13 (1999): 2415–2419.

51. Jakarta's Superblocks are large internally integrated downtown blocks developed by separate developers conforming to an extensive set of urban design guidelines intended to achieve a complementary mix of uses and high design standards. The Kuningan CBD Superblock features two five-star hotels, restaurants, spas, garaged parking, and office towers that boast of having the fastest Internet connections in Indonesia.

52. Gordon G. Benton, Lippo Karawaci Town Manager, interviewed by Robert Cowherd, Lippo Karawaci, Indonesia (29 March 2000).

53. Manuel Castells, *The Rise of the Network Society*, vol. 1 of *The Information Age: Economy, Society and Culture* (New York: St. Martin's Press, 1996); J. H. Mollenkopt and Manuel Castells, *Dual City: Restructuring New York* (New York: Russell Sage Foundation, 1991); Harvey, *Social Justice and the City*.

54. Stephen Graham and Simon Marvin, *Splintering Urbanism: Networked Infrastructures, Technological Mobilities and the Urban Condition* (London: Routledge, 2001).

55. Dick and Rimmer are writing from the near horizon of Australia. H. W. Dick and P. J. Rimmer, "Beyond the Third World City: The New Urban Geography of South-east Asia," *Urban Studies* 35, no. 12 (1998): 2316–2317.

56. Several newspapers gave attention to the issues raised by the Bukit Jonggol project in general and the controversy over its impact on the water supply and flooding problems of Jakarta in particular. Perhaps the best article on the topic is by environmentalist Bondan Winarno, "Jonggol Jangan Jadi Kota Asrama" (Jonggol Shouldn't Become a Bedroom Community), *Kompas* (25 January 1997).

57. Robert Matson, Transportation Planner with RBF & Associates, Laguna Beach, Calif., and Roger McErlane, Land Use Planner with McErlane Associates, Master Planning, Irvine, Calif., developed the plans for both the larger Jonggol area and Waskita. Both worked for the Irvine Company in the planning of Irvine Ranch. They were interviewed separately (1 May 1997).

58. This information is from the Robert Bein, William Frost & Associates, "Bukit Waskita Master Plan Transportation Analysis" Appendix 8.2 in the McErlane Associates, "Bukit Waskita Master Plan" (15 May 1996), 12.

Index

About the Contributors

DANIEL ABRAMSON is a postdoctoral research fellow at the University of British Columbia's Centre for Human Settlements, with degrees in Architecture and City Planning. He has conducted urban housing and neighborhood research, planning, design, and development projects in China, Poland, and the United States.

TRIDIB BANERJEE is Vice Dean and James Irvine Chair Professor of Urban and Regional Planning in the School of Policy, Planning, and Development at the University of Southern California.

MICHAEL CLOUGH is a Research Associate at the Institute of International Studies at the University of California at Berkeley.

ROBERT COWHERD is a Ph.D. Candidate in the History, Theory, and Criticism Section of the MIT School of Architecture and Planning. He received a Fulbright Grant in 2000 to conduct field research for his dissertation: "Cultural Construction of Jakarta: Planning and Development of the New Order New Towns."

GRACE DYRNESS is Associate Director of the Center for Religion and Civic Culture at the University of Southern California.

ERIC J. HEIKKILA is an Associate Professor at the School of Policy, Planning, and Development at the University of Southern California and Executive Secretary of the Pacific Rim Council for Urban Development. His scholarly work focuses on the myriad ways that metropolitan systems evolve, both as economic entities and as cultural phenomena.

MICHAEL LEAF is an Associate Professor in the University of British Columbia's School of Community and Regional Planning, a Faculty Associate of UBC's Centre for Human Settlements, and the Director of UBC's Centre for Southeast Asia Research. His research and publications are primarily concerned with issues of urbanization in Indonesia, China, and Vietnam.

DONALD E. MILLER is Executive Director of the Center for Religion and Civic Culture at the University of Southern California (USC).

JON MILLER is a Professor in the sociology department and director of research at USC's Center for Religion and Civic Culture. Together with Donald E. Miller, he is conducting a three-year study of religion and immigration in Southern California as part of the Gateway Cities Project funded by The Pew Charitable Trusts. He is also involved in comparative and historical research on the international missionary movement of the nineteenth century.

RAFAEL PIZARRO is a Ph.D. Candidate in the School of Policy, Planning, and Development at the University of Southern California. His research interest and Doctoral Dissertation relate to the effects of globalization on the urban form of Latin American cities.

STANLEY ROSEN is a professor of political science at the University of Southern California. His chapter in this book stems from a project to examine Hollywood films in China and the future of the Chinese film industry after China joins the World Trade Organization.

GREGORY F. TREVERTON is a senior policy analyst at RAND where he formerly directed the International Security and Defense Policy Center, and is on the faculty of the RAND Graduate School. He taught public management and foreign policy at Harvard's Kennedy School of Government, and he has been an adjunct professor at Columbia's School of International and Public Affairs. His current book projects are *Reshaping National Intelligence for an Age of Information*, Cambridge University Press, 2001, and *Making the Most of Southern California's Global Engagement*.

NIRAJ VERMA is Associate Professor of Planning and Management and Director of Doctoral Programs in Planning and Development in the School of Policy, Planning, and Development at the University of Southern California. His research interests are in planning and management theory. His chapter in this book stems from work with Professor Tridib Banerjee on a book titled *Probing the Soft Metropolis: From Chicago Models to Los Angeles*. Their goal is to study the limits of modeling in understanding cities and to propose ways of extending these limits by using metaphorical descriptions of important urban processes.